Home for the Friendless Chicago

The Home Cook Book

Compiled from Recipes Contributed by Ladies of Chicago and other Cities

Home for the Friendless Chicago

The Home Cook Book

Compiled from Recipes Contributed by Ladies of Chicago and other Cities

ISBN/EAN: 9783744781893

Printed in Europe, USA, Canada, Australia, Japan

Cover: Foto ©Andreas Hilbeck / pixelio.de

More available books at **www.hansebooks.com**

HOME COOK BOOK

COMPILED FROM RECIPES CONTRIBUTED BY LADIES OF CHICAGO AND
OTHER CITIES AND TOWNS : ORIGINALLY PUBLISHED FOR THE
BENEFIT OF THE HOME FOR THE FRIENDLESS, CHICAGO.

—— With dispatchful looks in haste
She turns, on hospitable thoughts intent,
What choice to chose for delicacy best,
What order, so contrived as not to mix
Taste not well joined, inelegant, but bring
Taste after taste upheld with kindliest change.
— *Paradise Lost.*

FORTY-FIRST THOUSAND.

CHICAGO
J. FRED. WAGGONER.
1877.

Oak Street

PREFACE.

In issuing this new edition of the HOME COOK
BOOK, the Publisher takes renewed pleasure in acknowl-
edging the kind favor with which the work has been
received by the intelligent housekeepers of the country,
by whose appreciative judgment alone it could have
attained to such extraordinary success. In accordance
with the promise made at the outset, improvements have
been made from time to time, each adding to the value
of the work, and increasing its just popularity. Pursuant
to the same policy, the present edition is still further
improved by the addition of articles on Servants, Marketing and the Kitchen, which have been prepared expressly
for this work, by one of the most prominent and experienced of American housekeepers, whose name would be
sufficient guaranty for the value of her suggestions. It
will be seen, that in its chief and distinctive character as
a collection of choice and valuable recipes, tried and
approved by housekeepers of first intelligence and most
ample experience, the work is unchanged.

INDEX.

(4)

HOME COOK BOOK

HOUSEKEEPING.

,Word of grace to women; word that makes her the earthly providence of her family, that wins gratitude and attachment from those at home, and a good report of those that are without. Success in housekeeping adds credit to the woman of intellect, and lustre to a woman's accomplishments. It is a knowledge which it is as discreditable for any woman to be without as for a man not to know how to make a living, or how to defend himself when attacked. He may be ever so good an artist, ever so polished a gentleman, if deficient in these points of self-preservation you set him down for a weakling, and his real weight in society goes for very little. So, no matter how talented a woman may be, or how useful in the church or society, if she is an indifferent house- . keeper it is fatal to her influence, a foil to her brilliancy and a blemish in her garments.

Housekeeping ought not to be taught in classes and by

professors; though when early training is lacking they
may be of use. It is one of those things to be imbibed
without effort in girlhood, instead of being taken up at
marriage and experimented on with varying certainty for
the rest of one's natural life. There is no earthly reason
why girls, from eight to eighteen, should not learn and
practice the whole round of housekeeping, from the first
beating of eggs to laying carpets and presiding at a dinner party, at the same time that they go on with music,
languages and philosophy. The lessons would be all the
better learned if, instead of sitting down at once out of
school hours, the girl was taught to take pride in keeping
her room nice, or in helping about such work as canning
fruit for the season, hanging clean curtains, or dusting
every day. The wealthiest women of the oldest families
society are not above seeing to these things themselves, in
and they know how it should be done. They were bred
to it as part of a lady's duty. But if a woman finds herself ignorant or half taught how to keep house, there is
nothing so difficult to learn that she may not be proficient
in a year or two at most. An intelligent woman will suc-
ceed in most duties at first trying. Housekeeping is an
exact science, and works like the multiplication table if
one only has learned it. But if one is shaky in figures
how is he ever to keep accounts? There is no chance
about housekeeping. If Mrs. Smith's sitting room is
always neat and fresh, it is because she sweeps it with tea
leaves, and sponges the carpet with ox gall, and dusts it
with a damp cloth, and keeps a door mat on the porch,
and sends the boys back every time to use till they get the

habit of keeping clean. While you hang a newspaper before the what-not and throw one over the work table, sweep with a soft broom, butting the broad side of it at every stroke against the moulding; instead of carrying all the dust clean from the crevice next the wall by one lengthwise sweep with the corner of the broom, you blow the dust off some places and give a hasty rub at others; pass the stove with a touch from the hearth brush instead of blacking it, and let the boys track in mud and dust enough to deface a new carpet its first season, while you take it out in scolding — which was never known to brighten rooms yet. So, when your feather cake fails, though you made it precisely by the rule which the other day came out like bleached sponge, there is a very good reason for it, you did not stir it as much as the first time, or you beat it a little too long and lost the best effervescence of your soda, or your baking powder had been left open a few minutes at a time on baking days and lost strength. By practicing the same recipe carefully all these and other points fix themselves in your mind, so that success is certain. Those clever cooks, whose success is so much a matter of instinct, observe all these points unconsciously each time, and lay it to luck! There's no such word in housekeeping.

This labor does not only mean keeping things clean, and having plenty to eat. It goes from the outside of the house to the inside of the traveling-bags of those who leave it. The mistress must observe the outside of her house regularly; on Saturday is the most convenient time to see if window-blinds need washing, if the catches are

in repair, if the shades inside hang straight, and the
curtains drape well, if the walks, steps, and piazzas are
neat, and the door knobs and paint in order, making a
note of every want, and having it attended to ‛*at once*.
Dexterity with tools is very convenient to any one, and I
have known accomplished women who would set a pane
of glass, put on a door knob, and hang a gate in the best
style.   One of the valued contributors to the New York
press is a woman who reads Horace in Latin, and Bastiat's
political economy, makes point-lace and embroiders beautifully, who at the gold mines with her husband, built the
chimney to her house, and finished most of the interior
with her own hands.   A little care, weekly, keeps a place
in that bright order that so attracts and welcomes one at
sight.   It looks as if whole people lived in it, with live
sensibilities and intelligence.   Indoors the same spirit is
reflected.   The bell-pull never is left for weeks after it
gets loose, the gas burners are never suffered to leak, or
grow dim ; the kerosene lamps are large enough to give
good light, and of the best pattern for safety, and for the
eye.   The stoves are the open "Fireside" kind, the
modern version of the old Franklin stoves—giving the
ventilation and delight of an open fire, burning either
coal or wood, with bars and fender like a grate ; yet,
capable of being shut up as tightly as any base-burning
heater by two tight fitting covers that may be removed
and put away at pleasure.   The health, the comfort, the
luxury of such an addition makes up for many a deficiency
beside.   The carpet was well-chosen at first in small figure
and warm colors of good quality, whether Brussels or

three-ply, and it looks well as long as it lasts, and kept
clean by shaking twice a year, laid straight and stretched
smooth over a soft lining, which saves the carpet and
saves noise; darned at the first break with wool, matching
the pattern, it will not be shabby in ten years. It is pleasant to have things last with the family, and grow to seem
a part of it. The true sentiment of the sharp, genteel
woman, was expressed by the housekeeper who "liked to
have her carpets wear out so she could have new ones."
She let lodgings to have company, and money to dress by,
against her husband's wish, and her only dread was that
of "settling down and having a lot of children with no
theatres, no opera, nobody to see." The home feeling,
the attachment that grows for the pleasant enduring
objects of daily use is one of the rare plants of sentiment
that the housekeeper does well to cherish. There should
be care at first to have things agreeable and handsome as
possible, that they need not be a daily eyesore, and there
need be no reason for wishing them to wear out. Manu-
factures constantly add service to trade by placing better
patterns in reach of moderate purses. Thus, the mottled
carpets in oak and brown, ash and crimson, maroon and
elm-leaf yellow, with borders to match, so admired in
velvet and Brussels, are found in fine three-plys and
ingrain, and in the newer Venetians of hemp and wool,
like the old-fashioned stair carpet that lasts so long. A
word for these new Venetians, which is on account of
their artistic quality, likely to be overlooked, because they
are so cheap. All the best colors and patterns of Brussels,
in two shades, in mottled, moss or leaf designs, are

afforded in this carpet, which is durable as the conscience
of a housekeeper could exáct. Two rules are enough for
the looks of a carpet; choose small figures and avoid
contrasts of color. Small figures, however, have different
meanings to different people. As a rule, a small figure is
not more than three inches at most, any way across.
Very, very few rooms there are, but look better with
carpets of small design. Then the oil-cloth under the
stove must match, if possible, and be bound with leather
strips to keep the edge from getting unsightly. The
woodbox or basket is covered with wool work on canvas,
or applique of bright cloth on Turkish toweling, making
a handsome bit of furniture. A scrap basket, with applique border, and bright lining, goes far toward keeping
a room tidy. The mistress will try to have her rooms in
keeping with the style by a few pieces of furniture in the
fashion of the day, a Turkish chair embroidered in wools,
a straight-backed one in unbleached toweling and applique
of crimson, blue, black and gold, a stand covered with
velvet, or a home-made easel with the single good picture
the house affords on it, a jardiniere of titles or wicker-
work in the window, or a bamboo lounge, things not
expensive in themselves, yet lending a graceful air to
quiet surroundings. As for chairs, sofas and lambrequins,
artists have been insisting on chintz for the last ten years,
and women have as steadily bought woolen reps, which
the doctors tell us harbors dust, absorbs vitiated matter
from the air, and is absolutely dangerous in disease from
the contagion it holds. But women of the best taste,
who like to have their rooms pretty, will choose chintz,

when they cannot afford silk and satin, and often when they can, for its intrinsic beauty.

It is of more account to have broad seats and deep cushions to chairs and sofas, than to have them covered with rich material. See that there are plenty of low seats in your sitting-room, for much of the furniture seen is of very little use for rest and ease, points essential to the health and comfort of women and children. If a woman will only start with the intention of making her house comfortable, she will gain all the admiration she wants. Many elegant rooms in private houses, where there were only one or two that came up to the idea of comfort. Now that is a very important word, one that cannot be infringed on without losing health. The mistress of a house must see that it is ventilated from top to bottom, by having every window and the skylight, if there is one, open at least once a day — if possible when the sun is shining. She is responsible for the health of the household, and must allow no scent of decay, whether from vegetables or meat, barrels or refuse in the cellar, no slops anywhere about the premises, no mouldering food in closets, no confined bed-rooms or closets with old clothes or soiled linen to taint the air, no dead, musty smell in any room however seldom used, no sickly smell escaping from rooms where there is illness. She must see that fires are started as early in the fall and kept as late in the spring as the weakest, chilliest of her family desires, for these slow chilly days take more life, and play more mischief with nerves and blood than she could bear to think of, could she see their effects. She must look after the cloth-

ing from a hygienic view, to see that her children and family are warm enough and cool enough, so warding off
many an attack of cramps, coughs and neuralgia. The
food must be of the best quality, and she must *know* that
it is. It pays to give an extra shilling on the half barrel
for selected potatoes and apples, as they go farther and
make more muscle than poor ones, and don't poison anybody. Sharp scrutiny of eggs, meat, butter, and milk, is
a benefit to others as well her own family, by raising the
standard of provisions, besides more direct gain. More
disease comes into the world in the shape of tainted butter and milk, than any one dreams of but the doctors. If
she gets the hygienic craze about food, don't let her carry
it to the verge of confounding things "healthful" with
things uneatable, for badly cooked oatmeal and graham
"gems" are as distressing to delicate organisms as the
richest mince pie and old cheese together. That slight
sour tinge, which nobody noticed, in the home-made
bread, that solid pudding, which yet was not quite rejected
at dessert, are responsible for the bad breath of the children, and the beginning of a sick headache in their elders.
Never be satisfied with any but the nicest cooking, with
variety enough to make your table a delight as well as a
necessity. And don't let anybody lay it to you that you
are pampering your family, and devoting yourself to a low
sphere of action. You are doing no such thing, but are
giving them strong, active bodies, steady nerves and tem-
pers, and clear brains to meet their work with. By just
so much as you neglect your part of the work, they will
fail in theirs. You are the engineer to feed the fires, and

keep the wheels oiled, and the whole family system depends on you. Don't dare to call such work low. There is a great work to be done in American kitchens. You may and ought to delegate as much· to hired helpers as you can, but you must see that all is done as it should be. And one receipt for training service is given, that is the whole secret in a nut-shell. If child or servant leaves anything undone, or ill-done, don't scold, but insist on having it done immediately as it ought to be. Put the badly ironed shirts in the basket to be done over, have the house-girl who left the china badly washed, take it out of the closet and do it right, time after time, and let her get tired of doing her work over before you get tired of telling her. It is no harder to do work nicely than to half do it. Indeed the careless way is the hardest. Finally, let your housekeeping be as liberal as you can. Whether well-to-do, or in narrow circumstances, you will hold that waste is a sin, against yourself and the world. By keeping strict account of every cent received and paid out, you can gauge your means, laying by what is proper, but within that limit be good to yourself and yours. Make the most of your money. It was no less a divine than the orthodox Doctor John Hall, who said that, of the two faults, he had far rather see people extravagant than penurious. Stint nowhere in cleanliness, light, and warmth, and let what you have be the best and prettiest for its cost. By these things men live, in body at least, and the soul is very dependent on its surroundings, or at any rate greatly assisted by favorable ones. It is an every-day wonder to see how little rich people get from their money.

The commonplace houses, with so little that is light or striking or original in them, the dull service, the narrow round of enjoyments. In some sense housekeeping is making the most of life, bringing taste and variety into it, compassing difficult ends with invention. Those who disdain it lower themselves. Never think that anything is too good for you and yours that you can obtain. Everywhere there are people living in small common ways, because they are absolutely afraid of the expense or the notice which a pleasanter life would bring. Half the niceties of life involve only care to secure them, without a dollar of expense. Good manners cost nothing, good taste is a saving, and good housekeeping actually makes money. Though this book is an aid to the ambitious housekeeper in one direction only, that is on the way to all the rest. People grow refined first in their eating. How is it that the most brilliant and cleverest nation in the world has also the best cooking? Put these things together, and do your best according to their result.

TABLE TALK.

In all attempts at refinement, one cardinal point should be kept in view — that manners were made for men, not men for manners. Nice customs, courtesy to great kings, and the greatest of these is convenience. Most rules will be found to serve convenience, and there is no good breeding where etiquette is not observed for this end, the order and comfort of all concerned, *not* for the sake of defining one's social position. When any one begins to study manners as a set of arbitrary rules, followed because every other desirable acquaintance does the same, politeness breeds a sort of pharisaism that the best bred persons look down on as supremely vulgar. If any mistress of a house looks here for rules that will aid her to affect a trifle more of style than her neighbors she will only be disappointed. If any woman wishes hints how to reduce her household to regularity and make her children neat and gentle in habits, it may be that she will not find this chapter in vain.

Martinet regularity as to hours and minutes is no longer held the saving virtue in a household. The rule in many families keeps all the rest waiting for a meal if one is tardy. Modern custom both for the family and for din-

ner parties takes the sensible course of sitting down to
table when the hour comes, and the principal part of
those expected. No guest should feel affronted, if he
is late, and finds the party at dinner, provided the
indispensable care has been shown to keep his portion
warm over dishes of hot water, by which they neither
grow cold or are dried up in the oven. Order the table
daily with the same care as for a dinner party. This is
the only way to insure success for hostess and servants
when one does come off, and gives mistress and waiter
the luxury of getting used to nice style; so that it is just
as easy as common ways, and no sudden visitor can put
them out. Home tables do not always compare to advantage with those at the restaurant or club, and the
housemother should see that a man finds as careful service at home as he does anywhere else. Unlimited laundry work should be one of the indulgences of one's own
house, and it should be of the utmost nicety. Why
should it be too much to provide clean napkins and table-
cloth daily at home as well as at a hotel? They would
cost half an hour's extra work a day, and this is not too
much for the refinement it gives. We should then expect
to see the table spread with a snowy cloth, less starched
than many housekeepers think necessary, finish and pli-
ancy given by plenty of wax in the starch, which will
keep it clean the longer. It should fall below the table
half a yard all round, and be pinned up at the corners to
keep it from the floor if necessary. For ceremonious
occasions a common white cloth is laid under the table-
cloth to protect a handsome table, keep the upper cloth

from wearing, and because dishes make less noise when set down on it.

For breakfast the coffee is set before the mistress, the cups and spoons ranged in their saucers ·in front of it, in two rows if there are many of them; the meat and plates, which should be warm, before the master; salt, butter and castor at the corner to the right of both, head and foot, if the table is a large one, when two sets of these things will be convenient. Otherwise put them in the center with the dishes in regular order around them, and relishes at the corners. To meet this order, it is a trifle to have dishes in pairs of the same size, and use them always together for different things. Fruit, whether berries, baked apples, or pears, is served first at breakfast, then oatmeal or wheaten grits, now found on every good table in cities at least, then meats and vegetables, with toast, hot cakes and coffee following. Hot rolls come wrapped in a napkin to keep them warm, griddle-cakes between two hot plates, and all meats covered. Baked potatoes are scrubbed with a manilla brush, the ends cut off, rinsed twice, and eaten without paring, as the best flavor goes with the skin. This is the custom with the best society in this country and abroad. Eggs are washed with a cloth in cold water before boiling, and eaten in egg cups from the shell, chipping the small end off, or broken into larger glasses, or held in the napkin and eaten from the shell with entire good form, in either method. Where individual salt-cellars are used they should be emptied after each meal, and the salt thrown away, that one person may not use it after another, and they should be

2

very small, that there be less wasted. Butter should be piled round a lump of ice in little pats. To be very nice, as many have learned to like it from living abroad, it should be churned daily from perfectly sweet cream, worked without being touched by the hands or with water, and without a particle of salt. Thus it has the delicate flavor of cream at its best. Honey is especially a breakfast delicacy, and so is maple syrup, which should be served in small saucers to be eaten with hot biscuit. A basket of crisp cakes, toasted rusk and crackers, will accompany coffee.

For lunch the colored table cloths may be used if ever, though their use is gradually dropped because the colors do not wash well. White cloths with striped border in colors, or fine gray or brown unbleached damask, with napkins to match, assist the easy half-dress style of this repast. Cups of broth and thick chocolate, with light meats, hashes, croquettes, and stews. Salad and fruit are the staple variety, and rather more attractive than the cold meat, tea and cracker fare too often set apart for this hurried meal. Nowhere is negligence more annoying than at luncheon, and the cloth, glasses, and arrangements should be fastidiously neat to do away with the disagreeable feeling that everybody is too busy with drudgery to look after comfort. Insist that the girl who waits on the table has her hair neat, her hands washed, and a clean apron and collar on. An unkempt servant will spoil the best dinner appetite was ever sharp-set for. Ceremonious lunches mean an hour's visit with a meal, at which salads, shell-fish, chops in paper frills, and broiled chicken play a part, with ices, tarts and fancy cakes for dessert. Mixed drinks, like Regent's punch, or claret sup, with ale and beer, are more in keeping at lunch than wines. These drinks are served from the side-board, the malt liquors in common goblets, the claret cup in tumblers, the punch in small cups. Beef tea is taken from cups held in very small saucers, or in small Chinese bowls, with little saucers. The absence of all ceremony with the presence of light charming detail makes the luncheon attractive.

For dinner, the family table wants to have less the air of hotel arrangements. More delicate napery and ware, whether the latter is only "seconds," or the finest egg-shell china; lighter, more convenient, knives and forks, and heavier teaspoons, nice thin glass for drinking, thick cut crystal for sweets, with above all things a well kept cruet stand, make the difference in favor of home taste and home comfort. Keep all cracked and nicked ware from the table. Buy nothing that cannot be replaced without regret, but let each article be the best of its material. There is choice in the quality of stone ware and blown glass as well as in the shapes of each. The plainest is always most satisfactory of inexpensive things. The old fashion of furnishing dining-rooms in dark and heavy styles is reversed. The room is light, cheerful, warm in color, the chairs broad and substantial, the table lower than it used to be, two points which add sensibly to the comfort of those who use them. Have the chair feet shod with rubber tips which come for the purpose, or if on castors, cover the wheel with rubber so that they can move without noise. See that the room is light and especially warm, for people want comfort at meals of all times, and they feel the cold more in sitting.

DINNER ETIQUETTE.

Directions for a ceremonious dinner naturally include those for the family table, as much form in serving being kept as may be convenient.

The number of guests for a state dinner, even such as are given by the President and Secretary of State, at Washington, rarely exceeds twelve.

Written invitations are always complimentary and in finer style than any other for small parties, but persons who entertain often, have engraved cards with blanks left for the name of guest, and date, for convenience. The following is the form adopted by Tiffany & Co. for dinner cards, a large, nearly square form being used:

MR. AND MRS. ARTHUR HOYT,

Request the pleasure of

....Company, (name.)

....date and No.

...........................o'clock.

The favor of an answer is requested.

(or) R. s. v. p.

For a gentleman's party the host's name alone appears on the invitation. An early answer must be sent in all cases, either to accept or to decline. Not to do so, is the grossest rudeness.

Invitations are always sent to persons in the same town by private messenger. Outside envelopes are necessary only when sent by mail to another city. No particular excuse need be sent. It is enough to say " Mr. and Mrs. —— regret that they are unable to accept Mr. and Mrs. —— kind invitation for the date named." When the dinner is to meet any particular guest or distinguished person, it is made known by the words, " To meet So and So," at the head of the invitation, or after the name of the invited person before the date.

Written invitations are on note sheets of mill-finished paper with side fold, the fancy rough and the highly glazed papers of eccentric shapes and fold being out of use. The large envelope, nearly square, allows the sheet to be doubled once to fit. Cards have the same finish, neither dull, nor highly polished. The cipher of initials entwined is preferred to the monogram, and occupies the corner of the note sheet

Guests arrive at any time during the half hour before dinner, and after leaving wraps in the dressing room, are met by the host and hostess at the door of the drawing-room. Introductions follow if the guest is a stranger. If the party is given in honor of any distinguished person, or favorite visitor, the other guests are brought up to him or her, and presented. It is an omen of success for her evening if the hostess can make conversation general before dinner. To this end, have some novelty at hand, either in the shape of a personage whom everybody wants to meet, or a new picture, a grotesque group, a rare plant in the drawing-room, the latest spice of news to tell, or a pretty girl to bring forward. Whatever the attraction, bring it on at once, to prevent that very stupid half hour. At the hour, the servant comes in and tells the hostess dinner is served. The arranging of the guests has all been considered beforehand. If she wishes people to think her dinner a pleasant one, the hostess will see that the likings of her guests are consulted in pairing off for the table. Host and hostess intimate to the gentlemen whom they are to escort. "Mr. Lance, will you be kind enough to take Miss Dart in to dinner. Mr. Curtis, be so good as to see Mrs. Vane. Jermingham, I know you'd prefer Miss Olney, she's such a good listener. Mr. King, if you want to finish telling that story to Mrs. Capron, suppose you give her your arm," and so on. If the guest to be honored is a lady, the host offers her his arm and goes out first, the hostess last. If a gentleman, he escorts the hostess and the host follows the company. Before dinner is announced, after the guests have arrived, the host has the names of each person written on a card and laid on the plates at the place where he or she is to sit. This does away with that awkward moment when the guests are in the dining room waiting to be told their places. The method long used at public dinners is now adopted for private ones in the best circles here and abroad.

The standard size for dinner tables is four and-a-half feet wide, by any length desired. Round tables for gentlemen's dinners, where all are wanted in the conversation are made seven feet across. For the costly dinner parties given in his white marble mansion, Mr. A. T. Stewart has a dining table five feet by twenty, and there are one or two larger held by dinner givers in the city. For his intimate parties, Mr. William Butler Duncan has a round table seven feet across, and we hear of English tables of twelve feet, the napery for which has to be woven to order. Dining chairs should have cushioned seats covered with fine leather, but no arms, or very low ones, that will not impede the flow of ladies' dresses. People who make a study of entertaining are particular on such points. Each gentleman offers his right arm to the lady he takes to dinner and seats her on his left, which gives occasion for a pretty piece of attention on his part. On reaching their places, he draws out her chair for her, and as her hand leaves his arm he takes the tips of her fingers and hands her to her seat, relinquishing his touch with a slight bow or glance of acknowledgement. Of course, the honored guest, if a lady, takes the right hand of the host; if a gentleman, he is at the right of the hostess.

Small can-shaped pitchers of engraved crystal, holding about a quart, are placed with ice water between each pair of guests. The napkins are folded flat, with a thick piece of bread on each, a cruet-stand and silver salt cellar is at each corner, and a silver butter dish at each end. The small individual-salt cellars and butter plates, have an air of hotel arrangements which it is desirable to avoid at home dinners, though entirely admissible and convenient at breakfast. If wax lights are used, there should be as many candles as guests, according to the old rule. These are in branches held by Sevres and Dresden figures, above the heads of the guests. Nor are wax lights by any means the extravagance they seem. Dinner napkins are from three-quarters to seven-eights of a yard square, and should match the cloth, for which Greek, Moresque, and Celtic filigrees and diaper patterns are preferred to large arabesques and fruit pieces. French napkins of fine fringed damask, with crimson figures of lobster and craw-fish woven in the centre, are sometimes used at first and removed with the fish. Decorations must be choice and used with discretion. Flowers should be fine but few, for cultivated senses find their odor does not mingle pleas-antly with that of food. All artificial contrivances, like epergnes and show-pieces, tin gutters lined with moss and filled with flowers for the edges of a table, or mirror plates to reflect baskets of blossoms, are banished by the latest and best taste. The finest fruit grouped in the centre of the table, set off with leaves, the garnished dishes, the lustre of glass and silver, and the colors of delicately painted china, need no improvement as a picture. A low silver basket of flowers at the sides, and a crystal bouquet holder with a delicate blossom and leaf, sparingly intro-duced, are all that is allowed for ornament's sake. Large dinner services of one pattern are no longer chosen. The meats and large dishes are in silver or electrotype ware, the sweets come in heavy English cut crystal, and each course brings with it plates of a different ware.

The order of wines is sometimes perplexing, and the novice should remember that Chablis or Sauterne comes with the small oysters before soup, and that Sherry is drank after soup and with fish. Claret may be taken by those who prefer it during a whole dinner with entire propriety. Champagne comes with the roast, and Burgundy with game. The French and Germans reserve champagne for a dessert wine, but we drink it with both roast and dessert. After dessert comes coffee, which with us is served at table, not in the drawing-room. Fingerbowls with warm water are placed on the napkin on the dessert plate, and removed by the guest to the left, to be used by dipping the fingers in lightly and drying them on the d'oylay. When the ladies are quite through with dessert the hostess catches the eye of each or raises her gloved hand slightly, as a signal, and they leave the table, the oldest lady going first, the youngest last, followed by the hostess — the youngest gentleman, or the one nearest the door, taking it on himself to hold the door open. After half an hour a guest is at liberty to withdraw, but a dinner party rarely breaks up till half past ten or later, if cards and dancing follow.

As to the individual etiquette of the table, on seating himself a guest draws off his gloves, and lays them in his lap under the napkin, which should be spread lightly, not tucked in the dress. The raw oysters are eaten with a fork; the soup, only a ladleful to each plate, is sipped from the side of the spoon, without noise, or tilting the plate. The head should never stoop toward the plate or cup, but the shoulders kept straight and the food lifted to the mouth, the head bent naturally a little. A quiet 'celerity in eating is preferable to the majestic deliberation which many people consider genteel. Bread should be

broken, never cut at table, and should be eaten morsel by
morsel, not crumbed into soup or gravy. Food should
not be mixed on the plate. Sweet corn is brought on, tied
in its husk by a strip of leaf, and should be eaten from the
cob, breaking the ear in two, and holding the piece in the
left hand. Asparagus should *not* be touched with the fingers, but the tender part cut up, and eaten with the fork.
Fish is eaten with the fork, asssisted by a piece of bread
in the left hand. Maccaroni is cut and taken with the
fork, unless served with the tomatoes, when a teaspoon is
allowed, as with green peas, and stewed tomatoes alone.
Cheese is crumbled with the fork and eaten with it, never
touched by the fingers. Pastry should be broken by the
fork without the aid of a knife. Game and chicken are
cut up, never picked with the fingers, unless in the indul-
gence of a family dinner, when the bone may be held in
one hand and eaten. Pears are held by the stem to be
paired, and then cut and eaten like apples, beginning to
remove the skin at the blossom end. Oranges are held on
a fork while peeled and divided without breaking the skin.
Cherries in pie, or natural, should have the stones passed
to the napkin held at the lips and returned to the plate,
and grape seeds and skins are disposed of .in the same
way. Salt is left on the edge of the plate, not on the
table. Ladies take but a single glass of any wine at most,
having their glasses half-filled with champagne a second
time. It is beginning to be the custom to take soft bread
as well as ice cream with cake. Cocoanut pudding looks
pie, but is helped and eaten with a spoon. Small meringues are best eaten with a spoon, though the practice is to
take them in the fingers.

SOCIAL OBSERVANCES.

THE simplest society duty is, that of making calls. A new comer should return each call within two weeks after it is made. After this, a call once in six months, or a year, serves to keep up acquaintance. Calls are due to a hostess two days after a dinner party, and two days after a ball, and a week after a small party, though these are amply fulfilled by leaving one's card in the case of a gentleman, a personal call being polite from a lady who has more time.

In town, leaving a card with the corner bent signifies that it was left by its owner in person, not sent by a servant. Bending the edges of a card, means that the visit was designed for the young ladies of the house, as well as the mistress of it. If there is a visitor with the family whom you wished to see, a separate card should be left for that person, naming him or her to the servant. A card should also be left for the host, if the call was designed as a family matter, but more than three are not left at one house.

Visits of condolence are paid within a week after the funeral, and are as well expressed by leaving a card and kind inquires of the servant. This is the only proper thing to do in case of sickness, beside asking if one can be of use. Visits of congratulation are paid in person. After the birth of a child, cards and inquiries are left at the door, when the lady is able to receive her friends, she sends her card in return "with thanks for kind inquiries," after which calls are made on her in person.

Bending the corners of the cards to signify "condolence." "felicitation," "to take leave," etc., is not used so much as a penciled word or two, to express one's "kind inquiries," if there is trouble in the house, or "best wishes," if there is a wedding, or engagement.

The P. P. C. card when one is going away, is a convenient way of letting friends know of your absence, the initials of "*pour pendre conge,*" being often relinquished for the plain English "to take leave." On returning, cards are sent to all the friends one wishes to see, with one's address, and receiving day, when one day of the week is set apart for company.

From three to six are proper calling hours, and a visit may be from five minutes to half an hour, never longer, unless with a very intimate friend. A gentleman leaves his umbrella in the hall, but carries hat and cane with him, keeping the former in his left hand, never venturing to lay it on table, or rack, unless invited to do so by the lady of the house. Her not doing so is a sign that it is not convenient for her to prolong his call.

The lady of the house rises to receive any guest, unless it be a very young one, and gives her hand. After the visit, she receives a gentleman's bow, and if disposed to be very polite, walks with him to the door of the room. She sees a lady visitor to the street door, if the parlor is on the same floor. If not, going to the head of the stairs is sufficient courtesy except to elderly guests. A gentleman must escort a lady who makes him a business call to the outer door, and to her carriage, if she has one. A caller should take leave as soon as possible on the arrival of another visitor, unless asked to stay.

Where a lady has a large acquaintance, it is most convenient for her to set apart a day for receiving their calls, of which she admonishes them by her visiting card on which the day of the week is pencilled, or engraved thus:

MRS. BRUCE-PERRINE.

23 W. 25th St.   Tuesdays.

Unless specially invited otherwise, her friends will confine their visits to that day of the week.

To these afternoons the hostess appears in usual afternoon dress, it is presumed is always choice and delightful; her rooms attractive with flowers and pictures, but no refreshments served. Her guests find her, not sitting at the receipt of customs, but busy with some elegant trifle of lace or wool-work, writing letters, or touching a sketch to be laid aside on the entrance of visitors.

The set afternoon reception is announced by this form of card, the hostess usually preferring to have some young lady with her to add to the attractions of her house.

MRS. L. PERSIFER,
MISS ARNOLD,
At Home,
Saturday, January thirteenth,
from three until six,
33 West 40th st.

If there is a card receiver in the hall, the visitor's card is left in it, that the hostess may have the pleasure afterward of recalling all the friends who favor her with their presence.

Coffee, chocolate, cake and ices, are to be found in a side room at such receptions.

The form of card for afternoon tea, which means ladies in visiting or carriage dress, a harlequin tea service, each cup different, or a set of choice East India china, rooms cosey with warm curtains, and signs of womanly occupation, everything in short, to have the daintiest home-look possible, are issued in this fashion:

MRS. BRADLEY COWLES,
Friday, January 18th,
Tea at 4 o clock.

39 W. 188th St.

Guests arrive in the five minutes before the hour, or the five minutes after. The tea is brought in punctually and placed on the hostess' table in the corner, where are the urns of black, green and Russian tea for those who like each, a basket of wafers, delicate sandwhiches of chicken or thin sliced meats, and a basket of fancy cake. If the English style is followed, the cups of tea are carried to the guests on a tray, and a tiny table to rest the cups on placed in reach of each group. Centennial enthusiasm has brought the customs of our grandmothers into honorable imitation, and the old fashioned tea party, such as Mrs. Washington used to give, are very successful, gathering ladies for a couple of hours gossip in afternoon dress, with hoods and cloaks laid aside, the gentlemen dropping in just before tea, which is served in hospitable fashion, all sitting at table, where chicken, oysters, preserves, compotes and cake appear in old fashioned plenty. The party breaks up by six, unless the old habit is carried farther by pretty girls and escorts coming in for a dance in the evening, to be home by half past ten. The style of these gatherings depends on the elegance in equipage and surrounding, where the choicest old china, silver, abundance of flowers, embroidered chairs, and fashionable nicknacks contrast with the easy, neighborly way of receiving.

Cards are issued for dinner parties and afternoon receptions in distinction from evening parties and weddings, invitations to which are engraved on notepaper. Written invitations are more complimentary than the printed ones, but the idea of cards and engraved requests is to save the labor of writing notes for a large party, or where one entertains continually. Thus the President, a member of the Cabinet, or any one in society who gives dinners and receptions weekly or oftener, will send cards to a party of a dozen, where it would be sheer affectation in a hostess who wishes to give a handsome party to a dozen of her best acquaintance, once a season, to have cards for it. Written invitations for the honor and style of the thing, cards and engraving for convenience, though this is perhaps contrary to the popular notion. Written invitations should be as fastidiously correct as printed one, on mill-finished side-fold note sheets with cipher in the corner, and written in the same form as cards, unless to a familiar friend, when such precision would be absurd. Outside envelopes are only used when invitations are sent by mail. And whether so requested in the note or not, answer to accept or to decline should be sent as soon as possible, no matter how slight the invitation may be, even to dine with a gentleman, or go to a picture gallery. It will not do to present ones self without a word to announce ones coming, or to stay away and apologize the first time of meeting. Good breeding is hardly shown in nicer points than this.

The person entering a room is the one to salute the company by a good morning, or how do you do, and to make his adieus, to which the rest respond. Where a stranger enters a small company, each one should be separately presented. The guest salutes hostess and host before speaking to any one else, and if the party is large, is introduced to two or three convenient persons that he may have somebody to talk to, though in a private house guests may accost each other without formal presentation. Near the close of a party, the host and hostess usually are to be found near the door of the parlor, and guests take leave of them with a bow and compliment for a pleasant evening, then pass to the dressing rooms after wraps and vanish without further ceremony. In small circles a bow should be given to each person about one, and leave taken of any special friend whose conversation has been particularly pleasant.

3

A gentleman does not shake hands with a lady not of his kindred, unless she offers to do so. Unmarried ladies do not give their hands in salute to any but gentlemen relations. Ladies in any case give the hand, the gentleman respectfully presses it without shaking. It is a piece of stupid bad-breeding, however, not to take the hand of any one offered in ignorance of the rule. The best breed‐ing always adapts itself to the customs of those about one.

New York etiquette prescribes that a lady shall not take the arm of a gentleman in the street by day unless engaged or married to him. But the English custom is much more sensible, which allows any gentleman to give a lady the support of his arm in a busy street. Invalids and persons in delicate health, who are easily fatigued, are exceptions to the strictest rule.

When a gentleman escorts a lady to a party, he waits for her near the door of the ladies' dressing-room till she shows herself, gives her his right arm, or gives it to the elder lady if he takes two, and goes up to the hostess with her to make salutations, then after a sentence or two, turn‐ing away to join the company. After a dance with any lady, it is proper to take half a turn round the room in promenade with her, and take her to the refreshment room if she wishes, always leaving her with her chaperone. An unmarried lady does not ask gentlemen to call, but the gentleman asks permission for the favor of her, or waits to be invited by her father or mother.

LITTLE HOUSEKEEPERS.

It often happens that a good deal of knowledge which we are not conscious of possessing—but which finds its way somehow into the brains of big and little people as well—comes very readily to hand when it is needed. It so happened with Annie and Jennie, whose first practical lessons in housekeeping began after breakfast, one morning when Bridget was absent, at her sister's funeral, and in consequence of an accident by which mamma sprained her ankle.

And the doctor had said, with a very wise shake of his head, and any amount of wisdom in his eye, that "Little Mother" must not step on that foot for three days, she grew still whiter with dismay, for Bridget would not be back until quite late in the day, and how was all the house work to be done and nobody to do it?

It was thus that Annie's and Jennie's first practical-experiences in housekeeping began, and as our object in telling you how and what they did is to give you some ideas how you should manage in similar circumstances, I must not pass over their mother's first caution: *Before commencing your work prepare yourselves for it.* This they did by putting long sleeved aprons over their dresses, rolling back their sleeves when it was very evident that the right place to begin with was

THE DINING ROOM.

The first thing here to do, was the clearing of the table. In this, all the clean silver, china, and dishes that had not been used, were first put away in the silver drawer, the china closet and on the side-board. Next, the dishes to be cleaned were collected together; the silver and the knives were first put into a pitcher of hot water, with the bowls and blades downwards. Next, the water was emptied from the glasses, and the coffee from the cups into a basin, and while Annie took these into the kitchen and placed them there on the table, Jennie gathered the plates in a pile, the cups and the saucers, each by themselves, in which, way they were quickly and easily carried to the kitchen.

They were careful not to take too many at once, as they would be liable to break them. Then the tablecloth was folded and laid in the side-board; the napkins were put in the napkin basket; the dining room floor was nicely swept and the furniture dusted; the coal stove was attended to, that the fire was not too lively and not too low; and then, after kissing and petting mamma a few minutes, the little housekeepers set about

THE WASHING OF THE DISHES.

This, of course, with "Little Mother" at the head of affairs, was no disagreeable work, you may be sure. The large tin dish-pan, as bright as silver, was placed in the sink; the hot and cold water faucets turned on until the temperature of the water was hot enough for cleansing the dishes, and not too hot for the hands; then the suds was made by stirring about in the water the soap-shaker (a little tin box with soap in it, and perforated with holes having a long handle like a dipper). Then the glasses were first washed and quickly wiped on clean dry towels; then the silver; then the pretty china cups, saucers, plates and other dishes, which were then rinsed by pouring clear hot water over them in another pan, from which they were wiped with the coarser towels. This finished, Jennie removed the dishes from the kitchen table, putting the silver, glass and china away, while Annie washed the sauce-pans and the tins, putting them in their places in the kitchen; then brushed the range and swept the kitchen floor; after which they washed their hands well and dried them on the roller-towel; and then our little housekeepers set themselves about preparations for

THE CHAMBER WORK.

First, the two little girls went into mamma's room, and put on over their bright glossy curls two little Martha Washington dusting-caps of pink and blue cambric, trimmed around the edges with scalloped ruffles, and ornamented with pretty little fanciful bows of pink and blue cambric, with scalloped edges. Then Annie took the pails and cloths, and Jennie the brushes and brooms, and went up stairs.

The first rule of chamber work is to open the windows and turn down the bed clothes to air them well; beating up the pillows and the mattress. As Annie and Jennie always did this the first thing after dressing in the morning, and before going down to breakfast, the first thing

now to do was to make up the bed.   While Annie went to
the further side, Jennie remained on the other, and thus,
each sheet and blanket was brought up and laid over
straight and smooth, with not a wrinkle in sheet or blanket,
or a single article out of line.   When all was done, the
spread and blankets were turned neatly back, with the
pretty ruffled sheet laying back on the nice white counter-
pane; the clothes were all neatly tucked and folded at
the sides and the corners, and the pillows put up against
the headboard.   Then, while Annie washed the bed-room
service, first emptying the waste water, and then washing
out the cleanest dishes in warm suds, Jennie brushed the
room, dusted the furniture and put the hair and clothes-
brushes in order, and arranged the bureau and toilet table.
They followed the same order in their brother John's
room, which was all of the chamber work to be done that
day, and then went down stairs.

By this time the little housekeepers began to feel tired,
and so they rested a while in their two little easy chairs
in mamma's room, talking to mamma and each other until
it came the time for getting ready for the

LUNCHEON.

As John took his dinner with him to school, and papa
ate his luncheon down town, and would not be home until
the five o'clock dinner, there was only mamma and the
two little girls to partake of this repast together; and as
mamma's luncheons were such cosy, tasteful, though simple meals, we may gain some suggestions from the way our
little housekeepers prepared them.   The first thing to do

in getting any meal, is to decide upon the various dishes
to be served. A look at the supply of prepared food was
quite disheartening to the ambitious desires of the little
housekeepers, as there was bread and cake and cold meat
in plenty, and it seemed as though there would be no
opportunity for practicing their skill in cooking. But
mamma, who saw the troubled look on the little faces,
made out the following

BILL OF FARE.

Tea.

White Bread.	Brown Bread.	Crackers.
	Ham.	
	Cheese Sandwiches.	
Jumbles.		Preserved Strawberries.
	Whipped Cream.	

Now, it must be remembered, that in this arrangement,
the bread was at hand ready to slice; the ham was boiled,
ready to cut; and the strawberries ready in the little glass
can to be opened. There remained, therefore, jumbles
and tea to make, and the cheese sandwiches to prepare.
Following mamma's advice, they first undertook the jumbles, of which they were to make but half the recipe.
They selected for this "Excellent Jumbles," in the Home
Cook Book, and while Jennie held the book and read the
ingredients, Annie collected them together. Thus : one-
half a cup of butter, one cup of sugar, and one-half
cup of cream, and one-half teaspoon of soda. When
Jennie came to the one egg of the recipe, they had some
trouble how they should manage to make it half an egg;
but after consultation with mamma, they concluded to

vary from the given rule, and put the whole egg in.   Then
Jennie read on : "A little nutmeg; flour enough to stiffen
it, so as to bake in rings; bake quickly."

The flour was sifted ; the butter and sugar first creamed
together by Annie, while Jennie beat the yolk of the egg,
and added it to the creamed sugar and butter ; then they
put in the nutmeg, the cream and the soda; then the
beaten white of the egg, and the sifted flour ; then they
put the jumbles into the buttered rings and baked them.
As the oven was quick and hot, I am happy to say these
jumbles were a success.   In taking them out of the tins
when done, they did not pile them on one another, but
placed them carefully about on a large plate to cool.   Then
the little housekeepers made the tea, according to the
directions in the Cook Book, and also the cheese sandwiches, which were a complete success.   The cutting of
the bread was a difficult task, since to be nice, the slices
should be even and thin, but it was managed nevertheless
with patience and care.   When all was ready, the cream
nicely whipped, the strawberries put in the preserve dish,
the little round table in mamma's room drawn out, and the
luncheon arranged, they were just ready to sit down to
enjoy the fruits of their labor, what should they hear but
Bridget's voice at the door.   So it came to pass, that with
the luncheon ended for this time the practical experi-
ments of our little housekeepers.   But it all goes to prove
that, if we live with our eyes open, we shall all of us find
that, with such help as our Home Cook Book, we shall be
ready for those emergencies which come to big as well as
the little housekeepers, when Bridget is not at hand.

MARKETING.

Every lady, whatever her position in life, ought to understand how to select and purchase such stores as are needed in her family. Possibly she may never be called upon to put this knowledge into practice. No matter. It is surely worth knowing; and if never brought into active use, it will do its possessor no harm. This kind of knowledge, more than almost any other of practical worth, must be acquired in girlhood.

All knowledge, and every acquirement for daily use, will be better and more thoroughly established through the mother's teachings and under her immediate supervision. As far as possible, let the daughters accompany their mother in their marketing, and watch her proceedings. Let the mother explain, as they pass from one stall to another, examining the various articles needed, the reasons that lead her to reject one while she accepts another of the same kind of article, but differing in quality. Domestic economy — that part of the daughter's education which is of more importance than almost any other, and on which they will be most dependent when called upon to build up a home of their own — is the one we are all most inclined to neglect or put off till a more "convenient season." "We are too much occupied," or "There is time enough by and bye," is an oft-repeated excuse, when in truth the real motive for procrastination is the

(41)

mother's own disinclination to take up this duty, because she thinks such teaching will be irksome.

To be of lasting benefit, or at all effective, instruction of this kind should not only commence early, but be systematically carried out, or else, before she is aware, the mother will find the little girl has discarded her dolls, and stands by her side a lovely woman; but, through that mother's neglect, utterly ignorant of the duties that are rising up before her.

Many wives leave all household purchases, and among them all the marketing, to their husbands. It is because we do not think this a wise arrangement that we would so earnestly enjoin on all mothers to give their daughters a perfect knowledge of the duties they must understand, if they expect to become the true mistresses of their own homes — the real "helpmeets" for their husbands. There are some articles, doubtless, that a man can buy for the family with better judgment than his wife will exercise; but this is seldom the case, and ought not to be. As he is not expected to superintend the use of the materials to be sent home, how is it possible that he can judge as correctly as the mistress of his house as to what and how much is needed, or what articles are best suited for each meal? To be sure, his wife may prepare a list of what she needs; but is she safe in trusting to his taking such list for his guide in his purchases? Is there not danger that some conversation with a friend, in going to the market, may put these instructions entirely out of his mind. These are but a small part of the many reasons why the housekeeper should, as far as possible, keep all that belongs to her special department in her own hands.

In the evening it is a good plan to take a few moments

of quiet, before retiring, to arrange the work for the coming day, and decide what must be done in the way of marketing the next morning.

As far as practicable, buy all imperishable stores by the wholesale. Tea, coffee, sugar, flour, spices and seasoning, salt beef, pork and hams, coal and wood, soap and starch, if bought in wholesale quantities, and paid for as soon as delivered, will save much money in the course of a year. If nothing more, one saves the retail commission by wholesale purchases, beside many small items, which in the course of a few months would amount to a larger sum than one could know until they had tried the experiment. The extra price charged, where small parcels are bought at retail, for the wrapping paper used, small as it may seem on first thought, will prove no trifling addition to the sum total at the end of a year. There need be no trouble in managing to buy by wholesale everything that will keep well, if one is blessed with suitable storage rooms; or, if thus favored, in securing many kinds of vegetables and fruit by this same practice. Of course, in this advice, it must be understood that to be truly economical everything must be paid for as soon as the articles are delivered and carefully examined, to be certain that the order has been correctly filled. This should never be neglected, for any error can be more readily righted if noticed at once, and before payment. By paying in this way, one has the benefit of the lowest market, and many other advantages which we have not space to enumerate.

All marketing, especially of vegetables and perishable articles, should be done early in the morning, because the earlier this work is done the surer are the prospects of securing what is needed in the best and freshest condition.

We should not advise roaming from store to store, or

from one market stall to another, after having become well
acquainted with what the city or village has to offer, and
having formed as correct a knowledge as possible of the
character of the vender and the quality of the goods
offered   Until this knowledge is well established, it is of
course necessary, for one's own security, to make a fair
trial of all, but having done this, we think it wise to hold
fast to that which, all things considered, is best.   The
grocer, butcher, fish and poultry dealer, as well as the dry
goods merchant, will take greater interest in faithfully
serving a regular customer, at the most reasonable rates,
than one who may not buy of him again.   This much is
certainly gained, aside from a great saving of time and
fatigue to the purchaser.   If those you thus patronize or
trust cannot supply your present needs, it is for their
interest to send out and procure what is needed; and this
they usually do with great cheerfulness, and with a hearty
wish to give the best they can.   But, having decided with
whom you think it most desirable to trade, do not feel
that you can lay on them the responsibility of selecting
the articles you need.   Accept gratefully such hints as
may be given, and which may be valuable, because of the
vender's larger experience; but every housekeeper should
know how to choose the best and most economical articles
herself, and to feel so certain of the correctness of her
judgment as to decide for herself.   We are sorry to say
that very few modern housekeepers do understand how
to select wisely, or how to buy economically, particularly
when buying meats, poultry, fish, etc.

It is not a difficult thing to secure such knowledge as
will make imposition almost impossible.   Careful obser-
vation, knowledge of certain rules to be observed in
selections, with some experience secured before marriage,

should enable any one to buy economically, as well as correctly.

Talking impatiently to and scolding those with whom one trades, aside from being unlady-like, is very poor policy. If not satisfactorily served, or if mistakes occur, seek an explanation at once. Name the grievance quietly, but so clearly that there can be no misunderstanding. Listen calmly to whatever excuse may be given, and, if possible, have it rectified. Firmness and gentleness can work together, and with more lasting effects than irritability and scolding. If the same mistakes occur a second time, probably it is from ignorance, or inability to supply the demand; and this being so, it will be advisable to transfer your custom elsewhere. But this can be done without argument or severity. Tradesmen who do a large business usually furnish articles of the best quality; and, as a general rule, they are not likely to charge exorbitantly. Their own interest, if no higher motive, will prompt them to supply their customers with the best, and at the most moderate rates.

There is no economy in buying an inferior article. Get the best, and let the economy be shown in the way it is used. Let no part that is suitable for use be wasted. What is left from the first serving of a piece of meat can be made into soups, hashes, *ragouts*, or croquettes, and be a most acceptable addition to the bill of fare.

This is not exactly the place to furnish rules for selecting the different articles needed in the household; but it may not be amiss to mention concisely some few points to be remembered when marketing, particularly in purchasing meat, fish, etc., although almost all books on domestic affairs are full of such directions. The "line upon line, and precept upon precept " principle is nowhere more needed, or more effective, than in domestic economy.

In choosing fish, of every variety, bear in mind that if they are perfectly rigid, and the eyes bright, there is no fear of their being stale. Fish that live chiefly or altogether on the surface of the water will keep but a very short time. They die almost as soon as they are taken; and the change is so sudden that they lose their best flavor in a very few hours. Mackerel and herring are of this class. The fish that lie near the bottom of the water, like the *cod*, can be kept alive longer after being taken from the water, and their flesh keeps fresh longer than those first mentioned. Some think the flesh better if kept a day or two. Crabs, lobsters, etc., are worthless if they are light and watery. When they feel solid and heavy, they are good. One will soon learn to judge of them by comparing the weight. If oysters are in the least degree open, discard them; they are always good when the shell is tightly closed. Ox beef is the best. The animal should be five or six years old. If well fed, the flesh will be fine-grained, of a bright red color, with plenty of yellow fat running through it, and sufficiently elastic to rise up quickly when pressed by the fingers. If this is not so, it will be tough and of poor flavor. Cow or heifer beef is paler than ox beef, the fat a clear white, firmer grained, and the bones smaller; but it is not so rich or juicy. Veal should be small and white, the kidneys well covered with fat, and the flesh dry. If coarse-grained, moist and clammy, have nothing to do with it. Mutton must be dark color and fat; the color determines the age, and age is the mark of excellence. Five or six years is the age that epicures demand in mutton. Lamb, small, pale red, and fat. If fresh killed,

the veins in the neck will be *bluish ;* if stale, *greenish.*
Never buy pork except from a butcher whose honesty is
undoubted, and who knows where the animal was fattened.
When good, the skin will be thin and smooth. Reject it
if the flesh be flabby or clammy to the touch; and if there
are kernels in the fat, it will be dangerous food. As soon
as meat is brought in from the butcher's, wipe it dry with
a clean cloth. Common fowls will be plump on the
breast and fat on the back if good; when young, the legs
and combs are smooth. Turkeys, when fresh killed, will
have clear, full eyes and moist feet. In old birds the legs
are rough and reddish; in the young, smooth and black.
When geese are old, the bills and feet are red; when
young, yellow. If fresh killed, the feet will be pliable;
if too long kept, they will be stiff. Ducks and pigeons,
when in good condition and fresh, will have plump breasts
and pliable feet.

These are simply general directions, but quite necessary
if one would be an expert in marketing. Without some
guide, by which to judge of the quality and value of
articles needed in the home department, and especially
of the food, on which so much of health and comfort for
the family depends, the most experienced would often
find their duties very trying; but for those just entering
the field, and too poorly fitted for the work before them,
there must be something definite and reliable, to assist
while learning the way.

SERVANTS.

There is, in this country, a foolish prejudice against the
term "Servant." Why? What is the true meaning of
the word? A slave? No. An inferior? Not necessa-
rily. The definiton is very simple : "One who serves or
labors for another." What is there, degrading in that?
Every one is, or should be, laboring for or serving others.
That there are different degrees of servitude, no one will
deny. The rank or position of each one who serves must
depend largely on the ability of the servitor, and the quality or character of the work he offers to his employer.
The President is the "servant" of the people ; the lawyer, of his client; the physician, of his patient ; the cler-
gyman, of his church and congregation; the mechanic,
of those needing his special services ; the laboring man,
of the farmer; and the cook, of the mistress of the
house. Each receives compensation in accordance with
the importance of the services rendered, and the terms
mutually agreed on.

This is true in every profession, in all business, from the
highest to the lowest. In every department there are certain stipulations to be accepted before service is rendered,
and each party, employer, as well as employee, is bound to
fullfil his part of the contract—the lawyer who demands and
receives his fifty thousand dollar fee, as much as the cook in
the kitchen, who has such wages as she herself demands;

not such as her mistress may be pleased to give. One is just as much the servant of the employer as the other, differing in degree and honors, according to the market value of the skill or talent they are able to bring to the market, and in nowise controlled by the caprice of the employer.

If this is a correct rendering of the term "servant," we fail to see any degradation in it. It is a more convenient, and, to our thinking, a more respectable term, than "Domestic" or "Help." It may have just as much honor in it as those to whom it is applied please to secure for it by their own acts; and with this explanation of our rendering of that word, we propose to say

A FEW THINGS ABOUT "SERVANTS."

The best way to select, and the surest way to secure, honest and faithful servants, is a matter which has always perplexed housekeepers, and seems to be a growing trouble. It must be remembered, however, that poor work is as often the fault of the mistress as of the maid. It is more common, of late years, than formerly, for young people to assume the cares and responsibilities of a home, when totally incompetent to superintend and secure the correct performance of domestic duties, and still less prepared to perform these duties themselves. To increase the perplexities of this class, they are met by like inefficiency on the part of many of those whom they employ. To mothers, chiefly, we must look for a more perfect system by which to secure more efficient service. If mothers could be made to see the importance of training their daughters to be conscientious, systematic housekeepers, as well as to excel in the less practical parts of an education, full one-half of our troubles would be mastered. This would

4

be more effective in training good servants than anything which could be devised. Let our daughters be taught that, as none are " fit to command until they have learned how to obey," so none are prepared to assume the care of a household or charge of servants until they are able, not only to arrange the work, and superintend its performance, but also able themselves to do all they would delegate to others.

In cases where several servants are employed, each one should have her appropriate work assigned, but with the full understanding that, if needed, she is to be called upon for work outside that which she considers her own. For this reason it is desirable that each one should have been early taught to be at home in all parts of household labor. No judicious housekeeper will be inclined to call a girl from her own regular work, unless there be real necessity for so doing. She will or should study the comfort of her servants, and exact from them no extra labor but such as under pressing circumstances they will see she is herself willing and capable of doing. If the mistress of the house shows herself ignorant of any of the duties belonging thereto, she has no reason to look for or expect satisfactory service from those in her employ. A firm, but kind, government, judicious rules, requiring implicit obedience, give larger promise of faithful and prompt work, and far more respectful service than an ignorant but exacting housekeeper can ever expect to find. While demanding prompt attention to the work to be done, those employed should receive such kindness and watchful care for their interest and comfort as employers would wish their children to have if similarly situated. Make their rooms as pleasant and comfortable as is possible. If the arrangements of the house will permit, see that those who have the hot and dirty work to do have the means for daily or frequent baths, which is as much for the employer's comfort as for theirs. Ample time should be allowed them for keeping their clothes in order. These things should be urged upon them for their own sakes; but if not attended to, should be required for the sake of their employers, and to secure the comfort of the family.

In making a contract with a girl for any position in the family, the mistress of the house should very carefully explain the rules by which she regulates the time and labors of those she employs, stating definitely in what part of the Sabbath each girl can go to church, or if they go on alternate Sundays, as must often be the case in large families. Then define exactly what privileges each may expect — how often they can visit their friends, and how late they may remain out. Give every privilege that can be allowed consistently with the duties to be performed, and for the girl's own best interests. These rules having been so distinctly stated that there can be no misapprehension, let it be as clearly understood that from these rules and regulations there can be allowed no deviation, except with the knowledge and consent of the mistress. One afternoon and evening of leisure each week is all the time that can be spared conveniently from household duties, and as much as the servant can have, and attend faithfully to her own sewing and keep her clothes in repair. All the other evenings, after the ordinary work is over, will be needed for this important attention to her own garments. Except in extreme cases, such leisure evenings as they can command should be scrupulously reserved for their social enjoyment and their personal affairs. To allow them more time would lead to idle habits, which those who must labor for their living can ill afford; while to give them less time would be unjust.

When two, three, or more girls are needed in one house, the question of how much company they can be allowed at the house is important. If one girl has the privilege of allowing her friends to call when they choose, the others will expect the same privilege, and justly. This will cause confusion and disorder in their regular duties. We think it should be settled, that visits cannot be permitted till after the day's important work is over, and that by ten o'clock visitors must leave, the kitchen and range . be put in order, and the girls all in and ready to retire to their needed· rest. Nor should a kitchen full of visitors be allowed at any time, nor the dining room be used for their guests. Their friends can easily be made to under- ' stand this. The kitchen ought to be in order before friends begin their calls, and the dining room carefully arranged for the morning's meal, the windows fastened and the doors closed. We do not approve the policy which permits the many visitors that naturally call where there are two or three girls, to be invited or expected to take their meals with them. On the contrary, it should be distinctly forbidden. If one feels at liberty to ask her friends to stop to meals, the others have good grounds for expecting the same privilege. If they may ask one, they must ask others, or act with great partiality. At first sight it seems mean and miserly to refuse this privilege to servants, but it is easy to see to what it leads. A room full every night. Simply in view of the expense of this kind of hospitality, it is a matter of grave consideration. It is also a bad custom — a real injury — for the employees, as well as the employer. We have been through a long experience of this kind of open hospitality, and confess

We did not find it either pleasant or profitable. It is bad every way, and no kindness to the servant. In all that increases the real comfort of those who labor, or tends to make them better and wiser, every housekeeper is bound to be as generous and thoughtful as circumstances will permit.

In engaging help, be slow to decide. Seek all the information possible. Be sure of substantial, reliable credentials, as to their worth and honesty; then, this once settled, let them see that it is the wish of their employer to trust them. Locking up closets where the food is, or putting aside the best part of the food from the first table, is a good recipe for making crafty, dishonest servants. If treated with kindness, courtesy and uniform gentleness, there are not many so rude and so low as not to be more faithful for these tokens of interest in their welfare. We recognize, to the fullest extent, the doubtful, unsatisfactory materials all housekeepers are exposed to have on their hands, if they are compelled to depend in any degree on "hired help." But the treatment which we have here recommended is, we believe, the surest way to transform them into useful, competent and honest friends.

THE KITCHEN.

Few things tend so much to peace and comfort, making all laboring for the family contented and comfortable, as a bright, pleasant, well furnished kitchen. In no other room in the house are sunlight and fresh, pure air so indispensable as in the room where some of the most important work must be done. We have not the least desire to be thought superior, as a general thing; but in building a house, no man, be he architect, brother, son, or husband, should have the control of planning the kitchen, store closets, or laundry. They are influenced in the construction by considerations for the beauty or artistic appearance of the house, as a whole, with little thought and no practical knowledge of what will make work easy and servants happy, or what will most conduce to the neatness of their work or the promptness of its execution. But a woman who understands what it is to ao the work, or arrange for others to do it, naturally realizes, as a man cannot, that in building a kitchen, whenever beauty, in the artist's sense of the word, and utility are not compatible, utility must be the major, and beauty the minor, consideration.

A long, narrow, dark kitchen is an abomination. In some city houses we suppose it cannot be avoided; at least so the architect will affirm. Ranges or cook stoves should not be placed opposite a door or window. A good ventilation is important over the range or cook stove, by which the steam and disagreeable odors from cooking can be carried off without pervading the house. Three large windows are always desirable, and for a very large kitchen four would be better. If the architect refuses so many, endeavor to compromise by having the outside door half glass. If possible, arrange to have the windows wide, with large panes of glass, and reaching down to the floor, so as to give more light. A sink should be on the left hand side of the range, and as near a window as possible, to secure good light. Porcelain washtubs are one of the last improvements, and if the inventor will now arrange for a porcelain sink, with the proper fixtures, it will be an improvement; but until that is done, marble or soapstone is the next best — far better than wood or iron. A large soapstone or marble bowl, for washing dishes, set perma-

nently at the left hand corner of the sink, with a very
fine drainer at the bottom, connected with the waste pipe
beneath the sink, is a greater convenience than any can
realize until they have tried it ; also, a marble or soapstone
drainer, with grooves, for rinsing and draining dishes.
It should be fixed to the table connected with the sink,
and set a little inclined, so that the water shall drain into
the sink. A moulding about an inch high will be needed
around the edges of the drainer, to prevent the rinsing
water from flowing over on the floor, and also to keep the
dishes from sliding off. With a sink thus furnished, no
dish pans are needed, except to wash pots and kettles.
It is a simple thing, but very useful, because it compels
the one washing to put her dishes into this drainer one
by one, as she washes them.

There are many more items connected with the kitchen
which we would like to notice, did space permit, as the
table adjoining the sink for washing game and vegetables,
the small drawers underneath, for scouring and polishing
material, and various little conveniences.

UTENSILS

WOODEN WARE.

Kitchen Table; Wash Bench; Wash Tubs, (three sizes); Wash Board; Skirt Board; Bosom Board; Bread Board; Towel Roll; Potatoe Masher; Wooden Spoons; Clothes Stick; Flour Barrel Cover; Flour Sieve; Chopping Bowl; Soap Bowl; Pails; Lemon Squeezer; Clothes Wringer; Clothes Bars; Clothes Pins; Clothes Baskets; Mop; Wood Boxes, (nests).

TIN WARE.

One Boiler for Clothes; one Boiler for Ham; one Bread Pan; two Dish Pans; one Preserving Pan; four Milk Pans; two Quart Basins; two Pint Basins; two quart covered Tin Pails; one four-quart covered Tin Pail; Sauce Pans with covers, two sizes; two Tin Cups with handles; four Jelly Moulds, (half-pint); two Pint Moulds for rice, blanc-mange, etc.; one Skimmer; two Dippers, different sizes; two Funnels, (one for jug and one for cruets); one quart measure, also, pint, half-pint and gill measures, (they should be broad and low as they are more easily kept clean); three Scoops; Bread Pans; two round

Jelly Cake Pans, and two long Pie Pans ; One Coffee Pot ; one Tea Steeper; one Colander ; one Steamer; one Horse Radish Grater ; one Nutmeg Grater ; one small Salt Sieve; one Hair Sieve for straining jelly; one Dover's Egg Beater ; One Cake Turner; one Cake Cutter; one Apple Corer ; one Potato Cutter ; one dozen Muffin Rings ; one Soap Shaker ; Ice Filter; Flour Dredge; Tea Canister; Coffee Canister ; Cake, Bread, Cracker, and Cheese Boxes; Crumb Tray; Dust Pans.

IRON WARE.

Range ; one Pot with steamer to fit; one Soup Kettle; Preserving Kettle (porcelain) ; Tea Kettle ; large and small Frying Pans; Dripping Pans; Gem Pans; Iron Spoons of different sizes ; one Gridiron ; one Griddle; one Waffle Iron; Toasting Rack; Meat Fork; Jagging Iron; Can Opener; Coffee Mill; Flat Irons; Hammer; Tack Hammer; Screw Driver; Ice Pick.

STONE WARE.

Crocks of various sizes; Bowls holding six quarts, four quarts, two quarts, and pint bowls; six Earthen Baking Dishes, different sizes.

BRUSHES.

Table Brush; two Dust Brushes; two Scrub Brushes; one Blacking Brush for stove; Shoe Brush; Hearth Brush; Brooms.

SOUPS.

" No useless dish our table crowds ;
Harmoniously ranged and consonantly just,
As in a concert instruments resound,
Our ordered dishes in their courses chime."

The basis of all good soups, is the broth of meat. This may be made by boiling the cracked joints of beef, veal or mutton, and is best when cooked the day before it is to be eaten. After putting the meat into the pot, cover it well with cold water and let it come to a boil, when it should be well skimmed. Set the pot where it will simmer slowly until it is thoroughly done, keeping the pot closely covered the while. The next day, when the soup is cold, remove the fat, which will harden on the top of the soup. After this, add the vegetables and the herbs you use for seasoning, cooking all well together. Before sending to the table, the soup should be strained. A good stock for soups may be made from shreds and bits of un-cooked meat and bones, poultry and the remains of game. When these are all put together and stewed down in the pot, the French term it *consomme*, and use it chiefly in the preparation of brown soups.

Soups may be varied in many ways, chiefly in the kinds of vegetables and different seasonings used, — as in herbs, burned caramel, eggs or slices of bread fried to a crisp in butter, which impart a savory relish.

BEEF SOUP.

Mrs. Wm. H. Low.

Cut all the lean off the shank, and with a little beef suet in the bottom of the kettle, fry it to a nice brown; put in the bones and cover with water; cover the kettle closely; let it cook slowly until the meat drops from the bones; strain through a colander and leave it in the dish during the night, which is the only way to get off all the fat. The day it is wanted for the table, fry as brown as possible a carrot, an onion and a very small turnip sliced thin. Just before taking up, put in half a teaspoonful of sugar, a blade of mace, six cloves, a dozen kernels of allspice, a small teaspoonful of celery seed. With the vegetables this must cook slowly in the soup an hour; then strain again for the table. If you use vermicelli or pear barley, soak in water.

JULIENNE SOUP.

M. A. T.

Shred two onions and fry brown in a half spoon of butter; add a little mace, salt and pepper; then a spoonful or so of stock; rub a tablespoonful of flour smooth with a little butter and let fry with the onions; strain through a colander, then add more stock as desired; cut turnip, carrot and celery in fillets; add a few green peas; boil tender in a little water and add both water and vegetables to the soup. If wished, the flour can be left out, and it will make a clear, light-colored soup.   In that case, the onions should be cut in fillets and boiled with the vegetables.

MUTTON SOUP.
Mrs. Whitehead.

Boil a leg of mutton three hours; season to your taste with salt and pepper, and add one teaspoon of summer savory; make a batter of one egg, two tablespoons of milk, two tablespoons of flour, all well beaten together; drop this batter into the soup with a spoon and boil for three minutes.

VEAL SOUP.

To about three pounds of a joint of veal, which must be well broken up, put four quarts of water and set it over to boil.   Prepare one-fourth pound of maccaroni by boiling it by itself, with sufficient water to cover it; add a little butter to the maccaroni when it is tender; strain the soup and season to taste with salt and pepper; then add the maccaroni in the water in which it is boiled. The addition of a pint of rich milk or cream and celery flavor is relished by many.

SWISS WHITE SOUP.
Anonymous.

Stock for six persons.   Beat up three eggs, two spoons of flour and one cup of milk, pour this slowly through a sieve into the boiling soup, adding salt and pepper.

TURKEY SOUP.
Anonymous.

Take the turkey bones and cook for one hour in water

enough to cover them; then stir in a little dressing and a beaten egg. Take from the fire and when the water has ceased boiling, add a little butter with pepper and salt.

OYSTER SOUP.

M. A. T.

Take one quart of water; one teacup of butter; one pint of milk; two teaspoons of salt; four crackers rolled fine, and one teaspoon of pepper; bring to full boiling heat as soon as possible, then add one quart of oysters; let the whole come to boiling heat quickly and remove from the fire.

OYSTER SOUP.

Mrs. T. V. Wadskier.

Pour one quart of boiling water into a skillet; then one quart of good rich milk; stir in one teacup of rolled cracker crumbs; seasoned with pepper and salt to taste. When all come to a boil, add one quart of good fresh oysters; stir well, so as to keep from scorching; then add a piece of good sweet butter, about the size of an egg; let it boil up once; then remove from the fire immediately; dish up and send to table.

CLAM SOUP.

Mrs. A. A. Carpenter.

Cut salt pork in very small squares and fry light brown; add one large or two small onions cut very fine and cook about ten minutes; add two quarts of water and one quart of raw potatoes sliced; let it boil. Then add one can of clams. Mix one tablespoonful of flour with water, put it with one pint of milk and pour into the soup and let it boil about five minutes. Butter, pepper, salt, Worcestershire sauce to taste.

LOBSTER SOUP.
Mrs. Robert Harris.

One large lobster or two small ones; pick all the meat from the shell and chop fine ; scald one quart of milk and one pint of water; then add the lobster, one pound of butter, a tablespoonful of flour, and salt and red pepper to taste. Boil ten minutes and serve hot.

PLAIN CALF'S HEAD SOUP.
Mrs. F. D. J.

Take a calf's head well cleaned, a knuckle of veal and put them both into a large kettle; put one onion and a large tablespoon of sweet herbs, into a cloth and into the kettle, with the meat over which you have poured about four quarts of water. If you wish the soup for a one o'clock dinner, put the meat over to boil as early as eight o'clock in the morning; let it boil steadily and slowly and season well with salt and pepper. About one hour before serving, take off the soup and pour it through a colander, pick out all the meat carefully, chop very fine and return to the soup, putting it again over the fire. Boil four eggs very hard, chop them fine, and slice one lemon very thin, adding at the very last.

VERMICELLI SOUP.
Anonymous.

A knuckle of lamb, a small piece of veal and water to

cover well; when well cooked, season with salt, pepper, herbs to your taste, and a small onion, to which you may add Halford or Worcestershire sauce, about a tablespoonful. Have ready one-quarter of a pound of vermicelli, which has been boiled tender; strain your soup from the meat, add the vermicelli, let it boil well and serve.

GUMBO SOUP.

Anonymous.

Put on half a peck of tomatoes in a porcelain kettle and let them stew; have half a peck of ochra cut in fine shreds; put them with thyme, parsley and an onion cut fine, into the tomatoes and let them cook until quite tender. Fricassee one chicken in ham gravy; then take the yolk of four eggs, a little vinegar, the juice of one lemon, and season to taste, beating the eggs into the vinegar; pour this over the chicken, and put all then into the tomatoes, letting the kettle be nearly filled with water. Boil all together four or five hours.

OCHRA GUMBO.

Mrs. Andrews.

Two quarts of ripe tomatoes and one quart of ochra cut in small rings; put them over the fire with about three quarts of water and let the mixture come to a boil; take one chicken; cut it up and fry brown, with plenty of gravy; put it in with the ochra and tomatoes; add several small onions chopped fine; salt and pepper to taste; a little corn and Lima beans are an improvement, if you have them. Let all simmer gently together for several hours. To be served with a tablespoonful of boiled rice and green garden pepper cut fine to each soup plate.

MOCK TURTLE SOUP.
Mrs. C. H. Wheeler.

One soup-bone, one quart of turtle beans, one large spoonful of powdered cloves, salt and pepper. Soak the beans over night, put them on with the soup-bone in nearly six quarts of water and cook five or six hours. When half done, add the cloves, salt and pepper; when done, strain through a colander, pressing the pulp of the beans through to make the soup the desired thickness, and serve with a few slices of hard-boiled egg and lemon sliced very thin. The turtle beans are black and can only be obtained from large grocers.

TOMATO SOUP.
Mrs. Whitehead.

Boil chicken or beef four hours; then strain; add to the soup one can of tomatoes and boil one hour. This. will make four quarts of soup.

TOMATO SOUP.
Mrs. Wheelock.

One pint tomatoes, two quarts water, one tablespoonful corn starch, beef bone, or cold steak.

TOMATO SOUP WITHOUT MEAT.
C. O. Van Cline, East Minneapolis.

One quart of tomatoes, one quart of water, one quart

of milk. Butter, salt and pepper to taste. Cook the tomatoes thoroughly in the water, have the milk scalding, (over water to prevent scorching.) When the tomatoes are done add a large teaspoonful of salaratus, which will cause a violent effervescence. It is best to set the vessel in a pan before adding it to prevent waste. When the commotion has ceased add the milk and seasoning. When it is possible it is best to use more milk than water, and cream instead of butter. The soup is eaten with crackers and is by some preferred to oyster soup. This recipe is very valuable for those who keep abstinence days.

TOMATO SOUP.
Mrs. B. J. Seward.

To one pint tomatoes canned, or four large raw ones, cut up fine, add one quart boiling water and let them boil. Then add one teaspoon of soda, when it will foam; immediately add one pint of sweet milk, with salt, pepper and plenty of butter. When this boils add eight small crackers rolled fine, and serve. Equal to oyster soup.

TOMATO SOUP.
Mrs. J. Hudson.

One quart of tomatoes, one soup-bone, one onion, one cucumber sliced, two ears of grated corn, salt, pepper and a trifle of cayenne pepper. Boil four hours, then add one tablespoon of corn starch dissolved in cold water; strain before serving.

TOMATO SOUP.
Mrs. G. W. Brayton.

For one gallon of soup, take two and a half quarts good

5

beef stock, one medium sized carrot, one turnip, one beet and two onions peeled and cut in pieces; boil the vegetables in the beef stock three-quarters of an hour; strain through a sieve; add a two quart can of tomatoes and boil fifteen minutes; strain again and add salt and pepper. While this is cooking, take a sauce-pan that will hold about six quarts and put in a quarter of a pound of butter and heat it to a light brown; add while hot three tablespoons of flour; take from the fire and mix thoroughly; add one dessert spoon of sugar and stir until it boils; boil fifteen minutes and strain.

TOMATO SOUP.

Mrs. L. H. Smith.

Make one gallon beef stock. Take half peck ripe tomatoes, cut in halves, two carrots, two onions, one turnip cut fine; boil all together for one hour and a half, then strain all through a fine sieve; take a sauce-pan large enough to hold it and put it on the fire with half pound of butter; heat it until of a light brown color, and add two spoons of flour, mixing well together; add to this two spoons of white sugar, salt and pepper to suit taste; stir well until it boils; let it boil and skim it for five minutes, and serve very hot. This recipe serves a large family; usually prepare two quarts of beef stock for a small family, using half the quantity of ingredients.

ASPARAGUS SOUP.

Mrs. D.

Three or four pounds of veal cut fine, a little salt pork,

two or three bunches of asparagus and three quarts of water. Boil one-half of the asparagus with the meat, leaving the rest in water until about twenty minutes before serving; then add the rest of the asparagus and boil just before serving; add one pint of milk; thicken with a little flour and season. The soup should boil about three hours before adding the last half of the asparagus.

GREEN PEA SOUP.

Anonymous.

Four pounds of lean beef cut in small pieces, one-half peck of green peas, one gallon of water; boil the empty pods of the peas in the water one hour; strain them out; add the beef and boil slowly one and a half hours. Half an hour before serving strain out the meat and add the peas; twenty minutes later add one-half cup of rice flour; salt and pepper to taste; and if you choose, one teaspoon of sugar. After adding the rice, stir frequently to prevent burning.

CORN SOUP.

Mrs. W. P. Nixon.

One small beef bone, two quarts of water, four tomatoes, eight ears of corn; let the meat boil a short time in the water; cut the corn from the cob and put in the cobs with the cut corn and tomatoes; let it boil about half an hour; remove the cobs; just before serving add milk, which allow to boil for a few moments only; season with salt and pepper.

CORN SOUP.

Anonymous.

One quart of corn cut from the cob in three pints of water; when the grain is quite tender, mix with them two ounces of sweet butter rolled in a tablespoon of flour; let it boil fifteen minutes longer; just before taking up the soup, beat up an egg and stir in with pepper and salt.

TURTLE BEAN SOUP.

Mrs. A. N. Arnold.

Take a quart of black beans, wash them and put them in a pot with three quarts of water; boil until-thoroughly soft; rub the pulp through a colander and return it to the pot; add some thyme in a clean cloth, and let it boil a few minutes for flavor; slice some hard boiled eggs and drop them into the soup.; add a little butter, pepper and salt.

BEAN SOUP.

Mrs. Whitehead.

One pint beans, four quarts water, small piece fat beef; boil three hours and strain. If too thin add one tablespoon flour.

BLACK BEAN SOUP.

Mrs. John B. Adams.

Boil the beans and strain them; at the same time make your stock (of any kind of meat,) saving the best for force meat balls; to be well seasoned and fried. Put the bean pulp in with the stock and boil; add red pepper, salt and a little thyme, tying it up in a bag to be taken out; cloves to your taste and a little wine. When ready to serve, put the fried balls into the tureen, with two or three sliced hard boiled eggs, and a lemon or two, according to the quantity of soup. Skim out bones and pieces of meat and pour over.

BLACK BEAN SOUP.
Mrs. H. L. Adams.

One pound of the round beef, one-half pound of salt pôrk, and one quart of black beans; soak the beans twenty-four hours; chop the beef and pork and boil with the beans, one grated carrot and one onion five or six hours; strain and add hard boiled eggs, salt, pepper and sliced lemon.

POTATO SOUP.
M. A. T.

Boil five or six potatoes with a small piece of salt pork and a little celery; pass through a colander and add milk or cream (if milk, a little butter,) to make the consistency of thick cream; chop a little parsley fine and throw in; let boil five minutes; cut some dry bread in small dice, fry brown in hot lard; drain them and place in the bottom of soup tureen, and pour the soup over; chop two onions and boil with the soup, if liked.

FORCE MEAT BALLS FOR BLACK BEAN SOUP.
Mrs. Baushar.

Take cold meat; chop very fine; add flour enough to

make it stick together in balls about the size of a walnut; roll in flour and fry until brown, and add to the
soup just before it is served.

FORCE MEAT BALLS.

Mrs. James S. Gibbs.

Mix with one pound of chopped veal or other meat,
one egg, a little butter or raw pork chopped fine, one cup
or less of bread crumbs; the whole well moistened with
warm water, or what is better, the water from stewed
meat; season with salt and pepper; make in small balls
and fry them brown.

EGG BALLS FOR SOUP.

M. A. T.

Boil four eggs; put into cold water; mash yolks with
yolk of one raw egg, and one teaspoon of flour; pepper,
salt and parsley; make into balls and boil two minutes.

NOODLES FOR SOUP.

Mrs. F. D. J.

Rub into two eggs as much sifted flour as they will
absorb; then roll out until thin as a wafer; dust over a
little flour, and then roll over and over into a roll; cut
off thin slices from the edge of the roll and shake out
into long strips; put them into the soup lightly and boil
for ten minutes; salt should be added while mixing with
the flour—about a saltspoonful.

CARAMEL, OR BURNED SUGAR.

Put two ounces of brown or white sugar in an old tin cup over a brisk fire, stir this until it is quite dark and gives forth a burned smell, then add a half a cup of cold water; let it boil gently a few minutes, stirring well and all the while. Take off, and when cold bottle for use. This keeps well, and may be used for flavoring gravies and soups.

CROUTONS.

These are simply pieces of bread fried brown and crisp to be used in soups.

FISH.

" The silvery fish,
Grazing at large in meadows submarine,
Fresh from the wave now cheers
Our festive board."
— ANON.

Fish are good, when the gills are red, eyes are full, and the body of the fish is firm and stiff. After washing them well, they should be allowed to remain for a short time in salt water sufficient to cover them; before cooking, wipe them dry, dredge lightly with flour, and season with salt and pepper. Salmon trout and other small fish are usually fried or broiled; all large fish should be put in a cloth, tied closely with twine, and placed in cold water, when they may be put over the fire to boil. When fish are baked, prepare the fish the same as for boiling, and put in the oven on a wire gridiron, over a dripping pan.

TO BOIL FISH.

Mrs. C. G. Smith.

Put a small onion inside your fish and tie it up in a towel, cover it with cold water, salt and a little vinegar, and let it heat to the boiling point; from two to three minutes' boiling is sufficient for the largest fish, and a small one will not require more than one minute. Fish boiled in this way is incomparably better than when cooked longer.

A SUGGESTION.— Boiling salt water is best for salmon, as it sets the color.— M. A. T.

BOILED WHITE FISH.

Mrs. Andrews.

Lay the fish open ; put it in a dripping pan, with the back down ; nearly cover with water; to one fish put two tablespoons salt ; cover tightly and simmer (not boil) one-half hour; dress with gravy, butter and pepper; garnish with sliced eggs.

For sauce use a piece of butter the size of an egg, one tablespoon of flour, one-half pint boiling water; boil a few minutes, and add three hard boiled eggs, sliced.

FISH A LA CREME.

Mrs. J. A. Ellis.

Take any firm salt water fish, rub it with salt and put it in a kettle with enough boiling water to cover it. As soon as it boils set it back where it will simmer, let it stand for an hour, then take it up and draw out all the bones. Put one ounce of flour into a sauce-pan, to which add by degrees one quart of cream or new milk, mixing it very smoothly, then add the juice of one lemon, one onion chopped fine, a bunch of parsley, a little nutmeg, salt and pepper. Put this on the fire, stirring it till it forms a thick sauce; stir in a quarter of a pound of butter; strain the sauce through a sieve. Put a little on a dish, then lay the fish on it and turn the remainder of the sauce over it. Beat to a froth the whites of six eggs, spread over the whole, and bake half an hour a light brown.

TURBOT A LA CREME.

Mrs. A. Keith.

Boil a large white fish; pick it up fine, taking out the bones; make a sauce of a quart of milk, a little thyme, a few sprigs of parsley, a little onion; simmer together till well flavored; wet two ounces of flour and stir in with a quarter of a pound of butter; stir until it thickens; then strain it on the yolks of two eggs; season with pepper and salt. Put some of the sauce in a pudding dish, then a layer of fish and so on until the dish is full, putting sauce on top; cover with rolled crackers and a little grated cheese, if to the taste; brown in the oven.

CODFISH A LA CREME.

Mrs. Baushar.

Take four pounds of codfish, let it come to a scald, pick it in pieces; four tablespoons Worcestershire sauce, two tablespoons anchovy sauce, one-fourth pound butter, one-half pint cream; boil one-half dozen large potatoes, mash them; put in the pudding dish, (except the potatoes,) then cover with the potatoes; bake fifteen or twenty minutes, or till nicely browned.

SAUCE FOR BOILED FISH.

To one teacup of milk, add one teacup of water; put it on the fire to scald, and when hot stir in a tablespoon of flour, previously wet with cold water; add two or three eggs; season with salt and pepper, a little celery, vinegar and three tablespoons of butter. Boil four or five eggs hard, take off the shells, and cut in slices, and lay over the dish. Then pour over the sauce and serve.

BAKED HALIBUT OR SALMON.

Let the fish remain in cold water, slightly salted, for an hour before it is time to cook it; place the gridiron on a dripping pan with a little hot water in it and bake in a hot oven; just before it is done, butter it well on the top, and brown it nicely. The time of baking depends upon the size of the fish. A small fish will bake in about half an hour, and a large one in an hour. They are very nice when cooked as above and served with a sauce which is made from the gravy in the dripping pan, to which is added a tablespoon of catsup and another of some pungent sauce and the juice of a lemon. Thicken with brown flour moistened with a little cold water. Garnish handsomely with sprigs of parsley and current jelly.

BAKED BLACK BASS.

Mrs. P. B. Ayer.

Eight good sized onions chopped fine; half that quantity of bread crumbs; butter size of hen's egg; plenty of pepper and salt, mix thoroughly with anchovy sauce until quite red. Stuff your fish with this compound and pour the rest over it, previously sprinkling it with a little red pepper. Shad, pickerel and trout are good the same way. Tomatoes can be used instead of anchovies, and are more economical. If using them, take pork in place of butter and chop fine.

BROILED WHITE FISH — FRESH.

Mrs. G. E. P.

Wash and drain the fish; sprinkle with pepper and lay with the inside down upon the gridiron, and broil over fresh bright coals. When a nice brown, turn for a moment on the other side, then take up and spread with butter. This is a very nice way of broiling all kinds of fish, fresh or salted. A little smoke under the fish adds to its flavor. This may be made by putting two or three cobs under the gridiron.

SALT MACKEREL.

Mrs. F. D. J.

Soak the fish for a few hours in lukewarm water, changing the water several times; then put into cold water loosely tied in cloths, and let the fish come to a boil, turning off the water once, and pouring over the fish hot water from the tea kettle; let this just come to a boil, then take them out and drain them, lay them on a platter, butter and pepper them, and place them for a few moments in the oven. Serve with sliced lemons, or with any nice fish sauce.

BOILED CODFISH—SALT.

Soak two pounds of codfish in lukewarm water over night or for several hours; change the water several times; about one hour before dinner put this into cold-fresh water, and set over the fire; let it come to a boil, or just simmer, for fifteen minutes but not to boil hard, then take out of the water, drain and serve with egg sauce, or with cold boiled eggs sliced and laid over it, with a drawn butter or cream gravy poured over all.

CROQUETTES OF FISH.

Take dressed fish of any kind; separate from the bone, mince it with a little seasoning, an egg beaten with a teaspoon of flour and one of milk; roll into balls, brush the outside with egg and dredge well with bread and cracker crumbs, and fry them of a nice color. The bones, head, tail, an onion, an anchovy and a pint of water will make the gravy.

EELS.

Mrs. P. B. Ayer.

Skin and parboil them; cleanse the back bone of all coagulations; cut them in pieces about three inches in length; dip in flour and cook in pork fat, brown.

TONGUES AND SOUNDS.

Mrs. P. B. Ayer.

Soak them thirty-six hours in cold water; scrape them thoroughly and boil tender; fry them brown or eat with butter and egg sauce.

CHOWDER.

Mrs. P. B. Ayer.

Five pounds of codfish cut in squares; fry plenty of

salt pork cut in thin slices; put a layer of pork in your kettle, then one of fish; one of potatoes in thick slices, and one of onions in slices; plenty of pepper and salt; repeat as long as your materials last, and finish with a layer of Boston crackers or crusts of bread. Water sufficient to cook with, or milk if you prefer. Cook one-half hour and turn over on your platter, disturbing as little as possible. Clams and eels the same way.

FISH CHOWDER.

Mrs. R. A. Sibley.

Four pounds of fresh fish skinned and cut in pieces; put in a pot some of the fish, then some crackers and sliced potatoes, salt and pepper; another layer of fish, crackers and potatoes; cover the whole with water; add a little onion, if liked, and some fried pork or butter; boil until the potatoes are done, then add a quart of milk and let it boil. When dishing for the table, take out all the large bones. Codfish or haddocks are the best; other fish will answer; use the head.

POTTED FISH.

Mrs. Gridley, Evanston.

Take out the backbone of the fish; for one weighing two pounds take a tablespoon of allspice and cloves mixed; these spices should be put into little bags of not too thick muslin; put sufficient salt directly upon each fish; then roll in a cloth, over which sprinkle a little cayenne pepper; put alternate layers of fish, spice and sago in an earthern jar; cover with the best cider vinegar;

cover the jar closely with a plate and over this put a covering of dough, rolled out to twice the thickness of pie crust. Make the edges of paste, to adhere closely to the sides of the jar, so as to make it air-tight. Put the jar into a pot of cold water and let it boil from three to five hours, according to quantity. Ready when cold.

Sauces for "Fish and Meat" will follow "Meats."

SHELL FISH.

OYSTERS ON THE SHELL.

Wash the shells and put them on hot coals or upon the top of a hot stove, or bake them in a hot oven; open the shells with an oyster knife, taking care to lose none of the liquor, and serve quickly on hot plates, with toast. Oysters may be steamed in the shells, and are excellent eaten in the same manner.

BROILED OYSTERS.

Drain the oysters well and dry them with a napkin. Have ready a griddle hot and well buttered; season the oysters; lay them to griddle and brown them on both sides. Serve them on a hot plate with plenty of butter.

CREAMED OYSTERS.

Clara E. Thatcher.

To one quart of oysters take one pint of cream or

sweet milk; thicken with a little flour, as if for gravy;
when cooked, pour in the oysters with liquor; pepper,
salt and butter the mixture. Have ready a platter with
slices of nicely browned toast, pour creamed oysters on
toast and serve hot.

OYSTERS A LA CREME.

Mrs. J. B. Lyon, Detroit.

One quart of oysters, one pint of cream; put the
oysters in a double kettle, cook until the milk juice begins
to flow out; drain the oysters in a colander; put the
cream on the same way; when it comes to a boil, thicken
with flour wet with milk as thick as corn starch ready to
mould; then put in the oysters and cook five minutes.
Serve hot on toast.

PANNED OYSTERS.

Mrs. J. B. Lyon, Detroit.

Drain the oysters from the liquor; put them in a hot
pan or spider; as soon as they begin to curl, add butter,
pepper and salt. Serve on toast, or without, if preferred.

STEWED OYSTERS.

Mrs. Andrews.

In all cases, unless shell oysters, wash and drain; mix
half a cup of butter and a tablespoon of corn starch;
put with the oysters in a porcelain kettle; stir until they
boil; add two cups of cream or milk; salt to taste; do
not use the liquor of the oysters in either stewing or
escaloping.

ESCALOPED OYSTERS.
Mrs. Andrews.

Butter the dish, (common earthern pie-plates are the best,) cover the bottom of the dish with very fine bread crumbs; add a layer of oysters; season with pepper and salt; alternate the crumbs and oysters until you have three layers; finish with crumbs; cover the top with small pieces of butter; finish around the edge with bread cut into small oblong pieces dipped in butter; bake half an hour; unless shell oysters, wash them thoroughly and strain.

ESCALOPED OYSTERS.
Mrs. D.

Crush and roll several handfuls of friable crackers; put a layer in the bottom of a buttered pudding dish; wet this with a mixture of the oyster liquor and milk, slightly warmed; next a layer of oysters; sprinkle with salt and pepper, and lay small bits of butter upon them then another layer of moistened crumbs, and so on until the dish is full. Let the top layer be of crumbs, thicker than the rest, and beat an egg into the milk you pour over them; put pieces of butter on top; cover the dish; bake half an hour.

ESCALOPED OYSTERS.
Mrs. Norcross.

Scald the oysters; butter the dish in which they are to be baked; put in first a layer of rolled crackers; take the oysters from the liquor one at a time, to be sure no shells

6

are on them; then add a layer of oysters with butter, a little pepper, and continue adding a layer of crackers and oysters until the dish is full; have the top layer crackers; strain over the whole the liquor; bake half an hour.

· OYSTER PIE.
Anonymous.

Take a large dish, butter it, and spread a rich paste over the sides and around the edge, but not on the bottom. The oysters should be as large and fine as possible; drain off part of the liquor from the oysters; put them into a pan, and season them with pepper, salt, spice and butter; have ready the yolks of three boiled eggs chopped fine, and grated bread crumbs; pour the oysters with as much of their liquor as you please into the dish with the paste, strew over them the chopped eggs and grated bread; roll out the lid of the pie and put it on, crimping the edges. Bake in a quick oven. Nice also, with a gill of cream added, and a little flour.

OYSTER PATTIES.
Aunt Maggie.

Make some rich puff paste and bake it in very small tin patty pans; when cool, turn them out upon a large dish; stew some large fresh oysters with a few cloves, a little mace and nutmeg; then add the yolk of one egg, boiled hard and grated; add a little butter, and as much of the oyster liquor as will cover them. When they have stewed a little while, take them out of the pan and set them to cool. When quite cold, lay two or three oysters in each shell of puff paste.

OYSTER PATTIES.

Mrs. Thos. Orton.

Stew the oysters; take the broth and allow the yolk of one egg to every dozen of oysters; turn off the broth and add the eggs; let it come to a boil; then turn back the oysters and fill the crust.

TO FRY OYSTERS.

Mrs. Edward Ely.

Roll a few crackers; beat two eggs; wash your oysters or not, according to your notion, but the bits of shell must be removed; dip your oysters into the egg, then into the rolled crackers; take half butter, and half lard in a spider, have it hot; (but not so hot that your oysters will burn;) fry them; then have a colander in a pan on the stove, and as soon as done, put into the colander to dry; when you have a dozen or so, take them out and put on a hot platter; salt to you taste.

TO FRY OYSTERS.

Mrs. D., and Mrs. T. V. Wadskier.

Use the largest and best oysters; lay them in rows upon a clean cloth and press another upon them, to absorb the moisture; have ready several beaten egg; and in another dish some finely crushed crackers; in the frying pan heat enough butter to entirely cover the oysters; dip the oysters first into the eggs, then into the crackers, rolling it or them over that they may become well incrusted; drop into the frying pan and fry quickly to a light brown. Serve dry and let the dish be warm. A chafing dish is best.

FRICASSEED OYSTERS.

Mrs. W. P. Brown.

For a quart can, drain the oysters dry as possible; put a piece of butter the size of an egg into your spider, and let it get quite brown; put in your oysters and as soon as they commence to cook, add as much more butter, which has been previously well mixed with a tablespoon of flour; let it cook a moment and add one egg, beaten with a tablespoon of cream; let this cook a moment and pour all over toasted bread.

MACARONI WITH OYSTERS.

Mrs. F. B. Orr.

Boil macaroni in salt water, after which drain through a colander; take a deep earthern dish or tin, put in alternate layers of macaroni and oysters; sprinkle the layers of macaroni with grated cheese; bake until brown. Delicious as a side dish at dinner.

MACARONI AND OYSTERS — AN ENTREE.

Mrs. Baushar.

Boil the macaroni first; place a layer of it in the bottom of the dish; dry the oysters and place around on the macaroni, then a layer of browned bread crumbs, then another layer of macaroni, then oysters as before, then bread crumbs, and so on, finishing off with bread crumbs, and bake; pepper, salt and butter to the taste; make a broth of the oyster juice and milk, and pour over it before baking; bake about twenty minutes.

PICKLED OYSTERS.

Mrs. C. G. Smith.

Wash them from their liquor and put them into a porcelain lined kettle, with strong salt and water to cover them ;
let them come to a boil, and then skim them into cold
water; scald whole peppers, mace and cloves in a little
vinegar ; the quantity of these must be determined by the
number of oysters; when the oysters are cold, put them
into a stone jar with layers of spice between them, and
make liquor enough to cover them from the liquor in
which they were cooked; spice your vinegar and cold
water to taste.

LOBSTER CHOWDER.

Mrs. Lamkin.

Four or five pounds of lobster, chopped fine; take the
green part and add to it four pounded crackers; stir this
into one quart of boiling milk; then add the lobster, a
piece of butter o..e-half the size of an egg, a little pepper
and salt, and bring it to a boil.

LOBSTER CROQUETTES.

M. A. T.

The same mixture as given for stuffed lobster, without
the cream; made into pointed balls, dipped in egg and
then rolled in cracker and fried in very hot lard; served
dry and garnished with parsley.

STUFFED CRABS OR LOBSTER.

M. A. T.

Boil crabs and pick out meat; carefully preserving the

shell whole; rub this with salad oil, add to meat one. fourth as much fine bread crumbs, very little nutmeg, cayenne pepper, grated rind and juice of lemon, butter and a little sweet cream, (if lobster, rub the coral with the cream,) replace in shells, dust lightly with bread crumbs, and butter and brown in oven. Garnish with parsley and lemon.

TO DRESS CRAB.

Mrs. Elia M. Walker.

Two or three shalots and a little parsley chopped very fine; one ounce of butter; a bunch of sweet herbs; a tea-cup of broth (or water); boil a few minutes, and take out the herbs; add the crumbs of a roll finely grated; one tablespoon of best sweet oil; one glass of sherry; the juice of half a lemon; cayenne pepper and salt to taste. Put in the crab to warm, then put all nicely into the shell. grate over some bread crumbs and put in the oven a few moments to brown.

CLAM STEW.

Mrs. M. L. S.

Lay the clams on a gridiron over hot coals, taking them out of the shells as soon as open, saving the juice; add a little hot water, pepper, a very little salt and butter rolled in flour sufficient for seasoning; cook for five minutes and pour over toast.

CLAM FRITTERS.

M. A. T.

Twelve clams chopped or not; one pint milk; three eggs; add liquor from clams; salt and pepper, and flour enough for thin batter. Fry in hot lard.

POULTRY AND GAME.

"Whoso seeks an audit here,
Propitious pays his tribute — game or fish,
Wild fowl or venison, and his errand speed."
— COWPER.

BOILED FOWL.

Take a young fowl and fill the inside with oysters; place in a jar and plunge into a kettle of water; boil for one and one-half hours; there will be a quantity of gravy in the jar from the juice of the fowl and the oysters; make this into a white sauce with the addition of egg, cream, or a little flour and butter; add oysters, or serve up plain with the fowl. This is very nice with the addition of a little parsley to the sauce.

ROAST TURKEY OR CHICKEN.

Having picked and drawn the fowls, wash them well in two or three waters; wipe them dry; dredge them with a little flour inside and out, and a little pepper and salt; prepare a dressing of bread and cracker crumbs, fill the bodies and crops of the fowls and then bake them from two to three hours; baste them frequently while roasting; stew the giblets in a sauce pan; just before serving, chop the giblets fine; after taking up the chicken, and the water in which the giblets were boiled, add the chopped giblets to the gravy of the roast fowl; thicken with a little flour, which has been previously wet with the water; boil up, and serve in a gravy-dish. Roast chickens and turkey should be accompanied with celery and jellies.

BAKED CHICKEN.

Anonymous.

Cut the fowls open and lay them flat in a pan, breaking down the breast and the back bones; dredge with flour and season well with salt and pepper, with bits of butter; put in a very hot oven until done, basting frequently with melted butter; or when half done take out the chicken and finish by broiling it upon a gridiron over bright coals; pour over it melted butter and the juices in the pan in which it was baked.

CHICKEN FRICASSEE.

Sarah Page, Albany, N. Y.

Cut up the chickens and put on the fire in a kettle with cold water sufficient to cover, add a little salt or salt pork sliced, if you like; boil until tender, and cut up and put in a part of a head of celery. When tender have ready hot baking-powder biscuits broken open and laid on a platter; on this place the chicken; thicken the gravy with flour moistened with water or milk, aud pour it over the chicken and biscuits. If you prefer, use a

good-sized piece of butter to season instead of the salt
pork. Oysters are an addition.

FRIED CHICKEN.

Mrs. Bausher.

Cut the chicken in pieces, lay it in salt and water,
which change several times; roll each piece in flour; fry
in very hot lard or butter, season with salt and pepper;
fry parsley with them also. Make a gravy of cream
seasoned with salt, pepper and a little mace, thickened
with a little flour in the pan in which the chickens were
fried, pouring off the lard.

DRESSING FOR CHICKENS OR TURKEY.

Mrs. F. D.

Chop bred crumbs quite fine, season well with pepper,
salt and plenty of butter; moisten with a very little water,
and add a few oysters with a little of the liquor, if you
please. The best authorities say the dressing is the
finest when it crumbles as the fowl is cut.

DRESSING FOR TURKEY.

C Kennicot.

One pint of soaked bread, two tablespoons of sage, two
tablespoons of summer savory, two teaspoons of salt, two
teaspoons pepper, butter size of an egg.

CHICKEN CHEESE.

Two chickens boiled tender, chop, but not too fine;
salt and pepper, three or four eggs boiled and sliced;

line dishes or moulds with them; pour in the chicken and the liquor they were boiled in; when cold slice. Should be boiled in as little water as possible.

JELLIED CHICKEN.

M. A. T. -

Boil a fowl until it will slip easily from the bones; let the water be reduced to about one pint in boiling; pick the meat from the bones in good sized pieces, taking out all gristle, fat and bones; place in a wet mould; skim the fat from the liquor; a little butter; pepper and salt to the taste and one-half ounce of gelatine. When this dissolves, pour it hot over the chicken. The liquor must be seasoned pretty high, for the chicken absorbes.

CHICKEN PIE.

Mrs. A. A. Carpenter.

Boil your chickens until they are tender and season highly, line deep pie plates with a rich crust, take the white meat and a little of the dark off from the bones, put into the pie plates, pour the gravy over the chicken, add butter and a little flour, cover with the crust, bake from half to three-quarters of an hour.

CHICKEN PIE.

Mrs. H.

Stew chickens until tender; line the sides of a deep pie dish, with nice pastry; put in the chicken, and the water in which it has boiled, (which should be but half a pint); season with a large piece of butter, salt and pepper, and then cover loosely with a crust. While this is baking, have ready a quart can of fine oysters; put on the fire a pint of rich milk, (or the liquor of the oysters will do;) let it come to a boil; thicken with a little flour, and season with butter, pepper and salt; pour this over the oysters boiling hot, and about fifteen minutes before the pie is done, lift the crust and pour the oysters and all into the pie; then return to the oven to finish.

CHICKEN LOAF.

Mrs. W. H. Low.

Take two chickens, boil them in as little water as possible until the meat will drop from the bones; cut it with a knife and fork; then put it back into the kettle; put in plenty of butter, pepper and salt; heat it thoroughly; boil an egg hard and slice it and place it in the bottom of a dish; pour it in hot, place a weight upon it, and put it away to cool; it will come out in a form.

CHICKEN CROQUETTES.

Mrs. P. B. Ayer.

Two well cooked chickens chopped fine; one pound rice boiled not more than twenty minutes; an onion, if preferred; one-half pound old cheese grated; parsley chopped fine; very little cloves, mace and thyme; cayenne and black pepper to season. Mix this thoroughly with the yolks of ten eggs, well beaten; one pint of sifted crackers; beat six eggs, separately; form the first compound in a pointed wine glass, dip first in the egg and then in the sifted cracker, and brown in hot lard. Heat before eating.

CHICKEN CROQUETTES.

Mrs. J. Young Scammon.

The proportions that we give below are for half a good sized chicken. After boiling, chop the meat fine, fry it with one ounce of butter; then add one half teaspoon of flour; stir for half a minute, adding the chopped meat and a little more than a gill of meat broth; salt, pepper and a pinch of nutmeg; stir for five minutes, then take it from the fire and mix the yolks of two eggs with it; put on the fire again for one minute, stirring the while. Lastly, you may or may not add four mushrooms chopped, or two truffles, or both, according to taste. Turn the mixture into a dish and set it away to cool. When perfectly cold mix it well, as the upper part is drier than the rest; put it in parts on the pasteboard, a tablespoon for each part. Have bread crumbs on the pasteboard, then make them into any form required. Dip each croquette in beaten egg; roll in bread crubs again and fry in hot fat. Garnish each croquette with a sprig of parsley.

CHICKEN CROQUETTES.

Marion Harland.

Minced chicken; about one-quarter as much fine bread crumbs as you have of meat; one egg beaten light to each cup of meat; gravy enough to moisten the crumbs and chicken; or, if you have no gravy, a little drawn butter; pepper and salt and chopped parsley to taste; yolks of two hard boiled eggs rubbed fine with the back of a silver spoon, added to the meat; mix up into a paste with as little handling as may be; nor must the paste be too

wet to mould readily; make with floured hands into rolls
or ovate balls, roll in flour until well coated, and fry a few
at a time, lest crowding should injure the shape, in nice
dripping, or a mixture half lard and half butter. As you
take them out lay in a hot colander, that every drop of
fat may be drained off. Serve in a heated dish with
cresses or parsley.

CHICKEN CROQUETTES.
Mrs. J. A. Ellis.

Four and one-half pounds chicken boiled and chopped
very fine; moisten to a thick pulp with the liquor in which
it has been boiled. Mix with this a pint and a half of
mashed potatoes, beaten to a cream; three eggs, one
teaspoon of mustard, sweet majoram, salt and pepper to
taste; a little celery chopped very fine; soften with milk
till very soft, and add a quarter of a pound of butter.
Mould into forms, dip in egg and cracker dust, and fry in
boiling lard.

CROQUETTES.
Mrs. I. N. Isham.

Take cold fowl or fresh meat of any kind, with slices
of ham, fat and lean; chop all together very fine ; add
half as much grated bread, and season with salt, pepper
and nutmeg; one tablespoon of catsup, one teaspoon of
made mustard and one lump of butter; mix well together,
make up in little rolls or balls, dip in beaten yolks of
eggs, cover with grated bread crumbs, and fry brown in
lard.

CHICKEN PATES.

Mince chicken that has been previously roasted or boiled, and season well; stir into this a sauce made of half a pint of milk, into which while boiling a teaspoonful of corn starch has been added to thicken; season with butter, about a tablespoonful, and salt and pepper to taste. Have ready small pate pans lined with a good puff paste. Bake the crust in a brisk oven; then fill the pans and set in the oven a few minutes to brown very slightly.

FORCE MEAT BALLS.

Mrs. James S. Gibbs.

Mix with one pound of chopped veal or other meat; one egg; a little butter or raw pork chopped fine; one cup or less of bread crumbs; the whole well moistened with warm water, or what is better, the water from stewed meat; season with salt and red pepper; do up in small balls, and fry them brown.

PILAN.

Mrs. J. S. Gibbs.

Place a full grown chicken and about one pound of pickled pork with a pod of red pepper and bunch of thyme, in a pot with water enough to cover. When perfectly tender, put the chicken and pork in a steamer which fits the pot; wash your rice carefully, and boil it seventeen minutes in the water from which the meat was taken; make a large gravy tureen full of drawn butter sauce, to which you add two hard boiled eggs sliced, and capers or chopped pickle; use about a pint of the water in which the meat has been boiled for the sauce, and if the food is very fat, skim the grease off the top and use instead of butter for the sauce. When you serve, place the rice on a large flat dish, and the chicken on top.

DUCKS.

Miss S. P., Albany, N. Y.

When roasted, use dressing as for turkey, with the addition of a few slices of onion. Many cooks lay over the game slices of onions, which takes away the fishy flavor, removing the onion before serving. Make a sauce with the drippings in the pan, in which the game is roasted, and to which are put the chopped giblets, which are previously well cooked; thicken the gravy with brown flour, moistened with water. Serve with currant jelly.

ROAST GOOSE.

Stuff and roast in the same manner as ducks. Many cooks cover poultry with a paste of flour and water while baking, removing it before it is served.

TO ROAST WILD FOWL.

M. A. T.

Put an onion, salt and hot water into a pan, and baste for ten or fifteen minutes; change the pan; put in a slice of salt pork and baste with butter and pork drippings very often; just before serving dredge lightly with flour and baste. Ducks take from twenty-five to thirty-five minutes to roast and woodcock and snipes fifteen to twenty-five

Do not draw or take off the heads of either. Garnish with fried or toasted bread, lemon, parsley and currant jelly.

PRAIRIE CHICKENS, PARTRIDGES AND QUAILS.

Miss Sarah Page, Albany, N. Y.

Clean nicely, using a little soda in the water in which they are washed; rinse them and dry, and then fill them with dressing, sewing them up nicely, and binding down the legs and wings with cords. Put them in a steamer over hot water, and let them cook until just done. Then place them in a pan with a little butter; set them in the oven and baste them frequently with melted butter until of a nice brown. They ought to brown nicely in about fifteen minutes. Serve them on a platter, with sprigs of parsley alternating with currant jelly.

QUAIL ON TOAST.

After the birds are nicely cleaned, cut them open down the back; salt and pepper them, and dredge with flour. Break down the breast and back-bones, so they will lie flat, and place them in a pan with a very little water and butter in a hot oven, covering them up tightly until nearly done. Then place them in a spider in hot butter, and fry a moment to a nice brown. Have ready slices of baker's bread toasted, and slightly buttered upon a platter. The toast should be broken down with a carving-knife, so that it will be tender. On this place the quails; make a sauce of the gravy in the pan, thicken lightly with browned flour, and pour over each quail and the toast.

7

A SUGGESTION.

M. A. T.

Singe all poultry with alcohol, and dip quails into clarified butter for broiling.

PRESSED CHICKEN.

Mrs. C. H. Wheeler.

Cut up the fowls and place in a kettle with a tight cover. so as to retain the steam; put about two teacups of water and plenty of salt and pepper over the chicken, then let it cook until the meat cleaves easily from the bones, cut or chop all the meat (freed from skin, bones and gristle) about as for chicken salad; season well, put into a dish and pour the remnant of the juice in which it was cooked over it. This will jelly when cold, and can then be sliced or set on the table in shape. Nice for tea or lunch. The knack of making this simple dish is not having too much water; it will not jelly if too weak, or if the water is allowed to boil away entirely while cooking.

PIGEON PIE.

Mrs. L.

Make a fine puff paste; lay a border of it around a large dish, and cover the bottom with a veal cutlet, or a very tender steak free from fat and bone; season with salt, cayenne pepper and mace. Prepare as many pigeons as can be put in one layer in the dish; put in each pigeon a small lump of butter, and season with pepper and salt; lay them in the dish breast downwards, and cut in slices a half dozen of hard-boiled eggs, and lay in with the birds; put in more butter, some veal broth, and cover the whole with crust   Bake slowly for an hour and a half.

MEATS.

GENERAL RULES FOR COOKING MEATS.

All salt meat should be put on in cold water, that the salt may be extracted while cooking. Fresh meat, which is boiled to be served with sauces at the table, should be put to cook in boiling water, when the outer fibres contract, the inner juices are preserved.

For making soup, put the meat over in cold water, to extract the juices for the broth.

In boiling meats, if more water is needed, add that which is hot, and be careful to keep the water on the meat constantly boiling.

Remove the scum when it first begins to boil. The more gently meat boils, the more tender it will become. Allow twenty minutes for boiling each pound of fresh meat.

Roast meats require a brisk fire. Baste often. Twenty minutes is required for roasting each pound of fresh meat.

The variation in roasted meats consists simply in the method of preparing them to cook, before putting in the oven. Some are to be larded, some stuffed with bread dressing, and others plain, only seasoning with pepper and salt.

A piece of red pepper, cooked in a boiled dinner, is very nice.   •

HINTS FOR COOKING MEATS.

E. E. Marcy, Evanston.

A tough piece of meat can be made tender by cooking for several hours, in water at a simmering heat. The fibre of meats is toughened by being subjected to a high temperature. It is upon this theory that Warren's Patent Cooker is constructed. The same results can be obtained by carefully watching the process of cooking, to prevent rapid boiling.

ROAST BEEF.

Prepare for the oven by dredging lightly with flour, and seasoning with salt and pepper; place in the oven, and baste frequently while roasting. Allow a quarter of an hour for a pound of meat, if you like it rare; longer if you like it well done. Serve with a sauce, made from the drippings in the pan, to which has been added a tablespoon of Harvey or Worcestershire sauce, and a tablespoon of tomato catsup. Thicken with browned flour, and serve in a gravy boat.

ROAST BEEF WITH YORKSHIRE PUDDING.

Set a piece of beef to roast upon a grating, or several

sticks laid across a dripping pan. Three-quarters of an hour before it is done, (allow fifteen minutes to a pound if you like it rare,) mix the pudding and pour into the pan. Continue to roast the beef, the dripping meanwhile falling upon the pudding below. When both are done cut the pudding into squares and lay around the meat when dished. If there is much fat in the dripping pan before the pudding is ready to be put in, drain it off, leaving just enough to prevent the batter from sticking to the bottom.

RECIPE FOR PUDDING.—One pint of milk; four eggs, whites and yolks beaten separately; two cups flour; one teaspoon salt. Be careful in mixing not to get the batter too stiff.

YORKSHIRE PUDDING.
Mrs. Joseph B. Leake.

To be eaten with roast beef, instead of a vegetable. Three tablespoons flour, mixed with one pint of milk, three eggs and a little salt. Pour into a shallow tin baking pan; put into oven, an hour before dinner, for ten minutes; then put it under the roasting beef and leave it till you take up the beef; leave it in about five minutes after you take up the beef; then pour off the fat and send it to the table.

BEEFSTEAK AND MUSHROOMS.
Mrs. Perry H. Smith.

Put in a sauce pan one ounce of butter, a small onion chopped fine, a little ground sage, and a little thyme, and put it over the fire; when hot, shake in two tablespoons of flour, and when it becomes brown, put in one gill of water, and let it boil for half an hour. Then add three tablespoons of beef stock, a little salt, a little nutmeg and one wine glass of sherry wine. Put in one can of mushrooms, and let it boil for ten minutes. Pour this over a nicely broiled beefsteak.

BROILED BEEFSTEAK.

Lay a thick tender steak upon a gridiron over hot coals, having greased the bars with butter before the steak has been put upon it; (a steel gridiron with slender bars is to be preferred, the broad flat iron bars of gridirons commonly used, fry and scorch the meat, imparting a disagreeable flavor.) When done on one side, have ready your platter warmed, with a little butter on it; lay the steak upon the platter with the cooked side down, that the juices which have gathered may run on the platter, but do not press the meat; then lay your beefsteak again upon the gridiron quickly and cook the other side. When done to your liking, put again on the platter, spread lightly with butter, place where it will keep warm for a few moments, but not to let the butter become oily, (over boiling steam is best;) and then serve on hot plates. Beefsteak should never be seasoned with salt and pepper while cooking. If your meat is tough, pound *well* with a steak mallet on both sides.

BEEF WITH TOMATOES.
Mrs. P. B. Ayer.

Eight pounds fresh plate beef, second cut broiled; boil tender two quarts tomatoes, three cloves, plenty butter.

pepper and salt; when cooked nicely and thick, strain through a colander and pour over your beef and serve hot or cold.

A LA MODE BEEF.

Miss Sarah Page.

Take a piece of beef four or five inches thick, and with a small knife make small holes entirely through it at small distances apart. Then take strips of fat salt pork, roll them in pepper and cloves. Lay on a pan, cover closely, and put over in a steamer, and steam for three hours. When done thicken the gravy in the pan with a little flour. This is excellent when eaten as cold meat.

MOCK DUCK.

Mrs. C. C. Stratton, Evanston.

Take the round of beef steak, salt and pepper either side; prepare bread or crackers with oysters or without, as for stuffing a turkey; lay your stuffing on the meat; sew up and roast about an hour; and if you do not see the wings and legs you will think you have roast duck.

BEEF OMELET.

Mrs. S. B. Adams.

Four pounds of round beef, uncooked, chopped fine; six eggs beaten together; five or six soda crackers rolled fine, little butter and suet, pepper, salt and sage, if you choose; make two loaves, roll in cracker; bake about an hour; slice when cold.

SPICED BEEF.

Mrs. E. R. Harmon.

Four pounds of round of beef chopped fine; take from it all fat; add to it three dozen small crackers rolled fine, four eggs, one cup of milk, one tablespoon ground mace, two tablespoons of black pepper, one tablespoon melted butter; mix well and put in any tin pan that it will just fill, packing it well; baste with butter and water, and bake two hours in a slow oven.

MEAT FROM SOUP BONES.

Mrs. DeForest, Freeport.

Before thickening the soup or putting in the vegetables, take out a large bowl of the liquor; take the meat from the bones, chop it fine, season with catsup and spices; pour over the liquor, which should be thick enough to jelly when cold; put into moulds and serve cold in slices.

BEEF CROQUETTES.

Mrs. J. B. R.

Chop fine some cold beef; beat two eggs and mix with the meat and add a little milk, melted butter, and salt and pepper. Make into rolls and fry.

TO BOIL CORNED BEEF.

Mrs. A. W. D.

Put the meat in cold water; boil from five to six hours, then take out the bones; wrap it tightly in a towel; put on ice, with a weight to press it.

BEEF OR VEAL LOAF.

Three pounds of meat chopped fine with one-fourth of a pound of salt pork, six Boston crackers powdered fine, one sheet of Cooper's isinglass dissolved in a coffee-cup of warm water, one tablespoon of butter, one tea-spoon of salt, and one of pepper, one of powdered cloves, or a nutmeg grated. Mix well together with two eggs; bake one hour. This will slice well when cold.

PRESERVED BEEF.

Mrs. Carter.

For preserving one hundred pounds beef: Six pounds salt, two ounces salt-petre, two tablespoons soda, two pounds sugar, four gallons water; mix well together; sprinkle the bottom of the barrel with salt; put in the beef with very little salt between each layer; pour over the brine and put on a weight to keep all well covered.

TO CORN BEEF.

Mrs. A. M. Gibbs.

To each gallon of cold water, put one quart of rock salt, one ounce of salt-petre and four ounces of brown sugar, (it need not be boiled,) as long as any salt remains undissolved, the meat will be sweet. If any scum should rise, scald and skim well; add more salt, salt-petre and sugar; as you put each piece of meat into the brine, rub over with salt. If the weather is hot, gash the meat to the bone, and put it in salt. Put a flat stone or some weight on the meat to keep it under the brine.

Or this: To every four gallons of water allow two

pounds of brown sugar and six pounds of salt, boil about twenty minutes, taking off the scum; the next day turn it on the meat packed in the pickling tub; pour off this brine; boil and strain every two months, adding three ounces of brown sugar and half a pound of common salt. It will keep good a year. Sprinkle the meat with salt the next day, wipe dry before turning the pickle over it. Let it entirely cover the meat; add four ounces salt-petre. Canvas lids are excellent for covering, as they admit the air and exclude flies. Mutton and beef may be kept sweet several weeks by simply rubbing well with dry salt and closely covering. Turn the pieces whenever the vessel is uncovered.

BOILED TONGUE WITH TOMATO SAUCE.

Mrs. J. A. Ellis.

Half boil a tongue, then stew it with a sauce made of a little broth, flour, parsley, one small onion, one small carrot, salt and pepper, and one can of tomatoes cooked and strained. Lay the tongue on a dish and strain the sauce over it.

BOILED TONGUE AND TOMATO SAUCE.

Mrs. A. L. Chetlain.

Boil a pickled tongue till well done, then peel. For the sauce, one can of tomatoes, boil half down, then strain; rub together one tablespoon of butter, one teaspoon of flour and a little salt, put these into the tomato, and let it come to a boil; then pour over the tongue and serve.

STEWED TONGUE.

Mrs. J. A. Ellis.

Cut square fillets of bacon, which dredge with a mixture of chopped parsley, salt, pepper and a little allspice. Lard the tongue with the fillets; put in a sauce-pan two ounces of bacon cut in slices, four sprigs of parsley, two of thyme, a little garlic, two cloves, two carrots cut in small pieces, two small onions, salt and pepper. Lay the tongue on the whole; wet with a glass of white wine and a glass of broth. Set it on a moderate fire and simmer about five hours, keeping it well covered. Put the tongue on a dish and strain the sauce over it.

BOILED LEG OF MUTTON.

Mrs. J. Brown.

Boil well in clear water until tender, seasoning the water with salt; serve with egg sauce, and garnish with parsley, sliced lemons, or some sour jelly.

MUTTON A LA VENISON.

Mrs. J. B. L.

Take a leg of mutton and lard it well with strips of salt pork inserted in deep slits in the meat, which has been previously rolled in pepper and cloves; bake two hours or according to the size of the roast, basting frequently while in the oven; about an hour before serving, spread over it currant jelly, return to the oven and let it brown.

MUTTON CHOPS.

Cut them nicely, clearing away all ragged ends and

edges; fry for a few moments covered closely, and then dip each piece in cracker crumbs and beaten egg, or you may prepare them as for frying; then, lay them in a dripping pan, and put into the oven to bake; baste frequently with a little melted butter and water.

ROAST VEAL.
Mrs. D. S. F.

Prepare a leg of veal for the oven, by washing, drying, and larding it with strips of fat bacon or ham, and dredging it well with flour, and seasoning with salt and pepper; baste frequently and serve with the gravy thickened. A roast fillet of veal should be prepared by stuffing it with bread crumbs, seasoned with chopped ham, summer savory, pepper and salt. Dredge lightly with flour and bake.

NECK PIECE OR SHOULDER OF VEAL.
Mrs. C. C. Stratton, Evanston.

Put a piece of butter the size of an egg into a kettle; put it on the stove; when it begins to fry, put in the veal, season it and let it fry until brown; then add water sufficient to cook it. When done take cream and flour well stirred, and thicken as for fricasseed chicken, and you have a nice dinner, very like chicken and much cheaper. Two pounds of veal will make a dinner for six or eight, providing it is not all bone.

VEAL PIE.
Mrs. Houghteling.

Three pounds of lean veal; two slices of salt pork,

chopped fine; one coffee cup of bread crumbs, two eggs, salt, pepper and herbs to taste; mix thoroughly and bake; use cold as a relish.

PATE OF VEAL.

Mrs. L. J. Tilton.

Three and one-half pounds of the leg of veal, fat and lean, chopped fine; six or eight small crackers rolled fine; two eggs, piece of butter the size of an egg, one table-spoon of salt, one of pepper and one of nutmeg; a slice of salt pork chopped fine. Work all together in the form of a loaf: put bits of butter and grate bread crumbs over the top. Bake two hours; to be cut in slices when cold.

VEAL PATE.

M. A. P.

Four pounds of veal and one and one-half pounds of salt pork chopped together, raw, and very fine, with four rolled crackers; two well beaten eggs, one lemon and one small onion; salt, pepper and sweet herbs to taste; mix well and bake in a pan as you would a loaf of bread; requires three hours.

VEAL CUTLETS,. A LA FRIED OYSTERS.

Mrs. A. M. Gibbs.

Cut the veal in small pieces three or four inches square; dry with a towel; season to taste; have ready a beaten egg and crackers rolled fine, each on separate dishes; dip each piece of the cutlet in the egg, then in the rolled cracker; have enough lard or butter hot in your spider so that it will nearly cover the cutlets when you put them in. A rich gravy can be made after the meat is done by adding a little boiling water.

VEAL LOAF.

Mrs. Lamkin.

Three and one-half pounds of lean and fat raw veal, chopped fine; one slice of salt pork, six small crackers rolled fine, butter the size of an egg, two eggs, one tablespoon of salt, one tablespoon of pepper, one of sage, three of extract of celery; mix thoroughly. Pack tightly in a deep square tin; cover with bits of butter and sprinkle fine cracker crumbs over the top; cover with another tin. Bake two hours, uncover and brown the top.

VEAL LOAF.

Mrs. Chas. Duffield.

Six Boston crackers, three eggs, one tablespoon of salt, pepper and sage, or summer savory; three pounds of veal. The veal must be raw and chopped fine; mix all well together and pack it hard in a deep tin pan; bake slowly for one hour; a tablespoon of butter improves it. This is a nice relish for tea, and should be sliced thin when cold.

VEAL LOAF.

Mrs. G. W. Brayton, and others.

Three pounds raw veal; one-half pound raw salt pork chopped fine; three Boston crackers rolled fine, or bread crumbs; three eggs, one teaspoon black pepper, little sage, little mace or nutmeg, one tablespoon of salt. Make in a loaf and baste while baking with butter size of an egg with water, and put on outside of loaf a small quantity of rolled crackers. Bake about three hours. Is very nice cold, cut in thin slices.

SPICED VEAL.
Mrs. C. E. Brown, Evanston.

Take four pounds veal, chop it fine and season highly with salt, pepper, cloves and cinnamon; add four small crackers rolled out, one egg, and a lump of butter nearly the size of an egg; mix thoroughly together and press it in a baking tin, and bake two and a half hours. When thoroughly cold, slice for tea. Some prefer it in rolls, convenient for slicing, and baked from one-half to three-quarters of an hour.

JELLIED VEAL.
M. A. T.

Boii the veal tender, pick it up fine, put in a mould, add the water it was boiled in, and set it in a cold place; season with salt and pepper to taste; a layer of hard boiled eggs improves it.

FRICANDEAU.
Mrs. J. M. Brown, and Mrs. M. L.

Three and one-half pounds of cold roast veal chopped fine, one tablespoon of salt and one of pepper, one-half a nutmeg, four or five rolled crackers, three eggs. If the veal is thin, add a piece of butter half as large as an egg, and tablespoon of cream. Form all this in a large roll, and spot the roll over with bits of butter; then strew over it the pounded crackers, (a little of the cracker should be mixed with the meat,) put it in the oven, and from time to time add a little water. Cook slowly two hours. When cold slice thin, and it makes an excellent relish.

CROQUETTES OF CHICKEN, VEAL OR SWEET BREAD.

Mrs. Gen. N. J. T. Dana.

Put in a stew pan a piece of butter size of an egg, one spoon of flour, a little pepper, salt and nutmeg; let it melt and mix well; chop the meat, but not too fine; put in the mixture and stir till well mixed; when cold add the yolks of two eggs to bind it; roll into oblong shape, dip it into egg beaten with a little pepper and salt; roll in crumbs of bread or powdered crackers and fry in boiling lard.

SWEET BREADS.

Scald in salt and water, take out the stringy parts; then put in cold water a few minutes; dry in a towel; dip in egg and bread crumbs, and fry brown in butter; when done place in a hot dish; pour into the pan a cup of sweet cream, a little pepper and salt, and a little parsley chopped fine; add flour, and when boiling pour over the sweet breads; add mushrooms, if desired.

SWEET BREADS — BROILED.

Mrs. Bates.

Parboil, rub them well with butter, and broil on a clean

gridiron; turn them often, and now and then roll them over in a plate containing hot melted butter, to prevent them from getting hard and dry.

CALF'S LIVER—FRIED.

Cut in thin slices; wash and drain them, roll them in corn meal or cracked crumbs, and fry in fresh or salt pork gravy or butter.

CALF'S LIVER—STEWED.

Boil till partly done; take out of the sauce-pan; chop in small pieces; put back in the sauce-pan; skim well; stew until tender; season with butter, pepper and salt; thicken with a little flour, and serve over slices of toasted bread.

CALF'S LIVER MARINE.
Mrs. J. M. Ayer.

Lard the liver; add pepper and salt sufficient to season it, then roll and tie it; cut two onions in thin slices and lay in the bottom of an earthen crock; add two slices of salt pork cut thin, and lay the liver on that; add more pepper and salt, a little vinegar and salad oil, and set in a cool place for twenty-four hours. Cook over a slow fire from half-past two until six; a wine-glass of claret added at half-past four is excellent. This is arranged for dinner at night; of course the rule for time will do for noon dinner. Easily mistaken for canvas-back duck.

TO ROAST VENISON.
Mrs. Porter.

Wash a saddle of venison thoroughly in several waters,

8

then rub it over with vinegar, red pepper and a little salt; lard with strips of salt pork rolled in seasoned bread crumbs; season if you like, with sweet marjoram and sweet basil, one teaspoon each, also pepper; then rub the whole over with current jelly, and pour over it one bottle of claret wine. Let it stand over night, and next morning cover the venison with a paste made of flour and water half an inch thick; then cover with soft paper, and secure well with strings; place it in the dripping-pan with some claret, butter and water, and baste very often; half an hour before you take it up, remove paste and paper, baste it with butter and dredge with flour to make it brown.

FOR SAUCE. — Take a pound and a half of scraps of venison, with three pints of water, a few cloves, a few blades of mace, one-half a nutmeg, and salt and cayenne pepper to taste; boil it down to a pint, skim off the fat and strain; add half a pint of current jelly, one pint of claret and one-quarter pound of butter, divided into bits and rolled in flour.

ROAST PIG.

See that the pig has been well scalded; put in the body a stuffing of dry bread crumbs, seasoned with sage, salt and pepper, and sew it up; skewer the legs back or the under part will not crisp; put in a hot oven after dredging well with flour, and baste it frequently with melted butter while roasting, or rub the pig with a cloth wet with melted butter. When done, serve whole on a platter, and garnish with parsley and celery tops alternately. Take off some of the fat from the gravy, set the rest on the top of the stove, thicken with a little flour, add a half glass of sherry wine, and the juice of half a lemon and serve in a gravy boat.

HEAD CHEESE.

Mrs. C. Bradley.

To one head add one heart, one-half liver and one tongue; first clean the head very nicely, then put it in a brine for twenty-four hours; then boil it until it is very soft, pick out the bones and chop very fine; then add salt, pepper, four small onions and a little sage, if you wish; mix it very thoroughly and put it in a colander and set it over a kettle of hot water over night; in the morning put in the press and press it as cheese.

SOUSE.

When the pig's feet and ears are well cleaned and scraped, put in cold water, and over the fire to boil; when • tender, put them in a jar; prepare a pickle of half a gallon of cider vinegar, whole black pepper, mace and cloves; boil up with the vinegar, and then pour over the pig's feet. Let them stand for two or three days, when they will be ready for use.

OXFORD SAUSAGE.

M. A. Sadler, Aurora.

Take one pound of young pork, fat and lean, without skin or gristle; one pound of lean veal; one pound of beef suet chopped very fine together. Put in half a pound of bread crumbs, six sage leaves, a teaspoon of pepper

and two of salt, some thyme, marjoram and savory shred
fine ; mix well together.

SAUSAGES.
Mrs. C. Bradley, and others.

Six pounds of lean fresh pork, three pounds of fat pork,
twelve teaspoons of sage, and six teaspoons of pepper, six
teaspoons of salt, (and two of cloves, and one nutmeg, if
you prefer,) grind or chop very fine ; mix these ingredients thoroughly, and pack in a jar, and pour hot lard over
the top.

HAM SANDWICHES.
Mrs. W. Butterfield.

Take some boiled ham and chop it very fine, mix it
with a dressing composed of one dessert spoon of mustard,
two of oil, one raw egg beaten very light, a little salt and
pepper; cut and spread the bread very thin.

HAM SANDWICHES.
Mrs. W. Butterfield.

Chop fine some cold boiled ham, a little fat with the
lean; add tongue and chicken also chopped fine; make a
dressing of one-half a pound of butter, three tablespoons
of salad oil, three of mustard, the yolk of one egg, and a
little salt; mix well together and spread over the meat
smoothly on thin slices of bread. Very nice.

TRAVELING LUNCH.
Mrs. J. L. B.

Chop sardines, ham and a few pickles quite fine ; mix

with mustard, pepper, catsup, salt and vinegar; spread between bread nicely buttered. This is to be cut crosswise, like jelly cake.

BOILED HAM.

Mrs. C. Waggoner, Toledo.

Take a ham weighing about eight or ten pounds; soak it for twelve or twenty-four hours in cold water; then cover it with boiling water, add one pint of vinegar, two or three bay-leaves, a little bunch of thyme and parsley (the dried and sifted will do, or even the seeds of parsley may be used, if the fresh cannot be procured); boil very slowly two hours and a half, take it out, skim it, remove all the fat, except a layer half an inch thick; cut off with a sharp knife all the black-looking outside; put the ham into your dripping pan, fat side uppermost, grate bread crust over it and sprinkle a teaspoon of powdered sugar over it; put it in the oven for half an hour, until it is a beautiful brown. Eat cold; cut the nicest portion in slices; the ragged parts and odds and ends can be chopped fine and used for sandwiches; or, by adding three eggs to one pint of chopped ham, and frying brown, you have a delicious omelet for breakfast or lunch. The bones should be put in a soup-kettle, the rind and fat should be rendered and strained for frying potatoes and crullers. Ham cooked in this way will go much farther than when cooked in the ordinary manner.

BOILED AND BAKED HAM.

Mrs. P. B. Ayer.

Boil your ham tender; cover it with the white of a raw

egg, and sprinkle sugar or bread crumbs over it; put it in the oven and brown; it is delicious also covered with a regular cake icing and browned.

TO BOIL A HAM.

M.

Wash and scrape the ham clean; put it on in cold water enough to cover it; put into the water two onions, two carrots, a head of celery, a dozen cloves and a handful of timothy hay; boil without stopping until the skin will readily peel from the ham; cover the ham with rolled crackers, or bread crumbs that have been browned and rolled, and bake in a slow oven for two hours.

A VALUABLE SUGGESTION.

Soak ham or salt pork (cut in slices for broiling or frying) in a quart or two of milk and water; over night for breakfast, and several hours for any other meal. The milk may be either fresh or sour, and diluted with equal parts of water. Rinse before cooking in water until it is clear. It will be found a very excellent method, and when once adopted will be invariably the choice of preparation.

SALTING PORK.

A. M. G.

Cover the bottom of the barrel with salt an inch deep; put down one layer of pork and cover that with salt half an inch thick; continue this until all your pork is disposed of; then cover the whole with strong brine; pack as tight as possible, the rind side down or next to the barrel; keep the pork always under the brine by using an inner cover and clean stones. Should any scum arise, pour off the brine, scald it, and add more salt. Old brine can be boiled down, well skimmed and used for a fresh supply.

CURING HAMS.

Mrs. Mulford.

Hang up the hams a week or ten days, the longer the tenderer and better, if kept perfectly sweet ; mix for each good sized ham, one teacup of salt, one tablespoon of molasses, one ounce of salt-petre ; lay the hams in a clean dry tub ; heat the mixture and rub well into the hams, especially around the bones and recesses ; repeat the process once or twice, or until all the mixture is used ; then let the hams lie two or three days, when they must be put for three weeks in brine strong enough to bear an egg ; then soak eight hours in cold water ; hang up to dry in the kitchen or other more convenient place for a week or more ; smoke from three to five days, being careful not to heat the hams. Corn cobs and apple-tree wood are good for smoking. The juices are better retained if smoked with the hock down. Tie up carefully in bags for the summer.

SALADS, SAUCES AND PICKLES,

"To make this condiment, your poet begs
The powdered yellow of two hard-boiled eggs ;
Two boiled potatoes, passed through the kitchen sieve,
Smoothness and softness to the salad give ;
Let onions atoms lurk within the bowl,
And, half suspected, animate the whole ;
Of mordant mustard, add a single spoon ;
Distrust the condiment that bites so soon ;
But, deem it not, thou man of herbs, a fault
To add a double quantity of salt ;
Four times the spoon with oil from Lucca crown,
And twice with vinegar, procured from town ;
And lastly, o'er the flavored compound toss
A magic *soup con* of anchovy sauce.
O, green and glorious ! O, herbaceous treat !
'Twould tempt the dying anchorite to eat ;
Back to the world he'd turn his fleeting soul,
And plunge his fingers in the salad bowl ;
Serenely full, the epicure would say,
'Fate cannot harm me, I have dined to-day.'"

—SIDNEY SMITH.

SUGGESTIONS.

Miss M. A. Ayer.

Chicken for salad should boil until it parts from the
bone easily.   It is also better to shred it, than to cut or

(120)

chop. Equal parts butter and salad oil are by many preferred to the entire quantity of either. The addition of the liquor the fowl is boiled in, is a great improvement, to moisten the salad with. Crisp celery and cabbage in ice cold water for an hour or two before using for salads.

CHICKEN SALAD.

Mrs. Morgan, Rockford, Ill.

Cut the white meat of chickens into small bits, the size of peas, (also the dark meat, if you like,) chop the whole parts of celery nearly as small. Prepare a dressing thus: Rub the yolks of hard boiled eggs smooth; to each yolk put half a teaspoon of mustard, the same quantity of salt, a tablespoon of oil, and a wine glass of vinegar; mix the chicken and celery in a large bowl and pour over this dressing with a little cream added. The dressing must not be put on till just before it is served.

CHICKEN SALAD.

Mrs. Higgins.

Two chickens, chopped coarse; eight heads of celery, three eggs, one pint vinegar, one tablespoon flour, one tablespoon sugar, rub the yolks of the eggs to a fine powder, then add the salt, mustard and oil, mixing well together; then add the cream; and after that the vinegar and raw egg.

CHICKEN SALAD.

Mrs. Hobbs.

Three chickens chopped fine, both light and dark meat;

the juice of two lemons; eight or ten eggs boiled hard; the whites chopped fine and the yolks mashed fine, moisten with six teaspoons melted butter, two of sweet oil; to which add one tablespoon of mustard, one of pepper, one of salt, one of sugar, three of cream; and last, add six large bunches of celery chopped fine, with sufficient vinegar to moisten the whole.

CHICKEN SALAD.

Mrs. Chas. Wheeler.

To one chicken use the same quantity of celery, three or four eggs, one tablespoon mixed mustard, one teaspoon of salt, two of celery seed, one tablespoon of hard butter; two-thirds teacup vinegar, four tablespoons table oil, two-thirds cup sweet cream. Process of making: Season your chicken in cooking, cut by hand th chicken and celery, then beat the yolks and whites of eggs separately, into that beat the oil slowly. Then mix all the ingredients in an earthen or new tin dish, except the cream, and set on the stove. Cook until as thick as pound-cake. When cold add the cream, stirring well, and pour over the chicken and celery one hour before eating. Do not be afraid of cooking too thick.

CHICKEN SALAD.

Mary Norton.

Take the breasts of four well boiled chickens, cut in small pieces, but not too fine; mix with the chicken e teacups of celery cut also in small pieces, and with above, the chopped whites of twelve hard boiled eggs.

For dressing, the yolks of four raw eggs; beat into them half of an ordinary sized bottle of olive oil, beginning with a teaspoon, and adding no more than that at a time, until it is all thoroughly mixed; then add the well mashed and pulverized yolks of twelve eggs, salt and pepper, three tablespoons mustard, a pinch of cayenne pepper, and a gill of vinegar; then stir this dressing thoroughly into the mixed chicken celery and whites of eggs.

SWEET BREAD SALAD.
Mrs. D. C. B.

Four hard boiled eggs, one raw egg, three tablespoons of salad-oil, one teaspoon of salt, one of pepper, two of sugar, two of mixed mustard, one-half a teacup of vinegar, one calf's sweet bread, and two heads of lettuce. For dressing, mash the yolks and mix the oils thoroughly in them; then add the raw egg well beaten; mix the other ingredients in slowly and thoroughly, adding the vinegar last. Boil the sweet bread thoroughly until tender; pick it up in small pieces; break the lettuce also in small pieces, and then put in a dish alternate layers of lettuce and sweet bread and dressing. Use the whites of the eggs sliced over the top.

For salmon salad, use the same dressing, omitting the sweet breads, and substituting salmon. Put the salmon on a platter, pour over it the dressing and garnish with celery leaves.

VEAL SALAD.
Mrs. G. E. P.

Boil veal until very tender, chop fine and stir into it a

nice salad dressing; put in a shallow dish and garnish with slices of lemon and celery ; a little chopped cabbage or lettuce may be added, if desired. Boiled ham chopped and seasoned and served in the same manner, is a very nice dish.

CHICKEN SALAD.

Mrs. Chas. Duffield.

The yolks of six eggs, well beaten; one-half pint of melted butter, or the same quantity of olive oil ; three tablespoons of mixed mustard (or more if it is not very strong); salt to taste; two teaspoons of celery seed ; mix thoroughly; then add three-fourths of a pint of strong vinegar; place over the fire, stirring constantly until it become thick, like boiled custard. Turn the mixture over the chickens, which have previously been chopped (not very fine). Just before bringing to the table, add four heads of chopped celery. If it is not strong enough of spice, add more mustard and cayenne pepper. This is enough for one boiled turkey, or three small chickens. The same dressing makes an excellent mixture for sandwiches, if used with finely chopped boiled ham or beef tongue, but should not be salted.

LOBSTER SALAD.

Mrs. S. I. D.

Two lobsters, picked fine ; four heads of fresh lettuce, cut fine ; put in a dish in layers with the lobsters ; boil your eggs, mash the yolks, add three tablespoons of melted butter, a teaspoon of mustard, cayenne pepper and salt;

two tablespoons of sugar, two cups of vinegar; heat to-gether and pour over when served.

FISH SALAD.

M. A. T.

Boil tender a white fish or trout; chop fine; add same quantity chopped celery, cabbage or lettuce; season same as chicken salad.

VEGETABLE SALAD.

Anonymous.

Take cold vegetables left from dinner, such as potatoes, peas, string beans, shell beans, beets, etc., and chill them on the ice; cover with mayonaise, and serve. You may use for this any salad dressing.

POTATO SALAD.

M. A. T.

Sliced cold boiled potatoes; almonds blanched and quartered; hickory-nuts, also, if liked (both of these may be omitted). A very small quantity of chopped onions; pour over this any good salad dressing, not too much, and garnish with chopped parsley; cold boiled beets, sliced lemon, and anchovies, may be added to the salad, if liked.

POTATO SALAD.

Mix a nice salad dressing of one teaspoonful of salt; a little pepper; two tablespoons of fine cut crisped parsley; grate onion, about two teaspoonsful, with four tablespoons of salad oil or butter. To this add eight tablespoons of vinegar; slice two quarts of cold boiled potatoes — have these slices not very thin; pour over the dressing, and let them stand half an hour before serving.

ASPARAGUS SALAD.

Boil the asparagus in a water until tender; cut off the hard ends, and set the rest away. When cool, cut in inch long pieces, and put it in your salad dish. Pour over a mayonaise dressing, and garnish with a few capers.

CUCUMBER SALAD.

Mrs. King.

Take a dozen ripe "white spine" cucumbers; wash, pare and cut into strips, taking out the seeds; cut into pieces, like small dice; to each dozen cucumbers, take twelve large white onions chopped; six large green peppers, also chopped; one-quarter pound each of black and white mustard seed, and a gill of celery seed; mix all well together; add a teacup of salt, and hang up in a cotton bag to drain for twenty-four hours. Then add enough clear cold vinegar to cover it; put into stone jars and fasten nearly air tight. In six weeks it will be fit for use. Excellent.

TOMATO SALAD.

Miss Spruance.

Twelve tomatoes, peeled and sliced; four eggs, boiled hard; one egg (raw) well beaten; one teaspoon salt; one-half teaspoon cayenne pepper; one teaspoon sugar; one teacup of vinegar; set on ice to become perfectly cold.

DRESSING FOR SALAD.

Mrs. Hoge.

Two raw eggs, one tablespoon of butter, eight table-spoons of vinegar; one-half teaspoon of mustard; put in a bowl over boiling water and stir until it becomes like cream; pepper and salt to your taste.

SALAD DRESSING.

Mrs. A. A. Carpenter.

The yolks of four eggs, two-thirds of a cup of oil, red pepper, salt and mustard to taste; the juice of two lemons, and last of all, one cup of thick cream. If the dressing is for chicken salad, use the oil or fat from the chicken instead of sweet oil. Be sure and put the cream in last, just before sending to table.

SALAD DRESSING.

M. A. T.

Take the yolks of two raw eggs, beat with them one teaspoon of made mustard; this mustard should be mixed with water, not vinegar; then add to this, drop by drop, olive oil, stirring constantly until the mixture becomes very thick; then add two teaspoons of powdered sugar and a scant one of salt; mix thoroughly; squeeze in the juice of one lemon; beat well, and if too thick, thin with a little sweet cream. If preferred, omit the lemon and cream, and use vinegar. This dressing with lettuce, celery or potato, makes a delicious salad. If needed for chicken salad, the yolks of hard boiled eggs added make it richer. Garnish lettuce with nasturtium blossoms and sliced lemon. Garnish potatoes with cold boiled beets, chopped parsley and sliced lemon.

SAUCES

FOR MEAT OR FISH.

DRAWN BUTTER.

Drawn butter forms the basis of most sauces. From this a great variety may be made, by adding to this different flavors — anchovies, ochra, onions, celery, parsley, mint and relishes — using those flavors, which are suitable for the meat, game or fish, with which the sauces are to be served. A good standard receipt for drawn butter is as follows:

Rub one tablespoon of flour with one-quarter of a pound of butter; when well mixed, put in a sauce pan with a tablespoon of milk or water; set it in a dish of boiling water, shaking it well until the butter melts and is near boiling. It should not be set directly on the stove or over the coals, as the heat will make the butter oily and spoil it.

MELTED BUTTER OR PARSLEY SAUCE.

Miss A. C.

One tablespoon of butter, one teaspoon of flour, rubbed together; one tablespoon chopped parsley, first boiled five minutes in water and squeezed out; two tablespoons water; shake over a clear fire, *one way*, until it boils; add the parsley gradually.

MINT SAUCE.

M. A. T.

Two tablespoons green mint, cut fine; two of sugar, and one-half teacup vinegar.

MINT SAUCE.

Mrs. J. M. B.

Mix one tablespoon of white sugar to half a teacup of good vinegar; add the mint and let it infuse for half an hour in a cool place before sending to the table. Serve with roast lamb or mutton.

CELERY SAUCE.

Mrs. J. B. L.

Mix two tablespoons of flour with half a teacup of butter; have ready a pint of boiling milk; stir the flour and butter into the milk; take three heads of celery, cut into small bits, and boil for a few minutes in water, which strain off; put the celery into the melted butter, and keep it stirred over the fire for five or ten minutes. This is very nice with boiled fowl or turkey.

CREAM SAUCE.

Anonymous.

Cream together a large tablespoon of butter with a little flour, and put over a gentle heat; add a little chopped

9

parsley, a little grated onion, pepper, salt and nutmeg; when these ingredients are well mixed, add half a pint of cream or milk and let it boil for fifteen minutes. If used with fresh fish, a little horse radish may be added.

EGG SAUCE.
Miss Hattie Buck, Adrian, Mich.

Take the yolks of two eggs boiled hard; mash them with a teaspoon of mustard, a little pepper and salt, three tablespoons of vinegar, and three cf salad oil. A tablespoon of catsup improves this for some. Nice for boiled fish.

EGG SAUCE.

Prepare drawn butter, and to this add three or four hard boiled eggs sliced or chopped.

FISH SAUCE.

One-quarter of a pound of fresh butter; one tablespoon of finely chopped parsley, a little salt and pepper and the juice of two lemons. Cream the butter; mix all well together, adding at the least a teaspoon of mayonaise. Less lemon juice may be used if preferred.

FISH SAUCE.
Mrs. Bausher.

Make a drawn butter very smoothly, mix with some finely cut pickle; add two tablespoonfuls of salad dressing well mixed, prepared from egg, oil and mustard, viz.: yolk one egg; one teaspoon mustard and oil, till thickens.

TOMATO SAUCE.

Mrs. C. S. Horseman, Rockford, Ill.

Thirty-six ripe tomatoes, six green peppers, two onions chopped fine, two cups of sugar, two tablespoons of salt, two teaspoons of ground cloves. two teaspoons of mustard, two teaspoons of cinnamon, two cups of vinegar, and boil half a day.

GREEN TOMATO SAUCE.

Mrs. Houghteling.

One peck of green tomatoes, cut in very thin slices; sprinkle with salt; press with a plate and leave to drain twenty-four hours. Then place in a porcelain kettle in layers with the following mixture : Six large onions cut in slices, one small bottle of mustard, one-quarter pound of mustard seed, two teaspoons cloves, four teaspoons black pepper, two teaspoons ginger, four teaspoons allspice. Cover with vinegar and simmer two hours, or until the tomato looks clear. All the spices should be ground.

OYSTER SAUCE.

Mrs. L. T.

Take oysters out of their liquor and throw them into cold water; put the liquor over the fire with the beards of the oysters, and boil with a bit of mace and lemon peel; then strain the liquor; take the oysters out of the water; drain, and put them with the strained liquor into a sauce-pan, with sufficient butter and milk for your sauce; dust into this flour; let it boil up; add a squeeze of lemon juice, and serve *hot*.

ONION SAUCE.

Boil three or four white onions until they are tender, and then mince them fine; put one-half pint of milk over to boil; add a piece of butter half size of egg, and a little salt and pepper; stir in the minced onion and a tablespoon of flour, which has been moistened with milk; let it cream over boiling water.

CHILI SAUCE.

Mrs. Henry M. Knickerbocker.

Twenty-four large ripe tomatoes, six green peppers, four large onions, three tablespoons salt, eight tablespoons brown sugar, six teacups vinegar. Chop the peppers and onions very-fine; peel the tomatoes and cut very small; put all into a kettle and boil gently one hour.

CHILI SAUCE.

Etta C. Springer.

One peck ripe tomatoes boiled one hour; add a cup of salt, one quart of vinegar, one ounce whole cloves, one ounce cinnamon, one ounce allspice, one ounce ground white mustard, one quart onions sliced, a little celery, a little horse radish, one-half pound of sugar, six red peppers.

CHILI SAUCE WITH SPICE.

Mrs. Lamkin.

Eighteen tomatoes (ripe ones); one green pepper chopped fine; three onions, if that flavor is desired; two tablespoons of salt; one-half cup of sugar, two cups of vinegar, one teaspoon of each kind of spice ; stew slowly; tomatoes to be sliced. Good without onion.

CHILI SAUCE.

Mrs. E. H. Dennison, Highland Park, Ill.

To nine large ripe tomatoes and three green peppers, add one onion chopped fine, two cups of vinegar, two tablespoons of sugar, and one of salt; steam one hour, then add one teaspoon of ginger, one of allspice, and one of cloves.

HORSE-RADISH SAUCE.

Two teaspoons of made mustard, two of white sugar, half a teaspoon of salt, and a .gill of vinegar; mix and pour over grated horse-radish. Excellent with beef.

MADE MUSTARD.

Pour a very little boiling water over three tablespoons of mustard; add one saltspoon of salt, a tablespoon of olive oil, stirred slowly in, and one teaspoon of sugar; add the yolk of an egg, beaten well together, and pour in vinegar to taste. It is best eaten next day.

SAUCE MAYONAISE.

Mrs. P. B. Ayer.

Yolks of two raw eggs, (not a particle of the white or your sauce will curdle,) and one and a half mustardspoons of mixed mustard beaten together; add very slowly the best salad oil, stirring constantly until you can reverse the dish without spilling; then add one tablespoon of vinegar and cayenne and black pepper to taste, one-half teaspoon salt; stir briskly until quite light colored, and serve on lobster, lettuce or fish.

CURRY POWDER.

Mrs. S. F. Page, Rockford, Ill.

Mix an ounce of ginger, one of mustard, one of black pepper, three of coriander seed, three of turmeric, quarter of an ounce of cayenne pepper, half an ounce of cardamon, half an ounce of cummin seed, and cinnamon; pound the whole very fine, sift and keep it in a bottle corked tight. To be used for gravies for ducks and other meats.

MAITRE D'HOTEL SAUCE.

Mrs. E. M. E.

Put one teacup of butter in an earthen dish; have ready two large tablespoons of parsley, which have been boiled for a few moments in water; chop fine and add to the butter the juice of two lemons; add cayenne pepper and salt to taste; let it boil a few moments. An excellent sauce for a variety of meats.

CELERY VINEGAR.

Soak one ounce of celery seed in half a pint of vinegar; bottle it and use to flavor soups and gravies.

GOOSEBERRY SOY.

M. A. Bingham, Elgin, Ill.

Take six pounds of gooseberries that are nearly ripe, and three pounds sugar, one pint best vinegar, and boil all together until quite thick. To be eaten with meats;

will keep good a long time; season to suit your taste with ground cloves and cinnamon.

CHERRY OR CURRANT SAUCE.

M. A. Bingham, Elgin, Ill.

Four pounds of cherries or currants, two pounds sugar, one cup vinegar, one-half ounce cinnamon; cook slowly about one hour.

GOOSEBERRY CATSUP.

Mrs. J. B. Adams, Mrs. Henry Stevens, and Mrs. R. Harris.

Eight pounds of ripe or partially ripe fruit, four pounds brown sugar, one pint good vinegar, two ounces each fine cloves and cinnamon tied in a bag; boil the berries and sugar for three or four hours, then add spice; boil a little more; put in a jar and cover well. Will keep two years by occasionally scalding and adding a little vinegar and spice.

CUCUMBER CATSUP.

Take a dozen large ripe cucumbers; pare and cut them open, and take out all the seeds; then grate them; make a bag like a jelly-bag of some thin muslin cotton, and hang them up to drain over night; chop two or three onions and two or three green peppers, a tablespoon of salt, and thin substance left in the bag, with a quart of best vinegar. If made of good vinegar will keep two or three years.

SWEET PICKLES.

PICKLED CHERRIES.

Five pounds of cherries, stoned or not; one quart of vinegar, two pounds of sugar, one-half ounce of cinnamon; one-half ounce of cloves, one-half ounce of mace; boil the sugar and vinegar and spices together, (grind the spices and tie them in a muslin bag,) and pour hot over the cherries.

PICKLED PLUMS.

Mrs. Meek.

To seven pounds plums, four pounds sugar, two ounces stick cinnamon, two ounces cloves, one quart vinegar, add a little mace; put in the jar first a layer of plums, then a layer of spices alternately; scald the vinegar and sugar together; pour it over the plums, repeat three times for plums (only once for cut apples and pears); the fourth time scald all together; put them into glass jars and they are ready for use.

PICKLED APPLES.

Mrs. Watson Thatcher.

For one peck of sweet apples take three pounds of sugar, two quarts of vinegar, one-half ounce of cinnamon, one-half ounce cloves; pare the apples, leaving them whole; boil them in part of the vinegar and sugar until you can put a fork through them; take them out, beat the remainder of vinegar and sugar and pour over them. Be careful not to boil them too long or they will break.

PICKLED APPLES.

Mrs. Henry Stevens.

Ten pounds fruit, four pounds sugar, one quart vinegar, cloves and cinnamon. Pare and core the apples. Boil apples in syrup until soft. Eat with pleasure, not with sauce.

PICKLED PEACHES.

Mrs. Dr. Evarts.

One quart sugar, one pint vinegar, one gallon fruit; let sugar and vinegar come to a boil; pour over the fruit, next day draw off and let the liquor come to a boil again; repeat till the ninth day, then boil fruit and syrup ten minutes. Spice to taste.

PICKLED PEACHES.

Mrs. C. D. Howard.

Take five pounds of brown sugar to one gallon of pure cider vinegar; boil it hard for thirty minutes, skimming off the scum till clear; rub off the peaches in the meantime out of boiling water (quickly); with a flannel cloth, sticking four cloves in each peach, and a bag of cinnamon put into the boiling syrup. If the peaches are clingstones, put them into the boiling syrup for fifteen or twenty minutes; if freestones, lay them in the jar in layers, and pour the syrup over them while hot; then put a small plate over to keep them from rising, and cover tightly

with cloth or paper. In four days look at them, and if
• necessary, boil the syrup again, and pour on while hot;
keep them in a cool place while the weather is hot to prevent their souring. . The White Sugar Cling is nice for
pickling, and the Blood Peach is very rich, but dark.
Small pears can be pickled in the same manner, if the
skin is taken off.

SOUR PICKLES.

" Who peppered the highest was surest to please."

PREPARED MUSTARD.

C. D. Adams.

Two tablespoons mustard, one teaspoon sugar, one-half
teaspoon salt, boiling water enough to mix it; when cold,
add one tablespoon salad oil, and vinegar enough to thin
it. This will keep a week or two.

TOMATO CATSUP.

Mrs. Monroe Heath.

Select good ripe tomatoes, scald and strain through a
coarse sieve to remove seeds and skins; then add to each
gallon when cold, four tablespoons of salt, three of ground
mustard, two of black pepper, one of ground allspice,
one-half of cloves, one-half of cayenne. pepper, and one
pint of white wine or cider vinegar; simmer slowly four
hours; bottle and cork tight.

PICKLED CUCUMBERS.

Mrs. A. P. Wightman.

Pick those that are small and of quick growth, wash well and pour boiling water over them with a little salt. Let them stand twelve hours; put them into cold vinegar. To a gallon of vinegar, put one tablespoon of pulverized alum, and a teacup of salt; let them remain in this until your vinegar is full of cucumbers, then scald them in it, and put them into new vinegar. Red peppers improve them.

OUDE SAUCE.

C. Kennicott.

One pint green tomatoes, six peppers (not large); four onions, chop together; add one cup salt, and let it stand over night; in the morning, drain off the water; add one cup sugar, one cup horse radish, one tablespoon ground cloves, one tablespoon cinnamon, cover with vinegar, and stew gently all day.

MY MOTHER'S FAVORITE PICKLES.

Mrs. Savage.

One quart raw cabbage chopped fine; one quart boiled beets chopped fine; two cups of sugar, tablespoon of salt, one teaspoon black pepper, one-fourth teaspoon red pepper, one teacup of grated horse radish; cover with cold vinegar, and keep from the air.

FRENCH PICKLES.

H. N. Jenks.

One peck of tomatoes sliced, six large onions, some

cauliflower (much or little as you prefer); a pint of salt thrown over them at night, the liquor drained off in the morning; then boil the tomatoes, onions, etc., in two quarts of water, and one quart of vinegar, fifteen or twenty minutes. After boiling, put it in a colander and drain it off; add seven pints of vinegar, two pounds brown sugar, one-half of white mustard seed, two tablespoons of ground allspice, two of cloves, two of ginger, two of cinnamon, two of ground mustard, one-half a tablespoon of cayenne; put all in a kettle and boil fifteen or twenty minutes; stir and be careful not to burn.

MIXED PICKLES.
Mrs. F. M. Cragin.

Three hundred small cucumbers, four green peppers sliced fine, two large or three small heads cauliflower, three heads of white cabbage shaved fine, nine large onions sliced, one large root horse radish, one quart of green beans cut one inch long, one quart green tomatoes sliced; put this mixture in a pretty strong brine twenty-four hours; drain three hours, then sprinkle in one-fourth pound black and one-fourth pound of white mustard seed; also one tablespoon black ground pepper; let it come to a good boil in just vinegar enough to cover it, adding a little alum. Drain again, and when cold, mix in one-half pint of ground mustard; cover the whole with good cider vinegar; 'add tumeric enough to color, if you like.

PICKLED CABBAGE.
Mrs. A. N. Arnold.

Select solid heads, slice very fine, put in a jar, then

cover with boiling water; when cold, drain off the water, and season with grated horse radish, salt, equal parts of black and red pepper, cinnamon, and cloves whole; cover with strong vinegar. This is convenient and always good.

WEST INDIA PICKLE.
Mrs. Edward Ely.

One white crisp cabbage, two heads cauliflower, three heads celery, one quart each of small green plums, peaches, grapes, radish pods, nasturtium seeds, artichokes, tomatoes and string beans. The green part of a.watermelon next to the rind; one quart small onions parboiled in milk; one hundred small cucumbers about an inch or so long, a few green peppers, and three limes or green lemons. Cut fine the cabbage, cauliflower, celery, pepper, and limes, and green ginger; mix well with the rest, then pour a strong hot brine over them, and let them stand three hours, then take out and let them drain over night. Mix one ounce tumeric powder, with a little cold vinegar, add one bottle French mustard, ground cinnamon, allspice, two nutmegs, black pepper, four pounds white sugar and one gallon vinegar, pour boiling hot over the pickle; if not sufficient liquid to moisten nicely, add more vinegar.

PICKLED ONIONS.
Mrs. Anna Marble.

Peel your onions and let them lie in a weak brine made of salt and water (over night); then put them in a jar, cover them with boiling white wine and vinegar. Cover close and tie down when cold.

PICKLED MELONS.

Mrs. Wicker.

Take ripe melons, wash, pare and take out the seeds, cut them in slices; put them in a stone jar, cover with vinegar, and let them stand twenty-four hours. Take out, and to each quart of fresh vinegar add three pounds brown sugar; for twelve melons take three ounces cinnamon, two of cloves, two of allspice; boil the sugar and spices in the vinegar; skim it well, then put in the melons and boil for twenty minutes; let the syrup boil a few minutes after taking them out, then pour it over them.

PICKLED CAULIFLOWER.

After cutting off all the green leaves, put the cauliflower into boiling water, with a good supply of salt, and boil from three to five minutes; take them out of the salt and water, dip them in clear cold water one minute, to send the heat to the heart of the cauliflower, cut them in pieces convenient to put in jars, then make a mixture of one tablespoon of mace, one of cloves, one of allspice, one of ginger, two of white mustard seed, and a red pepper pod, with each a gallon of vinegar. Let the mixture boil and pour it upon the cauliflower, cover them closely and let them stand one week, then pour off the vinegar, scald it, and return it hot again to the cauliflower; then put them in jars ready for use. The best cider vinegar should be used, and if it is not perfectly clear it will dissolve the cauliflower.

BRINE FOR CUCUMBERS.

Mrs. J. B. Adams.

Three pails water, two quarts coarse salt (rock is good,)

one pound alum, one pound black pepper, tied in a bag; dissolve the alum in a little hot water; put all into a jar or keg; wash the cucumbers with great care, and have none that are bruised ; throw them in and place a weight to keep them under. When wanted for pickling, soak a short time, changing the water as often as necessary.

CONGRESS PICKLES.
S. S. Pierce.

Wash the cucumbers; take one pint of fine salt to one hundred medium sized cucumbers, and sprinkle it over them ; pour on boiling hot water enough to cover them; let them stand forty-eight hours ; take them out of the brine, wipe them, put them in jars, and pour over them scalding hot vinegar with any spices you like. If the vinegar becomes tasteless, put them into fresh vinegar before using them. Keep them covered tight.

RECIPE FOR 600 PICKLES.
Mrs. F. D. Gray.

Make a brine of cold water and salt strong enough to bear an egg; heat boiling hot and pour over the cucumbers ; let them stand twenty-four hours, then take out and wipe dry ; scald vinegar and pour over them and let them stand twenty-four hours ; then pour off, and to fresh vinegar add one quart brown sugar, two large green peppers, one-half pint white mustard, six cents' worth of ginger-root, the same of cinnamon, allspice and cloves; one tablespoon celery seed, alum the size of a butternut ; scald these together and pour boiling hot on the cucumbers.

PICKLED CUCUMBERS.

Mrs. Packard.

Wash with care your cucumbers, and place in jars. Make a weak brine (a handful of salt to a gallon and a half of water.) When scalding hot, turn over the cucumbers and cover; repeat this process three mornings in succession, taking care to skim thoroughly. On the fourth day have ready a porcelain kettle of vinegar, to which has been added a piece of alum the size of a walnut. When scalding hot, put in as many cucumbers as may be covered with the vinegar; do not let them boil, but skim off as soon as scalded through, and replace with others, adding each time a small piece of alum. When this process is through, throw out the vinegar and replace with good cider or white wine vinegar; add spices, mustard seed and red peppers. Sort the pickles and place in stone or glass jars, turn over the hot spiced vinegar; seal and put away the jars not needed for immediate use. Pickles thus prepared are fine and crisp at the expiration of a year. Those that are kept in open-mouth jars may be covered with a cloth, which will need to be taken off and rinsed occasionally. I prefer green peppers, and prepare them with cucumbers in brine. They are not as apt to become soft.

GREEN TOMATO PICKLES.

Mrs. J. L. Harris, Keokuk, Iowa.

Chop one-half peck tomatoes, three onions, a gill of horse-radish, three green peppers; put them in a sieve and drain dry, salt in layers and let them stand one night;

drain the next day, scald vinegar and pour over it ; let it stand two or three days ; drain again, scald a pound of sugar to a quart of vinegar, a tablespoon black pepper, the same of allspice, three ounces of ground cloves, three ounces of mustard, a gill of mustard seed. Boil the spices in a little vinegar.

RIPE TOMATO PICKLES.
Mrs. C. M. Dickerman, Rockford, Ill.

To seven pounds of ripe tomatoes add three pounds sugar, one quart vinegar, boil them together fifteen minutes, skim out the tomatoes and boil the syrup a few minutes longer. Spice to suit the taste with cloves and cinnamon.

PICCALILLI.
Mrs. C. Bradley.

One peck of green tomatoes, slice them thin, add one pint of salt, cover with cold water, and let them stand twenty-four hours; then chop very fine one head of cab-bage, six onions, twelve green peppers; then cover it with hot vinegar, drain it through a sieve, add one pint of molasses, one tablespoon cloves, allspice, two ounces of white mustard seed, and cover with cold vinegar.

PICCALILLI.
Mrs. Lamkin.

One peck of green tomatoes; (if the flavor of onions is desired, take eight, but it is very nice without any,) four green peppers; slice all, and put in layers, sprinkle on

10

one cup of salt, and let them remain over night; in the morning press dry through a sieve, put it in a porcelain kettle and cover with vinegar; add one cup of sugar, a tablespoon of each kind of spice; put into a muslin bag; stew slowly about an hour, or until the tomatoes are as soft as you desire.

SWEET GREEN TOMATO PICKLES.

Mrs. P.

One peck of green tomatoes sliced, six large onions sliced; sprinkle through them one teacup of salt, let them stand over night; drain off in the morning; take two quarts of water and one of vinegar, boil the tomatoes and onions five minutes; drain through a colander, take four quarts of vinegar, two pounds of brown sugar, one-half pound of ground mustard, two tablespoons of cloves, two of ginger, two of cinnamon, one-half teaspoon of cayenne pepper, or instead five or six green peppers chopped; boil fifteen minutes. This will keep good a year, if prepared according to the recipe, and is generally liked.

PICKLED GREEN TOMATOES.

S. S. Pierce.

One peck tomatoes, two quarts small white onions, one dozen green peppers, one cup salt, one cup sugar, one tablespoon of cloves, allspice, stick of cinnamon; slice your tomatoes over night, and mix in the salt. In the morning drain off the water and throw it away; put all the ingredients together and let it come to a boil. Put away for use.

CHOW-CHOW.

Mrs. John Corthell.

Two heads of cabbage, two heads cauliflower, one dozen cucumbers, six roots of celery, six peppers, one quart or small white onions, two quarts green tomatoes; cut into small pieces, and boil each vegetable separately until tender, then strain them. Two gallons of vinegar, one-fourth pound of mustard, one-fourth pound of mustard seed, one pot of French mustard, one ounce of cloves, two ounces of turmeric; put the vinegar and spices into a kettle and let them come to a boil; mix the vegetables and pour over the dressing.

CHOW-CHOW.

Mrs. C. A. Rogers.

One-half bushel green tomatoes, one dozen onions, one dozen green peppers (chopped fine), sprinkle with salt, and let it stand over night; then drain off the lime, cover it with vinegar, and cook one hour slowly; drain again and pack closely in a jar; take two pounds sugar, two tablespoons of cinnamon, one pound of allspice, one each of cloves and pepper, one-half cup ground mustard, one pint horse-radish, and vinegar enough to mix them; then when boiling hot, pour it over the mixture in the jar, and cover tightly.

CHOW-CHOW.

Mrs. King.

Take a peck of cucumbers, one peck of onions, half a peck of string beans, three heads of cauliflower, three bunches of celery, a half dozen sweet peppers; soak the whole in strong salt and water over night; in the morning drain off the brine and scald them all in weak salt and water, but before scalding cut them into shape so that they will go easily into glass jars; add three-quarters of a pound of mustard, two packages of curry powder, and six quarts of good vinegar; put the mustard and curry powder into the vinegar, and let it come to a boil; put the pickles into the cans, and pour the liquid over them while hot. Do not cover while scalding.

CANTELOPE PICKLES.

Mrs. Earle.

Take fine ripe cantelopes, wash, pare and cut into small pieces, taking out the seeds; cover them with vinegar for twenty-four hours; throw away one quart of the vinegar to each quart remaining, allow three pounds sugar to a dozen cantelopes, three ounces stick cinnamon, two ounces cloves, two ounces of allspice (spices whole), boil them with the vinegar, when well skimmed put in the fruit, boil fifteen minutes, then take out, boil and skim ·▸syrup, and pour boiling hot over the fruit.

PICKLED OYSTERS.

Mrs. Carl Hammond.

Wash the oysters and scald them in strong salt and water; skim them out and throw into cold water; scald vinegar well and whole peppers; let it get cold. Put the oysters in a stone jar; make liquor to cover them of water they were scalded in, and vinegar. A cup of vinegar to one quart liquor, to be used cold.

TO PICKLE MARTINOES OR MARTYNIAS.

Mrs. E. S. Chesbrough.

Pick when soft enough to run a pin through, or from two to three inches long. Throw in brine till ready to put up. Soak in clear water one night or longer if very salt, then scald in weak vinegar; skim out and throw in cold water; then pour over them, (after draining from the water,) scalding hot vinegar and sugar in the proportion of five pounds of sugar to each gallon of vinegar, a handful of cloves and cinnamon, or whatever spices desired, scalded in the vinegar. If the martinoes are not tender enough the scalding can be repeated.

BREAKFAST AND SUPPER.

RELISHES.

OYSTER STEW

Mrs. A. S. Ewing.

Strain the juice from the oysters placed in the colander into a stew pan; let it come to a boil; remove the scum and a clear liquor will remain ; turn cold water upon the oysters, and rinse thoroughly; add them to the liquor, with a cup of cream or milk, butter, salt and cayenne pepper. Have ready buttered dice-shaped pieces of toast upon a meat dish; pour the oysters over, garnish with parsley, and serve hot.

TOAST.

Toast the bread very quickly, dip each slice in boiling

water (a little salt in the water); as soon as you have toasted it; then spread it with butter; cover and keep hot as you proceed. Make milk toast in the same way, keeping the milk at nearly boiling heat; it is better to spread the butter on the bread after it is dipped in hot milk, than to melt it in the milk; thicken what milk is left with a little corn starch, and pour over the toast when sent to the table.

FRENCH TOAST.
Mrs. M. J. Savage.

To one egg thoroughly beaten, put one cup of sweet milk and a little salt. Slice light bread, and dip into the mixture, allowing each slice to absorb some of the milk; then brown on a hot buttered griddle; spread with butter and serve hot.

TONGUE TOAST.
M. A. P.

Take cold boiled tongue, mince it fine; mix it with cream or milk, and to every half pint of the mixture, allow the well beaten yolks of two eggs; place over the fire and let it simmer a minute or two; have ready some nicely toasted bread; butter it; place it on a hot dish and pour the mixture over; send to the table hot.

LEMON TOAST.
E. A. Forsyth.

Take the yolks of six eggs, beat them well and add three cups of sweet milk; take baker's bread not too stale and cut into slices; dip them into the milk and eggs, and lay the slices into a spider, with sufficient melted butter hot to fry a nice delicate brown; take the whites of the six eggs, and beat them to a froth, adding a large cup of white sugar; add the juice of two lemons, heating well, and adding two cups boiling water; serve over the toast as a sauce, and you will find it a very delicious dish.

FRIED BREAD IN BATTER.

M. A. T.

Take one tablespoon sweet light dough; dissolve it in one cup sweet milk; add three or four eggs, one and a half cups flour, one teaspoon of salt; cut some thin slices of light bread, dip in this batter, and fry in hot lard; sprinkle with powdered sugar, and garnish with jelly.

CODFISH BALLS.

Mrs. Banks.

Take four cups of mashed potatoes; three cups of boiled codfish minced fine; add butter; mix well together; then add two well beaten eggs, beating it up again thoroughly; drop by spoonfuls into hot lard and fry the same as doughnuts. Are nice fried in croquette baskets.

CODFISH PUFF.

Mrs. Banks.

Recipe the same as for codfish balls put in an earthern baking plate; smooth over the top, and put over some butter. and then in a hot oven to bake.

CODFISH HASH.

Mrs. N. P. Wilder.

One pint boiled picked codfish well freshened, one quart cold boiled chopped potatoes mixed well together, three slices salt pork freshened, cut in very small pieces and fried brown; remove half the pork, and add your fish and potatoes to the remainder; let it stand and steam five minutes without stirring; be careful not to let it burn; then add one-third cup milk and stir thoroughly; put the remainder of the pork around the edge of the spider, and a little butter over it; simmer it over a slow fire for half an hour, until a brown crust is formed, when turn it over on a platter and serve.

BEEF HASH.

Chop fine cold beef, either boiled or baked; have ready cold boiled potatoes; to one pint of meat put one pint and a little more of potatoes, chopped fine; have ready a spider, with a good piece of butter in it; put in the hash; season with pepper and salt, and then add rich milk or cream. Milk is a very great improvement.

CORNED BEEF HASH.

One and one-half pounds nice corned beef, boiled tender and chopped fine; one-third more potatoes when chopped than meat; three large onions sliced fine and browned in butter, and when tender, add the meat and potatoes, well seasoned with salt and pepper; enough water to moisten. A small red pepper chopped fine is a great improvement. It is good without onions also.

BREAKFAST STEAK.

A nice steak of beef or veal; pound it with a steak mallet, if tough; lay in a baking tin, dredge it lightly with flour, season with salt and pepper, and if you like, a little chopped parsley; then put in the oven and bake for twenty or thirty minutes, or until sufficiently well done; take it up, put it on the platter, spread with butter, and dredge into the juices of the meat in the baking pan, a little flour, and season with butter; let this boil up, and pour over the steak. This is very nice.

SIDE DISH.

R. A. Sibley.

Chopped cold meat well seasoned; wet with gravy, if convenient, put it on a platter; then take cold rice made moist with milk and one egg, season with pepper and salt; if not sufficient rice, add powdered bread crumbs; place this around the platter quite thick; set in oven to heat and brown.

ANOTHER SIDE DISH.

R. A. Sibley.

Cold turkey, chicken or any cold meat, chopped fine, seasoned with salt, pepper and gravy; lay pie crust round the edge of the platter, and cover the same; bake a nice brown in the oven. Very little meat makes a dish for several persons.

HAM AND EGGS.

Anonymous.

Take pieces of cold ham chopped, and after cooking, add beaten eggs to suit your taste.

A NICE BREAKFAST DISH.

Harriet N. Jenks.

Mince cold beef or lamb ; if beef put in a pinch of pulverized cloves; if lamb, a pinch of summer savory to season it, very little pepper and some salt, and put it in a baking dish; mash potatoes and mix them with cream and butter and a little salt, and spread them over the meat ; beat up an egg with cream or milk, a very little; spread it over the potatoes, and bake it a short time, sufficient to warm it through and brown the potatoes.

POTATO PUFFS.

S. S. Pierce.

Take cold roast meat (either beef, veal or mutton); clear it from gristle ; chop fine; season with pepper and salt ; boil and mash some potatoes, and make them into a paste with one or two eggs; roll it out with a little flour; cut it round with a saucer; put your seasoned meat on one half; fold it over like a puff; turn it neatly round, and fry it a light brown. Nice for breakfast.

POTATO PUFF.

Anonymous.

Mealy potato, nicely mashed and seasoned with rich milk, butter, salt, pepper and two eggs ; the whites and yolks well beaten separately. Mix all lightly together, put in a pie dish and in the oven to brown. The crust is made richer by spreading with a little butter after putting in the oven.

RICE CAKES.

Mrs. A. M. Gibbs.

One teacup of soft boiled rice, the yolk of one egg, a pinch of salt, two tablespoons of sifted flour, beaten well together; add sweet milk until it is about the consistency of sponge cake or thick cream, and just before baking stir in lightly the beaten white of the egg. The less flour used the better for invalids.

CHICKEN CROQUETTES.

Mrs. Chaffee, Detroit.

One plump chicken, two pounds veal cut from the round. Boil chicken and veal separately in cold water, just enough to cover; pick to pieces and chop. Cut up one-third of a loaf of bread and soak in the broth of the chicken while warm; put all in a chopping bowl; season with salt, pepper, mace and nutmeg; beat three eggs light and mix with the above ingredients; make up in oblong balls; fry brown in hot lard and butter, equal parts.

VEAL STEW.

Two pounds of veal steak cut in strips. Put in cold water in a skillet or spider and over the fire. The water should be just sufficient to cover the meat. Pare, wash and slice one small potato and put in with the meat. Stew for twenty or thirty minutes gently, taking care that the water does not boil away. Have ready two or three eggs boiled in the shell. When the meat is tender add to the broth one cup of fresh milk and one heaping tablespoon of flour wet with milk; season all with butter, salt and

pepper, and, if you like, a little parsley. Cut the hard
boiled eggs in slices and put into the broth. Let all boil
up once, and serve with or without toast on the platter.
A very nice breakfast dish.

BAKED EGGS.
Mrs. L. M. Angle.

Break six or seven eggs into a buttered dish, taking care
that each is whole, and does not encroach upon the others
so much as to mix or disturb the yolks ; sprinkle with
pepper and salt, and put a bit of butter upon each. Put
into an oven and bake until the whites are set. This is
far superior to fried eggs, and very nice for breakfast,
served on toast or alone.

· POACHED EGGS.

Break as many eggs as you wish to use, one at a time,
and drop carefully into a spider filled with boiling water.
When the whites of the eggs are well set, slip a spoon
carefully under and take out, laying each upon a small
piece of buttered toast on the platter. Put a very small
piece of butter on each egg, a slight dash of pepper, and
serve immediately.

EGG BASKETS.
Mrs. F. M. Cragin.

Make these for breakfast the day after you have had
roast chicken, duck, or turkey for dinner. Boil six eggs
hard, cut neatly in half and extract the yolks; rub these
to a paste with some melted butter, pepper and salt and

set aside. Pound the minced meat of the cold fowl fine
in the same manner and mix with the egg paste, moistening with melted butter as you proceed, or with a little
gravy if you have it to spare; cut off a slice from the hol-
lowed whites of the egg to make them stand; fill in with
the paste; arrange close together upon a flat dish and
pour over them the gravy left from yesterday's roast,
heated boiling hot, and mellowed by a few spoons of
cream or rich milk.

ESCALOPED EGGS.

Put into a buttered baking dish a layer of bread-crumbs
moistened with milk or meat broth. Have ready some
hard boiled eggs; prepare a thick drawn butter gravy, to
which you must add a well-beaten egg. (There need be
but a small quantity of this, not more than half a teacup
for five eggs.) In the drawn butter dip each slice of egg
and place a layer upon the bread crumbs; sprinkle these
with minced meat of ham, veal, or chicken. Upon this
place another layer of bread crumbs and eggs and meat
until you have used all the eggs · cover with sifted bread
crumbs and heat well through.

OMELETS.

HOW TO MAKE AN OMELET.

A distinguished authority says: In preparing an omelet remember five things — a clean pan; the eggs must not be beaten too much; the omelet must not be too large; three eggs are better than six eggs, which make two omelets; they should not be too much cooked; they should be eaten immediately, or they become tough and more like a pancake. To which we would add that the finest omelets have no milk added to them. The eggs should be broken into a dish and beaten up with a little minced parsley. The butter should be melted in the saucepan, then the omelet poured in, and as soon as well set so the cook can raise the edges, should be folded and taken up.

OMELET.

With ham, cold tongue and other meats. Beat half a dozen eggs quite light, have ready minced meat of ham or tongue, cold chicken or veal; put this into a dish with a little butter to warm through, but not to fry. Then turn the eggs into a spider, in which you have previously heated two or three tablespoons of butter. Let the omelet brown lightly on the lower side and the upper, form-ing a thin custard, and season to taste. Then put in the meat, fold the omelet over and take up quickly. Serve immediately.

OMELET.

Miss E. C. Harris.

One cup of milk, one tablespoon flour stirred into the milk; four eggs, the yolks and whites beaten separately; one-half tablespoon melted butter stirred into the mixture;

a little salt. Stir in the whites before putting it into the spider. Cook on top of the stove about ten minutes, then set the spider in the oven to brown the top. To be eaten as soon as taken from the oven. Very nice.

OMELET SOUFFLE.
Mrs. Lamkin.

One pint boiled milk, three spoons flour, yolks of seven eggs, beaten with the flour; season with pepper and salt, and add a piece of butter size of egg; mix well, then add whites well beaten; bake twenty minutes.

FRIED OMELET.
Mrs. F. B. Orr.

Three eggs, two gills milk, two tablespoons flour, a little salt and pepper, fried on hot griddle.

FRIAR'S OMELET.
Mrs. DeForest, Freeport.

Boil a dozen apples, as for sauce; stir in one-fourth pound of butter, ditto white sugar; when cold, add four well beaten eggs, and a few spoons of cream; put it into a baking dish, well buttered, and thickly strewn with bread crumbs on the bottom and sides; strew currants over the top. Bake forty-five minutes; turn on a platter, and sift sugar over it. Serve with sugar and cream, or a boiled custard; the latter is much the nicer.

OMELET.
E. V. Case, Elmhurst.

Take three eggs, beat the whites and yolks separately;

to the yolks after they are beaten, add a half teaspoon of salt and a teacup of rich cream, in which a heaping teaspoon of flour has been smoothly rubbed; lastly stir in the whites which have been beaten as for cake; have ready a spider in which has been melted a tablespoon of lard, and which is as hot as can be and not be burned; pour in the mixture and let it stand till it is a rich brown on the bottom.

FRENCH OMELET.
M.

One cup boiling milk with one tablespoon of butter melted in it; pour this on one cup of bread crumbs (the bread must be light); add salt, pepper and the yolks of six eggs well beaten; mix thoroughly; and lastly, add the six whites cut to a stiff froth; mix lightly and fry with hot butter; this will make two; when almost done, turn together in shape of half moon.

BOILED OMELET.
E. M. Walker.

Four eggs well beaten up with a little pepper, salt, nutmeg, chopped parsley and chives; one-half pint of cream (or milk); half fill little well buttered cups or moulds and set them in boiling water; boil for ten minutes, then turn out. They may be served with a sauce.

BAKED OMELET.
Mrs. Edward Ely.

Six eggs, two tablespoons of flour, a little salt, one cup of milk. Take a little of the milk, and stir the flour into

11

it; add the rest of the milk, and the yolks of the eggs; then beat the whites of the eggs to a stiff froth, and pour into the flour, milk and yolks; put a piece of butter the size of a small egg into an iron spider, and let it get hot, but not so the butter will burn; then pour the mixture in and put in a moderate oven to bake in the spider. It takes about ten minutes to bake. Then slip a knife under and loosen, and slip off on a large plate or platter.

OMELET.

M. A. T.

Seven eggs beaten separately; add the yolks, one-half teacup sweet milk or cream, a tablespoon of flour, salt and pepper; after beating them very light, mix well; lastly, add the whites cut to a stiff froth; mix very lightly and only a little. Fry with butter on a quick fire. When brown, fold together and serve immediately. This will make two omelets.

VEAL OMELET.

Mrs. J. S. Gano.

Three pounds of lean veal, two eggs, six small butter crackers, one tablespoon of thyme, one of salt, one of pepper, two of milk; knead it like bread and bake it two hours in a slow oven, basting it with butter often, then slice for tea.

CHEESE SCALLOP.

Soak one cup of dry bread crumbs in fresh milk. Beat into this three eggs; add one tablespoon of butter and one-half a pound of grated cheese; strew upon the top sifted bread crumbs, and bake in the oven a delicate brown. An excellent relish when eaten with thin slices of bread and butter.

CHEESE SANDWICHES.
Anonymous.

One-half a pound of mild fresh cheese grated, a tablespoon of butter, the yolk of three hard boiled eggs and a teaspoon of mayonaise. Mash the yolks well, and mix with the other ingredients. Spread thinly cut slices of bread with butter, and spread with the dressing; then roll or fold together as sandwiches. Very nice for lunch.

WELSH RABBIT.
Mrs. Anna Marble.

One pound of cheese, melt; mix three tablespoons of olive oil, one tablespoon dry mustard, one teaspoon salt; pepper to taste. Put these in cheese when melted; add one-half pint ale.

CHEESE FONDU.
After Marion Harland.

Soak one cup of very dry fine bread crumbs in two scant cups of milk (rich and fresh, or it will curdle); beat into this three eggs whipped very light, add one small tablespoon of melted butter, pepper and salt, and lastly one-half a pound of old cheese grated. Butter a neat baking dish, pour the *fondu* into it; strew dry bread crumbs over the top, and bake in a quick oven a delicate brown. Serve immediately in the baking dish, as it soon falls. A delicious relish,

FISH RELISH.

After Marion Harland.

One cup of drawn butter with an egg beaten in, two hard boiled eggs, mashed potato (a cup will do), one cup of cold fish (cod, halibut or shad), roe of cod or shad and one teaspoon of butter, one teaspoon of minced parsley, pepper and salt to taste. Method: Dry the roe previously well boiled; mince the fish fine and season; wash up the roe with the butter and the yolks of the boiled eggs; cut the white into thin rings; put a layer of mashed potatoes at the bottom of a deep buttered dish; then alternate layers of fish; drawn butter with the rings of the whites embedded in this roe; more potato at top; cover and set in the oven until it smokes and bubbles; brown by removing the cover a few minutes. Send to table in the baking dish, and pass pickles with it.

LAPLANDERS FOR BREAKFAST.

Mrs. A. L. Chetlain.

Three eggs, three cups of flour, three cups of sweet milk, one teaspoon of melted butter, and a little salt; beat well together, then bake in iron moulds.

BREAKFAST GEMS.

Mrs. Brown.

One cup sweet milk, one and a half cups flour, one egg, one teaspoon salt, one teaspoon baking powder; beaten together five minutes; bake in *hot* gem pans, in a hot oven about fifteen minutes.

BREAKFAST BUNS.

Mrs. J. W. Preston.

Two cups of flour, three-fourths cup of corn meal, three-fourths cup of butter, one-half cup of sugar, two eggs beaten, one cup of milk, three teaspoons baking powder; bake in hot oven twenty minutes.

QUICK SALLY LUNN.

One cup of sugar, one-half a cup of butter; stir well together, and then add one or two eggs ; put in one good pint of sweet milk, and with sufficient flour to make a batter about as stiff as cake ; put in three teaspoons of baking powder; bake and eat hot with butter, for tea or breakfast.

BREAKFAST CAKE.

Mrs. C. Bradley.

One pint of flour, three tablespoons of butter, three tablespoons of sugar, one egg, one cup sweet milk, one teaspoon cream tartar, one-half teaspoon soda; to be eaten with butter.

RYE CAKES FOR TEA.

Harriet N. Jenks.

Two teacups of rye flour, one of wheat flour, one of sour milk, one teaspoon of soda, put in the sour milk, and while foaming stir it in the flour and rye, with one-half teaspoon of salt, one-half teacup of molasses ; make it stiff and turn it into a buttered pan ; spread it smooth with a spoon dipped in hot water ; bake one-half hour.

RYE GRIDDLE CAKES.

Stir into sour milk sufficient rye flour to make a batter for griddle cakes ; add salt and a little soda, and bake on a hot griddle. These are very simple, but very nice.

JOLLY BOYS.

Jeannie Brayton.

One quart corn meal; scald and cool; one pint of flour, two eggs, one teaspoon soda, two of cream tartar, a little milk, salt ; make as thick as pancakes, and fry in hot lard. Nice for breakfast..

GRAHAM BREAKFAST CAKES.

Mrs. A. M. Gibbs.

Two cups of Graham flour, one cup of wheat flour, two eggs well beaten ; mix with sweet milk, to make a very thin batter; bake in gem irons; have the irons hot, then set them on the upper grate in the oven; will bake in fifteen minutes.

TEA CAKE.

Mrs. H. P. Stowell.

One egg, one cup sugar, one cup sweet milk, piece of butter size of an egg, one teaspoon cream-tartar, one-half teaspoon soda, one pint of flour. Eaten warm.

COTTAGE CHEESE.

Mrs. A. M. Gibbs.

Pour boiling water on the thick milk in the pan in which it has turned, stirring while you pour; as soon as the milk separates from the whey and begins to appear cooked, let it settle ; in a minute or two most of the water and whcy can be poured off; if not sufficiently cooked, more hot water may be used ; set the pan on edge, and with your spoon or hand draw the curd to the upper side, pressing out as much water as possible; if desired, it can stand a few moments in cold water; when squeezed dry, work the curd fine, rolling it between the hands; add salt and cream to taste; in very warm weather when the milk has turned quickly, it is very palatable without the addition of cream.

WHITE CORN BREAD.

Mrs. E. S. Cheeseborough.

One pint of meal thoroughly scalded with hard-boiling water. Butter the size of an egg and one well-beaten egg; add milk to make it just thin enough to flow over the pan. Have the batter an inch thick, and then bake.

YPSILANTI EGG ROLLS.

Mrs. A. M. Gibbs.

Allow one egg for each person, two cups of milk for three eggs, four teaspoons of flour. Beat whites and yolks separately, and add the eggs last. Put a very little of the mixture into a hot frying pan well greased with butter; roll as you would omelet and put on a platter. Send in hot. For breakfast or tea. Can be eaten with sugar.

VEGETABLES.

BOILED POTATOES.

Old potatoes are better for being peeled and put in cold water an hour before being put over to boil. They should then be put into fresh cold water, when set over the fire. New potatoes should always be put into boiling water, and it is best to prepare them just in time for cooking. Are better steamed than boiled.

MASHED POTATOES.

Mrs. F. D. J.

Peel the potatoes, and let them stand in cold water for half an hour; then put in the steamer over boiling water and cook them until mealy and *quite tender*. Have ready an earthen basin, or a bright tin pan, into which you will put your potatoes, so that while mashing and preparing,

(168)

they can be kept on the stove and hot. Now mash well and finely with the potato-masher, and then season with salt; allow a generous piece of butter, and lastly, add a teacup of rich milk; mix altogether well, and then take up on a deep dish.

There will now be three or four ways to finish this, and which are, first by putting a little butter on the top, after smoothing nicely, and putting it a moment at the mouth of the oven, and then serving quite hot; or, you may put it into the oven, which should be quick and hot, and bake the crust of a rich brown. Or, again, the top may be scored a golden brown with steel bars made for this purpose. Or, lastly, after mashing the potato, put it into a mold and shape it; then loosen it from the mold and turn it on to a flat piece of sheet iron, large enough to cover the bottom of the mold with handles at the sides. Then have ready hot lard in which you immerse the molded potato and fry a rich golden brown. Take out and with a knife under, slide carefully on your platter. Garnish the dish around with curled parsley leaves. If the potato is put in the oven to brown, it should be put in a baking plate and may be sent to the table in the dish in which it is baked, with a knitted cover over.

POTATOES AND CREAM.

Mince cold boiled potatoes fine; put them into a spider with melted butter in it; let them fry a little in the butter well covered; then put in a fresh piece of butter, season with salt and pepper, and pour over cream or rich milk; let it boil up once and serve.

POTATOES FRIED.

Mrs. A.

Pare potatoes; cut in pieces one-half inch wide, and as long as the potato; keep them in cold water till wanted; drop in boiling lard; when nearly done, take them out with a skimmer and drain them; boil up the lard again, and drop them back, and fry till done; this makes them puff up; sprinkle with salt and serve very hot.

SARATOGA FRIED POTATOES.

Cut into thin slices; put them in cold water over night with a small piece of alum to make them crisp; rinse in cold water, and dry with crash towel; fry light brown in boiling lard

POTATO CROQUETTES.

Take finely mashed potato and mix through it sufficient salt, pepper and butter to season well, with sweet milk or cream to moisten; mix thoroughly with this one beaten egg, and then make up into small rolls, being careful to have the surface perfectly smooth. Have ready one plate with a beaten egg upon it, and another with cracker crumbs. Dip each roll into the egg and then into the crumbs, and fry of a rich golden brown in hot lard. Lay the croquettes on brown paper first, and serve on a napkin.

PARSNIPS.

Boil until tender in a little salted water; then take up; skim them, cut in strips, dip in beaten egg, and fry in melted butter or hot lard.

TURNIPS.

Boil until tender; mash and season with butter, pepper, salt and a little rich milk or cream. Serve with mutton.

BEETS.

Clean these nicely, but do not pare them, leaving on a short piece of the stalk. Then put over to boil in hot water. Young beets will cook tender in an hour; old beets require several hours boiling. When done, skin quickly while hot; slice thin into your vegetable dish, put on salt, pepper and a little butter; put over a little vinegar and serve hot or cold.

BAKED SQUASH.

Cut in pieces, scrape well, bake from one to one and a half hours, according to the thickness of the squash; to be eaten with salt and butter as sweet potatoes.

FRIED SQUASHES

Mrs. F. M. Cragin.

Cut the squash into thin slices, and sprinkle it with salt; let it stand a few moments; then beat two eggs, and dip the squash into the egg; then fry it brown in butter.

SUMMER SQUASHES.

Cook them whole; when tender, if large, skin and remove the seeds; if small, this will not be necessary; drain and press the water out with a plate; then put them in a stew-pan, and season well with butter, pepper and salt and a tablespoon of cream.

GREEN CORN—BOILED.

Throw the ears, when husked, into a kettle of boiling water, slightly salted, and boil thirty minutes.   Serve in a napkin.

GREEN CORN OYSTERS.

To a pint of grated corn add two well beaten eggs; one-half cup of cream, and a half cup of flour, with one-half spoon óf baking powder stirred in it; season with pepper and salt and fry in butter, dropping the batter in spoonfuls; serve a few at a time, very hot, as a relish with meats.

CORN OYSTERS.

Mrs. W. P. Nixon.

One dozen ears of corn; two eggs; salt, pepper and a dredging of flour; grate the raw corn, over which dredge a little flour; season well; add the beaten eggs and fry quickly in butter.

GREEN CORN PATTIES.

M.

Grate as much corn as will make one pint; one teacup flour, one teacup butter, one egg, pepper and salt to taste. If too thick, add a little milk, and fry in butter.

SOUTHERN WAY OF BOILING RICE.

Mrs. James S. Gibbs.

Pick over the rice; rinse it in cold water until perfectly clean, then put it in a pot of boiling water, allowing a quart of water to less than a teacup of rice; boil ᴊard seventeen minutes; drain off the water very close, and let it steam fifteen minutes with the lid off. When carefully done in this way, each kernel of rice stands out by itself, while it is perfectly tender. The water in which the rice has been boiled, makes, it is said, good starch for muslin, if boiled a few minutes by itself.

SUCCOTASH.

One pint of green corn cut from the cob, and two-thirds of a pint of Lima beans; let them stew in just enough water to cover them until tender, then season with butter, pepper, salt and a little milk; simmer together a few moments and serve.

BOSTON BAKED BEANS.

Soak over night one pint of beans in clear water; in the morning parboil the beans, and at the same time, in another dish, parboil a piece of salt pork, about three inches long and wide and thick; drain off the water from the beans and pork; put both together in a deep pan with the pork at top; season with one tablespoon of molasses, and bake for several hours. Add a little water when they are put in to bake.

YANKEE BAKED BEANS.

Mrs. Higgins.

Boil the beans until they begin to crack, with a pound or two of salt fat pork; put the beans in the baking pan; score the pork across the top, and settle in the middle;

add two tablespoons of sugar or molasses, and bake in a moderate oven two hours; they should be very moist when first put into the oven, or they will grow too dry in baking; do not forget the sweetening if you want Yankee baked beans.

LIMA BEANS.

Shell and put into cold water and let them stand awhile; then drain and put them into boiling water and cook until tender. Pour off the water and season with a little rich milk, butter, pepper and salt, and let them simmer in this dressing a few minutes before serving. Soak dried Lima beans over night, and allow them over two hours for cooking next day for dinner.

STRING BEANS.

The yellow butter bean is the preferred variety. Cut off each end and the strings from both sides of the pod; then cut the beans in strips lengthwise or across; put into boiling water and cook until perfectly tender. It is well to allow two or three hours to these, as they can be kept hot if done before you wish to serve them. Before sending to the table drain them and pour over them one-half a teacup of rich milk or cream, and season with butter, pepper and salt.

GREEN PEAS.

Shell and put into boiling water, cook from thirty to thirty-five minutes; drain and season with rich milk or cream, butter, pepper and salt; some cooks also add a little flour or corn starch to thicken the gravy, but which should be used very sparingly, not more than a teaspoon. Be sure the peas are young; old peas are fit for nothing but soup.

ASPARAGUS.

Cut off the green ends, and chop up the remainder of the stalks; boil until tender, and season with salt and pepper; have ready some toasted bread in a deep dish; mix together equal parts of flour and butter to a cream; add to this slowly, enough of the asparagus water or clear hot water, to make a sauce; boil this up once; put the asparagus on the toast, and pour over all the sauce.

BAKED CABBAGE.

Boil a cabbage, then put in a colander and drain it until perfectly dry; then chop fine; put in pepper, salt and a little cream, and put in an earthern baking pan, and into the oven. Bake one hour.

COLD SLAW.

One-half a head of cabbage chopped fine; rub to a paste the yolks of three hard boiled eggs; add a table-spoon of melted butter, one teaspoon of dry mustard, one tablespoon of sugar, and one gill of vinegar; mix thoroughly with the cabbage, and garnish with the whites of eggs cut in rings.

DRESSED CABBAGE.

Mrs. B. J. Seward.

One small teacup of vinegar, one egg, two tablespoon,

of sugar, one teaspoon of salt, and butter half the size of an egg; beat the egg before mixing with the other ingredients, which should be previously put over the fire, then put in the egg; stir until it boils; cool and pour over chopped or shaved cabbage.

CABBAGE.

Mrs. A. A. Carpenter.

Cut cabbage as fine as you can slice it; boil in milk thirty minutes, then add butter, pepper and salt, and a little flour to thicken.

CAULIFLOWER.

Remove the leaves; cut the main stalk close to the flower; lay it in boiling milk and water slightly salted, with the stalk down; when done, take out carefully and drain in a colander, then place in the vegetable dish and pour over it a rich drawn butter dressing.

ESCALOPED TOMATOES.

Put in an earthern baking dish, a layer of cracker crumbs and small bits of butter; then a layer of tomatoes with a very little sugar sprinkled over them; then another layer of cracker crumbs seasoned with butter, and a layer of tomatoes, until your dish is full, with the cracker crumbs at the top; pour over all this a little water to moisten, and bake half hour.

STEWED TOMATOES.

Put ripe tomatoes into hot water and skin them; then throw them into an *earthen* stew pan (a new tin will do,

but not so good) ; cut up and let the tomatoes cook gently
a few minutes; season with butter, pepper, salt, and
serve. Or, you may add bread crumbs and sugar to the
tomatoes if preferred. Some cooks stew tomatoes for a
long time, but the flavor is finer if allowed to simmer but
a few moments, just sufficient time to heat well through.

BAKED TOMATOES.

Wash, wipe and then cut in two ; place them in a baking
tin with the skin side down, and season with pepper and
salt, and place in a hot oven; take up carefully when
done, and put bits of butter on each piece of tomato.

FRIED TOMATOES.

Cut a large Feejee tomato in half, flour the cut side,
heat very hot, and put the floured side down ; when brown
on one side, turn ; when done, pour over a teacup of hot
cream or rich milk.

TOMATO HASH.

Butter the dish well; put in a layer of sliced tomatoes,
a layer of cold meat, sliced thin ; then a layer of bread
and butter, and so on until the dish is full, seasoning well
with pepper and salt, and beaten eggs poured over the
top. Bake brown.

FRIED EGG PLANT.

Mrs. F. M. Cragin.

Slice the egg plant, at least half an inch thick ; pare
each piece carefully, and lay in salt and water, putting a

12

plate upon the topmost, to keep it under the brine, and let them remain for an hour or more. Wipe each slice, dip in beaten egg, then in cracker crumbs, and fry in hot lard until well done and nicely browned.

EGG PLANT STEWED.

Put the egg plants into cold water slightly salted, and boil until they can be pierced with a fork, having changed the water once in the meantime. Peel and mash and season with salt water, pepper and butter. Serve hot.

EGG PLANT FRITTERS.

Cook as above until very tender; then drain, skin and mash finely; mix with it butter, salt, and an egg, with two or three tablespoons of flour, and drop by spoonfuls into hot lard.

MACARONI.

Mrs. M. C. Gridley, Evanston.

Cook macaroni in water until soft; then put in a deep dish with alternate layers of grated crackers and cheese, a little salt; fill up the dish with milk and bake one hour.

MACARONI.

Pour over one-half a pound of macaroni one quart of boiling water and let it stand for half an hour; then drain and pour cold water over it; in a few minutes, drain again and put it in a kettle of boiling milk and water; when tender, which will be in a few minutes, drain it and season with butter, cream, salt and pepper. Serve hot. If liked, add grated cheese to season.

ONIONS — BOILED.

Select those of uniform size; remove the outer skin, then boil until tender in a large quantity of milk and water; the flavor will be more delicate. Drain them when tender, and season with butter, salt and pepper.

ONIONS — FRIED.

Peel and slice and fry in lard or butter; season with pepper and salt, and serve hot.

MUSHROOMS FRIED.

When peeled put them into hot butter and let them heat thoroughly through — too much cooking toughens them. Season well with butter, pepper and salt. Serve on buttered toast; a teaspoon of wine or vinegar on each mushroom, is a choice method.

MUSHROOMS STEWED.

If fresh, let them lie in salt and water about one hour, then put them in the stewpan, cover with water and let them cook two hours gently. Dress them with cream, butter and flour as oysters, and season to taste.

SALSIFY STEWED.

Scrape well and then cut in round slices; stew it in sufficient water to cover. When tender turn off nearly all the water; add cream and butter, salt and pepper and a little flour rubbed smooth in a tablespoon of milk. Salsify when boiled tender is excellent scalloped or made into croquettes in the same manner as potatoes,

SCALLOPED OYSTER PLANT.

Boil the oyster plant until perfectly tender, then take out of water and rub through a colander ; add butter, pepper, salt and milk, and mix well. Put in a baking dish and cover the top with bread crumbs, with here and there small pieces of butter. Set in the oven and bake a delicate brown. Celery salt may be used with this for flavor, not using quite the quantity of common salt.

SALSIFY CROQUETTES.

Are made prepared as above before baking. The mixture should be made thin into balls, dipped in beaten egg and rolled in bread crumbs, and fried as croquettes in wire baskets, always deep in hot lard until of a golden brown.

PUDDINGS.

"And solid pudding against empty praise."

EVE'S PUDDING.

If you want a good pudding, mind what you are taught ;
Take eggs, six in number, when bought for a groat ;
The fruit with which Eve her husband did cozen,
Well pared, and well chopped, at least half a dozen ;
Six ounces of bread, let Moll eat the crust,
And crumble the rest as fine as the dust ;
Six ounces of currants, from the stem you must sort,
Lest you break out your teeth, and spoil all the sport ;
Six ounces of sugar won't make it too sweet,
Some salt and some nutmeg will make it complete ;
Three hours let it boil without any flutter,
But Adam won't like it without wine and butter.

SUET PUDDING.

Mrs. E. R. Harmon.

One cup of suet chopped fine, one cup chopped raisins, one cup of molasses, one cup of sweet milk, three teaspoons baking powder; spice to your taste; four cups of flour; mix and steam three hours.

(181)

SUET PUDDING.

Mrs. Bartlett.

One cup suet, one cup sugar, one cup milk, one cup chopped raisins, three cups flour, one teaspoon salt, one teaspoon soda; spice to taste; boil three hours.

SUET PUDDING.

Mrs. J. H. Brown.

Two cups of chopped suet, two of raisins, two of molasses, four of flour, one of milk, three teaspoons of baking powder; boil three and one-half hours; eat while hot. Sauce for same: One cup of sugar, one-half of butter, one egg, one tablespoon of wine or vinegar; beat fifteen minutes and heat to a scald.

SUET PUDDING.

Mrs. Henry Stevens.

One teacup of suet chopped fine, one teacup of molasses, one teacup of sweet milk, three and a half teacups of flour, one cup fruit, one teaspoon soda; steam two hours. Sauce for same : One coffee cup pulverized sugar, one-half teacup butter: stir these to a cream; place the dish in a kettle of boiling water; stir in white of one egg beaten to a stiff froth: one teaspoon of vanilla; serve hot.

SUET PUDDING.

Mrs. Banks.

Three cups flour, one cup suet, one cup molasses, one cup sweet milk, one cup raisins, one and a half teaspoons soda; three hours hard boiling in a bag or pudding dish.

SUET PUDDING.

Mrs. W. Butterfield.

One cup of suet, one cup of molasses, one cup of milk, one cup of raisins, three and a half cups of flour, one egg, one tablespoon of cloves, one tablespoon of cinnamon, one nutmeg, a little salt, one teaspoon of soda (dissolve in the milk); steam three hours.

FRUIT PUDDING.

Mrs. Taylor, Ft. Wayne.

One quart of flour, two tablespoons of butter, one teaspoon of salt, two teaspoons of baking powder; make a soft dough of milk or water, roll out thin and spread with fruit; roll it up and boil three-quarters of an hour.

STEAMED PLUM PUDDING.

Mrs. J. W. Farlin.

One and one-fourth cup beef suet, two cups raisins, four cups flour, one cup milk, one cup molasses, one teaspoon soda, one teaspoon salt. Season with nutmeg, cloves, cinnamon and allspice to taste; steam four hours. Do not uncover the steamer, but raise occasionally to fill the kettle with boiling water.

PLUM PUDDING.

Mrs. H. E. Houghton.

One cup suet, one cup sweet milk, one cup molasses, one cup sugar, one cup currants, two and a half cups raisins, four cups flour, one teaspoon cinnamon, one teaspoon cloves, one teaspoon spice, one teaspoon soda; boil three hours.

PLUM PUDDING.

Mrs. H. S. Towle.

One pint chopped suet, one pint sour apples, one pint raisins, one pint currants, one-half pint sugar, one-half pint sweet milk, one cup of citron; beat eight eggs and mix with the above, and add sufficient flour to make it stick together; boil three hours in a cloth bag. Serve with brandy sauce.

ENGLISH FRUIT PUDDING.

Mrs. H. S. Bristol.

One pound currants, one pound stoned raisins, one pound sugar, one pound suet, two pounds of grated or soaked bread, six eggs, one-half teaspoon saleratus, one teaspoon salt, and one grated nutmeg; crumb the soft part of the bread fine; soak the crust with boiling milk, or water will do; beat up the eggs and put all together, mixing thoroughly with the hands, take a square piece of cotton cloth and lay it in a tin pan, put the pudding into the cloth and tie down close; put into a pot of boiling water, and boil five hours; as the water boils away, keep adding more.

ENGLISH PLUM PUDDING.

M. Walker.

One pound raisins (stoned), one pound of currants, one pound suet very finely chopped, one pound flour, seven eggs, two wineglasses brandy, three of sweet wine, sugar and spice to taste (it may require a little sweet milk); tie it tightly in a well floured cloth, which should be first dipped in hot water, and boil four hours, or it may be boiled in a-pudding form.

PLUM PUDDING.

Mrs. E. Hempstead.

One pint raisins, one pint currants, one pint suet, one pint flour, one-half pint bread crumbs, one cup milk, five eggs, spices to taste, a little candied orange and lemon; mix all together and boil three hours. To be eaten with wine sauce.

BLACK PUDDING.

Mrs. H. M. Kidder, Evanston, Ill.

One teacup of molasses, one teacup of butter, one tea-cup of sugar, two teacups of flour, one teacup sour milk; four eggs, one nutmeg, one teaspoon soda; mix butter and sugar to a cream, add eggs well beaten, then molasses, then nutmeg, then flour and sour milk; last, soda dissolved in a little warm water; steam three hours. This pudding can be made Saturday and heated over again for Sunday. Sauce for same: Half cup butter, one of sugar, worked thoroughly together to a cream; put a teacup and a half of water in a saucepan, and when it boils, thicken with flour to the consistency of cream; take from the fire, and stir rapidly into it the butter and sugar; it will be like white foam; flavor to taste. This is an excellent sauce for all puddings.

BIRD'S NEST.

Mrs. F. M. Cragin.

Pare six or eight large apples (Spitzenbergs or Greenings are best), and remove the core by cutting from the end down into the middle, so as to leave the apple whole, except where the core has been removed; place them as near together as they can stand with the open part up- ward in a deep pie-dish; next make a thin batter, using one quart sweet milk, three eggs with sufficient flour, and pour it into the dish around the apples, also filling the cavities in them; bake them in a quick oven: eat them with butter and sugar.

CHOCOLATE PUDDING.

Mrs. Packard.

One quart milk, three tablespoons sugar, four table- spoons corn starch, two and a half tablespoons chocolate; scald the milk over boiling water; dissolve the corn starch in a little scalded milk, and before it thickens add the chocolate dissolved in boiling water; stir until sufficiently cooked. Use with cream, or sauce of butter and sugar stirred to a cream.

COCOANUT PUDDING.

C. A. Tinkham.

One quart sweet milk, ten tablespoons grated cocoanut, one cup powdered sugar, and whites of ten eggs; bake one hour, evenly and slowly; to be served cold, with sugar and cream.

ALMOND CUSTARD PUDDING.

Mrs. D.

Make a delicate sponge cake and stick it full of blanched

almonds. Pour over a little wine, and then a rich vanilla custard.

POTATO PUDDING.

Boil until white, mealy and very tender some potatoes; rub this finely washed through a colander; to a pint bowl of this while hot add one-quarter of a pound of butter, and mix well; beat the yolks of six eggs well with one pound of fine sugar; add the grated rind and juice of one lemon, and then the beaten whites; stir lightly in, and bake in pie plates lined with paste; eat cold.

A DELMONICO PUDDING.

Mrs. De Forest.

Three tablespoons of corn starch, the yolks of five eggs, six tablespoons of sugar; beat the eggs light, then add the sugar, and beat again till very light; mix the corn starch with a little cold milk; mix all together, and stir into it one quart of milk, just as it is about to boil, having added a little salt; stir it until it has thickened well; pour it into a dish for the table, and place it in the oven until it will bear icing; place over the top a layer of canned peaches, and it improves it to mix the syrup of the peaches with the custard part; beat the whites to a stiff froth, with two tablespoons white sugar to an egg, then put it into the oven till it is a light brown.

QUEEN'S PUDDING.

Mrs. A. P. Wightman, Evanston.

One quart of sweet milk, one pint of bread crumbs, five

eggs, one teaspoon of corn starch, one large or two small lemons, one cup of common sugar, and one of pulverized sugar; bring the milk to a scald, pour it over the bread crumbs and let it cool; beat the yolks of the eggs and one cup of common sugar together, and mix in the corn starch also; just before putting in to bake, add the grated rind of the lemon, and bake twenty minutes. Beat the whites of the eggs and one cup of pulverized sugar together, and add the lemon juice; when the pudding is done, put this on the top and set it in the oven again for a few minutes; to be eaten cold.

ROLY - POLY.
M.

Take one quart of flour; make good buscuit crust; roll out one-half inch thick and spread with any kind of fruit, fresh or preserved; fold so that the fruit will not run out; dip cloth into boiling water, and flour it and lay around the pudding closely, leaving room to swell; steam one or one and one-half hours; serve with boiled sauce; or lay in steamer without a cloth, and steam for one hour.

RAILROAD PUDDING.
E. Gage.

Cook a dozen apples soft, then stir in about a pint of Graham flour; salt it; then eat with sugar, cream and butter; it is very simple, and good for people troubled with dyspepsia.

RICE PUDDING.
E. Gage.

One quart of milk, with two tablespoons of rice; let it

come to a boil, then pour it over two tablespoons of sugar, one-half cup of raisins, a little lump of butter, flavor with ground cinnamon. Bake until thick.

RICE PUDDING WITHOUT EGGS.
Mrs. C. H. Wheeler, and others.

Two quarts of milk, half a teacup of rice, a little less than a teacup of sugar, the same quantity of raisins, a teaspoon of cinnamon or allspice; wash the rice, and put it with the rest of the ingredients into the milk; bake rather slowly from two to three hours; stir two or three times the first hour of baking. If properly done, this pudding is delicious.

COTTAGE PUDDING. ·
Mr. G. S. Whitaker.

One cup of sugar, one cup of sweet milk, one pint of flour, two tablespoons of melted butter, one teaspoon of soda, two teaspoons of cream tartar, one egg.

COTTAGE PUDDING.
M. G. Rand.

One teacup of white sugar, one-half cup of butter (or little less); one cup sweet milk, one egg, a little nutmeg, one pint of flour, three teaspoons of baking powder: rub the butter, sugar and egg together until light, add the nutmeg and milk, stir the baking powder into the flour while dry, and add just as the pudding is to be put in the oven; bake in a quart basin, very slowly; bring to the table hot, cut like cake, and serve with sauce made according to the following directions: Rub one tablespoon of flour in a little cold water until smooth, then turn it into one pint of boiling water, letting it cook five minutes, stirring constantly; add sugar, salt and nutmeg to suit the taste.

COTTAGE PUDDING.
Mrs. D. C. Norton.

One cup of sugar, butter the size of a large egg, one cup sour milk, one teaspoon saleratus (sweet milk is just as good if two teaspoons of baking powder is used instead of saleratus); two eggs, two heaping cups of flour, a little salt.

ESTELLE PUDDING.
Anonymous.

Three eggs well beaten, two and one-half tablespoons of sugar, two tablespoons butter, three-fourths cup sweet milk, one cup raisins chopped fine; one tablespoon baking powder, flour to make the consistency of pound cake; steam thirty-five minutes.

PUDDING IN HASTE.
Mrs. F. E. Stearns.

Three eggs, three cups of milk, and three cups of flour; bake in patty tins or cups, and serve with hot sauce.

MINUTE PUDDING.
C. Kennicott.

One-half cup milk, five large spoons flour, three eggs, one-half teaspoon of salt, stirred smoothly together; stir this into one pint of boiling milk,

A QUICK PUDDING.

Mrs. A. W. D.

One-half pint of milk, one-half pint of cream, three eggs beaten separately, little over one-half pint flour; season with lemon or vanilla.

BAKED INDIAN PUDDING—SPLENDID.

Two quarts scalded milk with salt, one and one-half cups Indian meal (yellow)· one tablespoon of ginger, letting this stand twenty minutes; one cup molasses, two eggs (saleratus, if no eggs) a piece of butter the size of a common walnut; bake two hours.

BAKED INDIAN PUDDING.

Mrs. A. W. D.

Three cups of raisins, one cup of chopped suet or butter, one pint of Indian meal, four sour apples, one quart of milk, one egg, and a little salt.

BAKED INDIAN PUDDING.

Mrs. A. W. D.

Seven spoons of Indian meal, two spoons of butter, one-half teaspoon salt, one teacup molasses; ginger or cinnamon to your taste; pour into these a quart of milk while boiling hot; mix well and put in a buttered dish; just as you put it in the oven, stir in a teacup of cold water, which will produce the same effect as eggs. Bake three-quarters of an hour.

CORN MEAL PUDDING.

Etta C. Springer.

One quart of sweet milk, boiled; stir in four table-spoons of corn meal; stand till cool; put in four beaten eggs, sweeten to taste, two tablespoons of butter; bake two hours.

BOILED INDIAN PUDDING.

Mrs. DeForrest.

One quart of good buttermilk or thick sour milk, two tablespoons of sweet cream, three eggs, one teaspoon soda, three handfuls of flour, a little salt, Indian meal to make a rather thin batter.

INDIAN PUDDING.

Mrs. Benham.

One quart of milk, four tablespoons (heaping) of Indian meal, one tablespoon of flour, one teaspoon of ginger, one of cinnamon, one lemon peel, one teaspoon salt, two eggs, one cup molasses; bake three hours, not in too hot an oven; boil the meal in half the quantity of milk, one cup raisins, one cup of suet (not too full); add the remainder of milk before the eggs.

GRAHAM PUDDING.

Mrs. G. F. DeForest.

One and a half coffee cups Graham flour, one-half coffee cup molasses, one-fourth coffee cup butter, one-half coffee cup sweet milk, one egg, one even teaspoon soda, one good half cup raisins, one good half cup currants;

salt and spice to taste; steam two and a half or three hours; serve with liquid sauce.

SUNDERLAND PUDDING.

Mrs. C. M. Dickerman, Rockford.

Eight tablespoons flour, four eggs, three pints sweet milk, one tablespoon melted butter, one-half nutmeg; bake in a pie tin; serve with pudding sauee.

DANDY JACK.

Mrs. Benham.

One pint milk, yolks of three eggs, two heaping table-spoons corn starch, one-half cup sugar; flavor as you like; for top, the whites of the eggs and a little sugar.

PRETTY PUDDING.

Mrs. Charles Bradbury.

One tablespoon flour wet with one-half cup of cold milk, the yolks of three eggs beaten, one small cup sugar; mix these together; put one quart of milk in a kettle and set it in boiling water; when the milk is at the boiling point, stir in the above mixture with vanilla or rose flavoring; stir till it begins to thicken, then take it off and let it cool a little; pour it into a pudding dish or cups; then beat the whites of the eggs to a stiff froth, add a teaspoon of fine white sugar, and drop it on the top of the custard in rounds about as large as an egg; put a small spoon of currant or other tart jelly on the middle of each round; serve cold.

13

WEBSTER PUDDING.

Mrs. O. L. Wheelock.

One cup molasses, one cup milk, one cup suet, one-half cup brandy, or wine if you like, one teaspoon saleratus, one teaspoon cloves, one teaspoon cinnamon, one-half nutmeg, two cups currants, one teaspoon salt; mix as soft as pound cake, and steam it two hours. Serve with hard sauce.

SPONGE PUDDING.

Mrs. Ada Sturtevant, Delaware, Wis.

One-half cup of butter, or one cup of chopped suet, one-third cup molasses, one-half cup wine, one-half cup sweet milk, three cups flour, one teaspoon soda, raisins and such spices as you prefer, about one-half spoon of each; dried cherries are nice instead of raisins, or it is good without any fruit; steam two hours and serve hot with sauce.

POUND CAKE PUDDING.

Mrs. E. L. Nichols.

One cup sugar, one-half of butter, rub to a cream, add one cup of milk, three eggs, the yolks and whites beaten separately, one teaspoon of soda in the milk, two teaspoons of cream tartar in the flour; fruit; bake or steam an hour.

ROME PUDDING.

Mrs. M. J. Woodworth.

Eight good sized apples stewed and strained, the yolks

of five eggs, one-quarter pound of butter, one lemon chopped fine, one-half pound sugar, one gill of cream; put a thin paste on a plate, as for custard pie, and bake.

ASTOR HOUSE PUDDING.

Mrs. Lamkin.

Two-thirds of a cup of rice, three pints of milk, one cup of sugar, a little salt, a piece of butter one-half the size of an egg; let it come to a boil; bake one and one-half hours in a slow oven.

BATTER PUDDING.

Mrs. H. L. Bristol.

One pint of milk, four eggs, the yolks and whites beaten separately, ten tablespoons of sifted flour, a little salt; beat in the whites of the eggs the last thing before baking; bake half an hour.

BAKED BATTER PUDDING.

One quart of sweet milk, seven tablespoons of flour (heaping), six eggs well beaten (whites separated), one tablespoon brandy; put the whites of the eggs in the last thing, and bake half an hour. Serve with brandy sauce.

STEAMED BATTER PUDDING.

Mrs. M. G. Hubbell, Cornton, Ill.

Two eggs to two teacups of sour milk, two teaspoons saleratus and salt; stir very thick or it will be heavy; then add any fruit you wish; steam two hours; eaten with sweetened cream.

STEAMED BATTER PUDDING.

Mrs. L. H. Davis.

Two eggs and one tablespoon of sugar beaten together, one cup of milk, two cups flour, one tablespoon melted butter, half teaspoon soda, one teaspoon cream tartar; beat well, and pour the batter over either sliced apples or peaches, and steam one hour and a quarter; this will fill a three pint basin. Serve with hot sauce.

BATTER PUDDING.

One quart of milk, twelve tablespoons of flour, nine eggs, a teaspoon of salt; beat the yolks thoroughly; stir in the flour and add the milk slowly; beat the whites of the eggs to a froth, and add the last thing; put in a tin pudding mould, having a tight cover, and boil two hours; the mould should not be full as the pudding will swell; the water must not stop boiling. Eat with liquid sauce.

AMHERST PUDDING.

Mrs. F. M. Cragin.

Three cups of flour, one of suet, one of milk, one of molasses, two of raisins; salt and spice to your taste; one teaspoon saleratus; boil in a bag three hours. For sauce: One cup of sugar, one-half of butter, one egg.

CORN PUDDING.

Mrs. F. M. Cragin.

One dozen ears of corn, one pint of milk, two eggs, salt, two teaspoons of sugar, two of flour; bake one hour in quick oven.

BREAD PUDDING.

Mrs. Freeman.

Soak a pint of bread crumbs in milk for an hour, then squeeze with the hands to a pulp, and mix well with a gill of milk, then add three tablespoons of sugar, one-quarter pound raisins, one-quarter pound of melted butter, and the yolks of four eggs; then beat the whites of the eggs to a froth and mix with the rest; turn the mixture into a dish and bake about forty minutes. Serve with wine sauce, hot or cold, according to taste.

BREAD PUDDING.

Mrs. C. M., Winnetka, Ill.

Put a pint of scalded milk to a pint of bread crumbs, and add the yolks of four eggs well beaten, a teacup of sugar, butter the size of an egg, and the grated rind of a lemon; bake, and then beat the whites of the eggs into a cup of powdered sugar and the juice of one lemon; cover the pudding with it, and set it in the oven till it is a brownish yellow.

BROWN BETTY.

Mrs. L. M. Angle.

One cup of bread crumbs, two of chopped apples (tart) one-half cup of sugar, one teaspoon of cinnamon, two tablespoons of butter cut into small bits; butter a deep dish and put a layer of chopped apple at the bottom, sprinkle with sugar, a few bits of butter and cinnamon. Proceed in this order until the dish is full, having a layer of crumbs on the top; cover closely and steam three-quarters of an hour in a moderate oven; then uncover and brown quickly; eat with sugar and cream. This is a plain, but very good pudding, especially for the children's table.

BREAD PUDDING WITHOUT MILK.
Mrs. A. M. Gibbs.

Take dry bread pieces, a half pint more or less, and pour boiling water on them; when soft, mix with this a cup of fruit of any kind, stewed or fresh, and add two tablespoons melted butter, the yolks of two eggs, spice and sugar to taste; bake twenty minutes; just before it is done spread on the beaten whites of the eggs, and brown nicely. To be eaten with wine sauce.

OXFORD PUDDING.
M. A. Sadler, Aurora.

A quarter of a pound of crackers pounded, a quarter of a pound of currants washed, a quarter of a pound of suet shred fine, half a large spoon of fine sugar; some grated nutmeg; mince it all together, then take the yolks of four eggs and make it up into balls as big as turkey egg; fry them in fresh butter of a fine light brown.

BAKED CRACKER PUDDING.
Mrs. H. P. Stowell.

Two quarts of sweet milk, seven Boston butter crackers rolled, three eggs, a little nutmeg, a little salt, sweeten with sugar to taste. Bake two hours and a half in a moderate oven.

APPLE BREAD PUDDING.
Mrs. O. L. Wheelock.

Pare, core and chop one-half dozen sour apples; drj bread in the oven until crisp, then roll; butter a deef dish and place in it a layer of crumbs and apples altef· nately, with spice, and one-half cup of beef suet chopped fine; pour in one-half pint of sweet milk, and bake till nicely browned; serve with hard sauce.

APPLE PUDDING.
Mrs. W. Guthrie.

Five eggs, one pint milk, four tablespoons flour, four apples grated; bake one hour and a quarter. Serve with sweetened cream or pudding sauce.

APPLE PUDDING.
Etta C. Springer.

Five large sour apples chopped, one cup raisins, one cup sugar, one cup sweet milk, one cup flour, one-half cup butter, two eggs, little salt, butter and sugar worked together; bake one hour; any sauce you please.

APPLE SAGO PUDDING.·
Mrs. K.

One cup sago in a quart of tepid water, with a pinch of salt, soaked for one hour; six or eight apples, pared and cored, or quartered, and steamed tender, and put in the pudding dish, boil and stir the sago until clear, adding water to make it thin, and pour it over the apples; this is good hot with butter and sugar, or cold with cream and sugar.

HUCKLEBERRY PUDDING.

Mrs. B. J. Seward.

One teacup molasses, one dessert spoon saleratus, stirred thoroughly in the molasses; as much flour as can be stirred in with one quart of huckleberries. To be steamed four hours in a basin, or boiled in a pudding bag. Serve with liquid sauce. An excellent dessert.

HUCKLEBERRY PUDDING.

Mrs. Bartlett.

One brick loaf, wet it with boiling milk, say one pint, four eggs, little salt, and one quart of berries. Boil one and a half hours. Serve with wine sauce.

BLACKBERRY PUDDING OR OTHER BER-RIES.

M.

One and one-half pints sifted flour; put a little of this into one and one-half pints of fresh berries. To the balance of the flour add salt sufficient to season, one even teaspoon soda dissolved in one-half teacup of sweet milk, then fill the cup three-fourths full of syrup or molasses, stir all into a smooth batter, lastly add the berries; mix lightly so as not to break. Put into a buttered mould and place in boiling water that does not quite reach the top of the mould. Do not let it stop boiling for an instant. It must boil *at least* two hours. Serve with boiled sauce.

FIG PUDDING.

E. M. Walker.

One-half pound figs, one-quarter pound grated bread,

two and a half ounces powdered sugar, three ounces butter, two eggs, one teacup of milk. Chop the figs small
and mix first with the butter, then all the other ingredients
by degrees; butter a mould, sprinkle with bread crumbs,
cover it tight and boil for three hours.

FIG PUDDING.

Mrs. E. Wood.

One pound suet chopped fine, one pound wheat flour,
one-half loaf of wheat bread, one pound figs chopped,
one and a half cups molasses, one teaspoon soda, one teaspoon cream tartar. To be eaten with sauce.

CURRANT PUDDING

Mrs. Bartlett.

Slice a baker's loaf, add butter, stew and sweeten three
pints of currants, turn over the bread, and set away until
cold. Serve without sauce, slice the bread thin.

MUSKMELON PUDDING.

Mrs. De Forest.

One-half cup butter, one pint of milk, two eggs, three
teaspoons baking powder, nearly one quart of flour.
Steam two hours. Serve with liquid sauce.

SWEETMEATS PUDDING.

Mrs. C. E. Browne.

Make a nice pie crust, little or much, as you may desire,
and roll it out in a long oval shape; spread thickly with
raspberry or currant jam, or with stewed fruit, cherries or

plums, then wet the edges of the dough with cold water, and roll it up, closing the edges tightly. Steam it for an hour or more, and serve in slices with a sauce of butter and sugar beaten well together, with nutmeg or other flavoring.

FRUIT PUDDING.

Mrs. S. W. Cheever, Ottawa, Ill.

One cup milk, one cup sugar, two eggs, two teaspoons cream tartar, one teaspoon soda, flour, dried fruit steam two hours. Sauce : To a pint of milk, add a lump of butter size of a small egg, let this come near to a boil ; save out from the pudding half teacup batter, thin it, stir it into the hot milk, stir all the time till it begins to thicken; sweeten and flavor to the taste.

FRUIT PUDDING.

Place in a tin basin fruit of any kind (raspberries, peaches and apples are the best), put sugar over them, and a little water; if peaches are used put them in after paring them, whole; have ready a biscuit crust, made of one pint of flour, with a small piece of butter or lard, a little salt, two teaspoons of baking powder, and water or milk to make a dough ; then roll out crust, and place over the top of your fruit in the tin ; cover with another two quart basin, to give room for the crust to rise, and set it on the stove ; as the fruit stews the crust will steam done. Serve with cream and sugar.

CHERRY PUDDING.

Mrs. H. S. Towle.

One pint flour, one pint sweet milk, one quart cherries, four eggs, a little butter and salt, baking powder; steamed. Serve with cream and sugar.

CHERRY PUDDING.

H. N. Jenks.

A pint of bread crusts or soft crackers, scalded in a quart of boiling milk, piece of butter the size of an egg, one teaspoon of salt, three eggs, one and a half teacups of sugar if eaten without sauce, and if with sauce a table spoon of sugar; a pinch of pulverized cinnamon, and a quart of stoned cherries; bake quickly.

JELLY PUDDING.

Mrs. C. H. Wheeler.

One quart of milk, one pint of bread crumbs, yolks of four beaten eggs, one-half cup of sugar; bake about half an hour; when cool, spread jelly over the pudding, beat the whites with a little sugar, and spread on top for frosting; set back in the oven a few minutes after the whites have been spread on the pudding; excellent for Sunday dinners, as it may be eaten cold.

BAKEWELL PUDDING.

E. M. Walker.

Cover a dish with thin puff paste, and put over it a layer of any kind of firm jelly, one-half inch thick; take - the yolks of four eggs, and one white, one-quarter pound sugar, one-quarter pound butter, twelve sweet and eight bitter almonds, well pounded; beat all together to a froth, pour over the jelly and bake one-half hour in a moderate oven.

KISS PUDDING.

Mrs. F. B. Cole.

One quart milk, three tablespoons of corn starch, yolks of four eggs, half cup sugar, and a little salt; put part of the milk, salt and sugar on the stove and let it boil; dissolve the corn starch in the rest of the milk; stir into the milk, and while boiling add the yolks. Flavor with vanilla.

FROSTING.—Whites of four eggs beaten to a stiff froth, half a cup of sugar; flavor with lemon, spread it on the pudding, and put it into the oven to brown, saving a little of the frosting to moisten the top; then put on grated cocoanut to give it the appearanco of snow flake.

SARATOGA PUDDING.

Mrs. A. G. Beardsley.

Mix four tablespoons of corn starch in one quart of cold milk; stir until it boils. When cool, stir in two tablespoons white sugar, six eggs, whites and yolks beaten separately. Put in a large pudding dish, place in a pan of water; bake one and a half hours. Sauce: One cup sugar, half cup butter, the yolks of two eggs, one glass wine. Rub sugar and butter to a cream, add eggs and half the wine. Put the dish in boiling water, stir ten minutes, add the rest of the wine and serve.

MERINGUE PUDDING.

Mrs. C. A. Rogers.

One pint of stale bread crumbs, one quart of milk, the yolks of four eggs, butter the size of an egg, a small cup of sugar, salt, the grated rind of one lemon; bake three-quarters of an hour. When cool, spread the top with preserves or jelly; beat the whites of the eggs with five tablespoons of pulverized sugar; spread on the pudding and brown in a quick oven; eat with cream.

OSWEGO PUDDING.

Kingford's Starch Company.

One quart of milk, three tablespoons of corn starch, four eggs; beat the yolks and mix them with a little of the milk and flour; sweeten and flavor with vanilla. Scald the milk and add the other ingredients, boil three minutes, pour into a dish and set away to cool. Beat the whites with four teaspoons of sugar. Cover the pudding with a layer of currant jelly, and spread the beaten whites over the whole.

BAKED PUDDING.

Mrs. E. C. Chapin.

Three tablespoons of corn starch to one quart of milk. Prepare and cook the same as for blanc mange. After it is cool, stir up with it *thoroughly* two or three eggs, well beaten, and bake half an hour.

CORN STARCH LEMON PUDDING.

Glen Cove Starch Company.

Grate the rind of two lemons, add the juice and rind

to six ounces of sugar and three ounces of the improved
corn starch. Stir this well into some cold water, sufficient
to make it smooth. Place three pints of milk on the fire;
when boiling add the above, stirring all the time until it
thickens. Remove it from the fire and add one ounce of
butter and four eggs. Stir again while on the fire, taking
care not to allow it to burn; as soon as it becoms thick,
remove it and fill out some small cups or forms, previously dipped in cold water. Place them aside; in one
hour they will be fit to turn out. Cream and sugar or any
sauce preferred.

SAUCE.—One ounce of the improved corn starch in a
little cold milk; blend till smooth; then pour a pint of
boiling milk on it. Beat the whites of four eggs in three
ounces of sugar, one glass of brandy; add this to the
sauce, and allow it to remain on the fire a short time,
stirring all the while. The sauce can be served hot or
cold. May be flavored with anything to fancy.

ORANGE PUDDING.

Nellie.

Line the bottom of a pudding dish with stale sponge
cake, slice upon the cake six oranges; make a custard of
one quart of milk and five eggs, leaving out the whites of
four; beat the whites to a stiff froth, adding sugar, put on
top of pudding, and put in the oven until brown,

ORANGE PUDDING.

Mrs. J. G. Hamilton.

Peel and cut five sweet oranges into thin slices, taking

out the seeds ; pour over them a coffee cup of white sugar; let a pint of milk get boiling hot, by setting it in a pot of boiling water; add the yolks of three eggs, well beaten, one tablespoon of corn starch, made smooth with a little cold milk ; stir all the time ; as soon as thickened, pour over the fruit. Beat the whites to a stiff froth, adding a tablespoon of sugar, and spread over the top for frosting; set it in the oven for a few minutes to harden; eat cold or hot (better cold), for dinner or supper. Berries or peaches can be substituted for oranges.

LEMON PUDDING.
Mrs. White.

Put in a basin one-fourth pound of flour, the same of sugar, same of bread crumbs and chopped suet, the juice of one good-sized lemon, and the peel grated; two eggs, and enough milk to make it the consistency of porridge ; boil in a basin for one hour ; serve with or without sauce.

PINE-APPLE PUDDING.
From choice recipes by M. S. W., Boston.

A grated pine-apple and its weight in sugar ; half its weight in butter; five eggs; the whites beat to a stiff froth ; one cup of cream ; cream the butter and beat it with the sugar and yolks until very light; add the cream, the pine-apple and the whites of the eggs. Bake in pie plates lined with pastry. To be eaten cold.

GIPSY PUDDING.
L. Osgood.

·Cut stale sponge cake into thin slices; spread them

with currant jelly or preserves; put two pieces together like sandwiches, and lay them in a dish; make a soft custard, pour over while it is hot, let cool before serving.

CRACKED WHEAT PUDDING.

Mrs. A. M. Lewis.

Cook cracked wheat enough for two meals; stir in a few minutes before taking up, raisins, dates, or any dried fruit; next day prepare a custard as usual, and stir thoroughly through the wheat, and bake just long enough to bake the custard; thus you have two desserts with but little trouble. Very palatable and nutritious.

GERMAN PUDDING.

A. S. Ewing.

Beat six eggs separately until very light; add one pint milk to the yolks, six tablespoons flour, one-half spoon butter, one-half nutmeg and salt spoon salt; stir in whites of eggs last. Bake half an hour.

SAUCE.—Six tablespoons sugar, one-half pound butter worked to a cream, one egg, one wineglass wine, one-half nutmeg; put on the fire and let it come to a boil.

CHOCOLATE PUDDING.

Mrs. E. Wood.

One and a half quarts milk, boiled, one-half cake of chocolate stirred in milk, small cup of corn starch dissolved in little water, add two eggs, with one cup sugar, a little salt. Cream for sauce.

COLD TAPIOCA PUDDING.

Mrs. H. F. Waite.

One cup tapioca in five cups water, one cup sugar and one lemon. Wash the tapioca; add the water; put it in a tin pail, in a kettle of water; let it boil two hours or more and until it is perfectly clear; just before taking up, add a teaspoon of salt, one cup of sugar and rind and juice of a lemon; stir thoroughly; place to cool; eat with cream and sugar.

TAPIOCA PUDDING.

Mrs. Rice.

Cover three tablespoons tapioca with water; stand over night; add one quart milk, a small piece of butter, a little salt, and boil; beat the yolks of three eggs with a cup of sugar, and boil the whole to a very thick custard; flavor with vanilla; when cold cover with whites of eggs beaten.

TAPIOCA PUDDING.

Mrs. Francis M. Thatcher.

Soak one cup of tapioca in milk; add one quart of milk, one cup of white sugar, two eggs, butter the size of an egg, nutmeg and raisins to suit taste; steam two hours.

CREAM TAPIOCA PUDDING.

Mrs. A. T. Hall.

Soak three tablespoons of tapioca in water over night; put the tapioca into a quart of boiling milk, and boil half an hour: beat the yolks of four eggs with a cup of sugar; add three tablespoons of prepared cocoanut; stir in and

14

boil ten minutes longer; pour into a pudding dish; beat
the whites of the four eggs to a stiff froth, stir in three
tablespoons of sugar; put this over the top and sprinkle
cocoanut over the top and brown for five minutes,

APPLE TAPIOCA PUDDING.

Mrs. C. Duffield.

One cup of tapioca soaked over night in six cups of
water; next morning add about six large tart apples,
chopped very fine, (or more, according to the size,) then
one cup of white sugar; bake slowly about four hours;
to be eaten either warm or cold, with cream. Very delicate for invalids.

SNOW PUDDING.

Mrs. D.

One-half package Coxe's gelatine; pour over it a cup
of cold water and add one and one-half cups of sugar;
when soft, add one cup boiling water, juice of one lemon
and the whites of four well beaten eggs; beat all together
until very light; put in glass dish and pour over it custard
made as follows: One pint milk, yolks of four eggs and
grated rind of one lemon; boil.   Splendid.

RICE SNOW BALLS.

Boil a pint of rice in two quarts of water, with a teaspoon of salt, until quite soft, then put it in small cups,
having them quite full; when perfectly cold, turn them
into a dish, take the yolks of three eggs, one pint of milk,
one teaspoon corn starch; flavor with lemon, and cook as

you do soft custard; turn over the rice half an hour previous to eating it. This is a nice dessert in hot weather. Sweet meats are a good accompaniment.

CHOCOLATE PUFFS.

Mrs. O. L. Parker.

One pound sugar sifted, one of chocolate chopped very fine; mix together; beat the white of an egg, and stir in your chocolate and sugar; continue to beat until stiff paste; sugar your paper, drop them on it, and bake in a slow oven.

CREAM PUFFS.

Mrs. Watson Thatcher.

One and one-half cups of flour, two-thirds of a cup of butter, one-half pint of boiling water; boil butter and water together, and stir in the flour while boiling; let it cool, and add five well-beaten eggs; drop on tins, and bake thirty minutes in a quick oven. Fill them with the following: One pint of milk, one cup of sugar, two-thirds of a cup of flour, two eggs; beat the eggs, flour and sugar together, and stir them in the milk while it is boiling. When partially cool flavor with lemon. These are favorites in bake shops.

DESSERT PUFFS.

Mrs. N. C. Gridley, Evanston.

One pint sweet milk, scant pint flour, three eggs (whites and yolks beaten separately); bake in cups. To be eaten with liquid sauce.

PUFF PUDDING.

Mrs. C. A. Rogers.

Five tablespoons of flour, five tablespoons of milk, five eggs stirred smooth ; turn on a pint of boiling milk, and bake twenty minutes.   To be eaten with hard sauce.

MOLLY PUFFS.

Mrs. George B. Cushing.

One cup Indian meal scalded; when it cools add two cups of rye meal, two eggs, one tablespoon of brown sugar, and a small half teaspoon of soda; fry them, dropped from a spoon in boiling lard.

GERMAN PUFFS.

H. M. Brewer.

One pint sweet milk, five tablespoons flour, one table-spoon melted butter, six eggs, leaving out the whites of three ; bake in buttered cups, half filled, twenty minutes in hot oven.

For Sauce. — Beat the whites of five eggs to a stiff froth, and one coffee cup powdered sugar, and the juice of two oranges; turn the pudding from the cups on to a platter, and cover with the sauce just before sending to the table.

GERMAN PUFFS.

Mrs. E. P. Thomas, Rockford, Ill.

One pint sweet milk, four eggs, five tablespoons flour, and a little salt.   Bake three quarters of an hour.

LEMON FRITTERS.

After Marion Harland.

Beat up the whipped and strained yolks of five eggs with one-half a cup of powdered sugar; add the grated peel of half a lemon, one teaspoon of mingled nutmeg and cinnamon, a little salt, and one-half a cup of cream; then the whites of the eggs, and then two heaping cups of prepared flour; work all together quickly and lightly into a soft paste, just stiff enough to roll out; pass the rolling-pin over it until it be about three-quarters of an inch thick; cut into small circular cakes with a tumbler or cake-cutter, and fry in hot lard. They ought to puff up like crullers. Drain on clean hot paper, and eat warm with a sauce made of the juice of two lemons and the grated peel of one, one cup of powdered sugar, one glass of wine, and the whites of two eggs beaten stiff.

PUDDING SAUCES.

" I crack my brains to find out tempting sauces,
And raise fortifications in the pastry."

PUDDING SAUCE.

Anonymous.

One cup of butter, one cup of milk, one cup of sugar, three eggs, flavor to taste.

PUDDING SAUCE.

Mrs. Dunham.

One-half cup of butter, one cup of sugar, two eggs well beaten, and pour on one cup of boiling water; flavor with nutmeg or other flavor.

PUDDING SAUCE.

Mrs. A. R. Scranton.

Four tablespoons of white sugar, two tablespoons of butter, one tablespoon of flour; beat all to a cream and add the white of one egg well beaten; then add one gill boiling water; stir well; flavor to taste.

(214)

FOAMING SAUCE.

Mrs. King.

One-half teacup of butter, the same of sugar; beat to a froth; put into a dish and set in a pan of hot water; add a tablespoon of hot water, or if preferred, a little vanilla; stir one way until it comes to a very light foam.

WINE PUDDING SAUCE.

One cup of sugar, one-half cup of butter, one-half cup of wine, one egg; beat butter, sugar and eggs together; set it on the stove and heat, pour in the wine, add a little nutmeg; pour from one dish to another a few times, and send to the table.

WINE SAUCE.

M. A. T.

Two teacups of sugar, one teacup of butter; stir to a cream; beat two eggs very light, and stir all together; add one teacup of wine; mix and set on top of tea-kettle of boiling water. It must not be put on the stove, nor boil.

PUDDING SAUCE.

Mrs. B. P. Hutchinson.

Two eggs well beaten, one cup pulverized sugar; when mixed pour over one cup of boiling milk, and stir rapidly; flavor as you please.

PUDDING SAUCE.

Mrs. Andrews.

One cup of sugar, one-half cup of butter, yolks of three eggs; one teaspoon of corn starch or arrow root; stir the whole until very light; add sufficient boiling water to make the consistency of thick cream; wine or brandy to suit the taste.

SAUCE FOR APPLE PUDDING

M.

Boil good molasses with a little butter, and serve hot.

HARD SAUCE FOR PUDDINGS, RICE, ETC.

M.

Take one teacup sugar, one-half teacup butter; stir together until light; flavor with wine or essence of lemon; smooth the top with a knife, and grate nutmeg over it.

WINE SAUCE.

Brown one cup of sugar and a piece of butter the size of a hen's egg, in a saucepan; pour two-thirds of a teacup of boiling water slowly over the mixture; when ready to serve, add one-half cup of currant wine.

WINE SAUCE.

Mrs. Pulsifer.

Two ounces of butter, two teaspoons of flour, one-quarter of a pound of sugar, one gill of wine, and half a nutmeg grated; mix the flour and butter together, add one-half pint boiling water and the sugar and wine; just before serving, add the grated nutmeg. Serve hot.

GERMAN SAUCE.

M. D. Harris.

The whites of two eggs, the juice of one lemon, sugar enough to beat up to a proper consistency for serving.

PIES.

PASTRY.

Drink now the strong beer,
Cut the white loaf here,
The while the meat is a shredding
For the rare mince pie,
And the plums stand by
To fill the paste that's a kneading.
— OLD SONG.

FINE PUFF PASTRY.

One pound of flour, a little more for rolling pin and board, and half a pound of butter and half a pound of lard. Cut the butter and lard through the flour (which should be sifted) into small thin shells and mix with sufficient ice water to roll easily. Avoid kneading it and use the hands as little as possible in mixing.

PLAINER PASTRY.

One cup of butter, one cup of lard, a little salt, cut through the flour and mix lightly together. Some cooks mix the lard through the flour and mix with water and then roll out; when in a sheet cut the batter into thin sheets, fold over and lay aside, cutting off from the roll what is used for the bottom or top crust as wanted.

PASTRY OF GRAHAM FLOUR.

Half a pound of Graham flour, one cup of sweet cream, a little salt; mix and roll and bake in the usual way with fruit between the crusts.

RICE PIE.

Mrs. A. S. Ewing.

One quart of milk, boiled; one small teacup of rice flour mixed in a little cold milk; add to the boiling milk two tablespoons of butter; when cold, add five eggs well beaten; sweeten to taste; flavor with vanilla, and bake.

FRUIT PIE.

Mrs. M. P. Carroll.

Must be baked in a two quart tin basin; to give it the right shape the basin must be of nearly the same size top and bottom; first make a nice pie crust; put a layer of it in the bottom, but not around the side of the dish; then a layer of chopped sour apples, two inches thick; then a layer of chopped raisins; sprinkle sugar over this, pieces of butter, and any spice you like — cloves and nutmeg are nice; another layer of crust and fruit, etc., until your dish is full; put a crust on top; bake slowly for two hours; when done, turn bottom upwards on a plate, and before putting it on the table sprinkle fine sugar over it. It is quite as good when warmed again as when first

baked. It takes one pound of raisins, ten or twelve
- good sized apples, two large cups of sugar, more if you
like.

TRANSPARENT PUDDING.
Mrs. P. H. Smith.

Five eggs, one-half pound sugar, one-third pound butter, three tablespoons of cream; divide the sugar, and
beat half of it in the butter, and the other half with the
yolk of the eggs, and then add the whites and the cream,
and one-half teaspoon of vanilla. Prepare crust in two
pie plates, and pour the mixture in and bake in a slow
oven.

ACID PIE.
M. A. Bingham, Elgin, Ill.

One cup of soft bread or crackers, one cup of sugar,
two cups of water, little lemon, one egg, one teaspoon of
tartaric acid.

LEMON PIE.
Mrs. H. L. Adams, and others.

One tablespoon of corn starch, boiled in a cup of water;
one egg, one cup of sugar, juice and rind of one lemon;
bake in a crust. This will fill one shallow plate.

LEMON PIE.
Miss Sophia Brownsberg.

The rind and juice of one lemon, one cup sugar, the
yolks of three eggs; mix these well together; two cups

of milk, little salt, one tablespoon corn starch; thicken the milk with the corn starch and let it come to a boil; then stir it into the other ingredients, pour it into a pie plate covered with a good paste and bake it. Beat the whites of three eggs to a froth, with a tablespoon of sugar, lay it over the top of the pie and set it again in the oven for a few seconds, to brown.

LEMON PIE.
Mrs. J. W. Preston.

Six eggs, (less two whites,) two cups of white sugar, a little salt, one cup of sweet milk, two tablespoons of corn starch dissolved in the milk; two large lemons, juice and rind; bake slowly until set. Meringue for the top: Whites of two eggs beaten with six tablespoons of powdered sugar; bake to a light brown, after having spread over the surface of the pie.

LEMON PIE.
Mrs. G. L. Dunlap.

Yolks of six eggs, two cups of pulverized sugar, beaten well together, two and a half cups of milk, three lemons, (only juice,) a little salt, mix well, bake; then take the whites of the eggs, add one-half cup of pulverized sugar, beaten well together, then spread over the top of pies and brown. This recipe will make two good sized pies.

LEMON PIE.
Miss Annie Slocum.

Two lemons, five eggs, one cup of sugar, one cup of

water, two tablespoons corn starch; grate the outside of
the lemon rinds into a dish, then cut in half and remove
the seeds, scooping the pulp and juice into the dish with
a silver spoon; add the sugar and water, wetting the
starch with some of the water; mix it in with the yolks
and one white of an egg, (the eggs well beaten first,) pour
into two tins lined with pastry, and bake; beat the remaining whites; gradually stir in ten tablespoons of pulverized sugar, and when the pies are done, spread the
snow over them, and place in the oven until brown.

LEMON PIE.
M.

For three pies, take the rind and juice of four lemons,
the yolks of nine eggs, the whites of three, nearly one
cup of butter, two cups of sugar, one-half cup of sweet
milk; beat the whites of six eggs with six ounces of
sugar; put on the top, after baking, and brown slightly.
Very rich.

LEMON PIE.
Mrs. Beyer, and others.

For one pie, take one large lemon, the yolks of two
eggs, one cup of sugar, one-half cup of cold water, one
teaspoon of bttter. Icing for the same: Whites of two
eggs, two tablespoons of pulverized sugar; brown it
nicely in the oven.

LEMON RAISIN PIE.
Anonymous.

On cup of sugar, one lemon, one cup of raisins, one

cup water; chop lemon and raisins fine, cook in the water
three-quarters of an hour.

LEMON PIE.

Mrs. A. L. Chetlain.

One tablespoon of corn starch stirred in a little cold
water; add one cup of boiling w ter, let it come to a boil,
then add seven tablespoons of sugar, yolks of four eggs,
grated rind and juice of two lemons; bake with a bottom
crust, then beat the whites of four eggs and a little sugar,
pour this over the top, and then brown.

LEMON PIE.

Mrs. L. Bradley.

One lemon, grate the rind and squeeze the juice; three
eggs, one tablespoon of butter, three tablespoons of sugar,
one cup of milk; beat the whites of eggs and stir in after
the rest are mixed.

MINCE PIES.

Six pounds of lean fresh beef boiled tender, when
cold, chopped fine, a pound of beef suet chopped fine,
five pounds of apples chopped, two pounds of raisins,
seeded, two pounds of currants, half a pound of citron,
two tablespoons of cinnamon, one of grated nutmeg, one
tablespoon of cloves, one tablespoon of allspice, one
tablespoon of salt, three pounds of brown sugar, a quart
of wine, pint of brandy, and the liquor the meat is boiled
in. Keep in a stone jar tied over with a double paper.
It should be made, at least, the day before it is used, and

when you make pies add a little more wine to what you take out for the pies, and more chopped apples,

MINCE MEAT.

Mrs. Higgins.

Six pounds of beef and six pounds of apples, chopped fine; four pounds of sugar, two of citron, three of raisins, three of currants, one of suet, two quarts of boiled cider, one-half cup, of salt, two nutmegs, two tablespoons of ground cloves, two of allspice, two of cinnamon; when used, enough sweet cider should be added to make the mixture quite moist.

MINCE MEAT.

Mrs. J. M. Durand.

Two pounds of raisins, one of currants, one of suet, two and one-half of sugar, one-quarter of citron, one-eighth of cinnamon; two chopped pippins, three lemons, two nutmegs; wine, brandy and cloves to taste.

MINCE PIE.

Mrs. Pulsifer.

Two pounds of suet chopped fine, four pounds of mince meat, three cups raisins, three cups of currants, two pieces of citron, twelve cups of fine chopped apples, five large teaspoons of cloves, four large teaspoons ginger, four nutmegs, one quart syrup, four quarts of cider, five teaspoons cinnamon, one teaspoon of pepper, salt to taste, one cup of sugar, two lemons (juice and rind grated); stir all together; let come to a boil, then put in a jar; when making pies put a tablespoon of brandy to a pie.

MINCE PIE.

Mrs. James Morgan.

Boil beef until tender (three pounds after it is boiled); when cold, chop fine; add three pounds of fine chopped suet, and mix with the beef; add a tablespoon of salt, six pounds of apples, four pounds of currants, six pounds of raisins, two pounds of citron; season to taste with pow-.dered cinnamon, mace, cloves and nutmeg; add boiled cider, brandy and wine until quite soft; mix well and pack in stone jars, pour brandy over the top and cover tightly. This will make about five gallons; add two pounds sugar.

MINCE PIE.

C. Kennicott.

Three pints apples, one pint boiled beef, one-half pint of butter or beef drippings, one pint molasses, one-half pint of water, one and a half teaspoons allspice, one teaspoon cinnamon, one teaspoon salt, three-fourths teaspoon cloves, two and a half large spoons of vinegar, one-half of a nutmeg. Young housekeepers will find this recipe a great comfort.

MOCK MINCE PIE.

Mrs. G. F. DeForest, Freeport, Ill.

One egg, three or four large crackers, or six or eight small ones, one-half cup of molasses, one-half cup sugar, one-half cup vinegar, one-half cup strong tea, one cup chopped raisins, a small piece butter, spice and salt.

SHAM MINCE PIE.
Eliza Wormley.

Ten crackers made fine, two cups of water, one of vinegar, one-half of butter, one of molasses, five eggs; add raisins; beat the eggs, butter and sugar together; spices and sugar to taste.

MINCE PIE.
Mrs. J. R. Adams.

Boil and chop three pounds of lean beef, two pounds of suet, four of good raisins, four of currants, one of citron, four of sugar, grated rind and juice of three lemons, and two sweet oranges, three large tablespoons of cinnamon, three grated nutmegs, two tablespoons of cloves, two of mace, one quart of cooking brandy, some wine, four tablespoons salt; pack it down tightly in a jar, and stir well before using. In making a pie, take nearly two-thirds of apples and more than one-third meat; add enough cider to make very juicy, and enough sugar to make very sweet.

VINEGAR PIE.
Ella Guild.

One cup of sugar, one-half of vinegar, two teaspoons of flour, one of butter, one of cinnamon, two cups of water; boil all together till thick, and bake as you would a custard pie. This is very nice.

CREAM PIE.
Mrs. M. A. Green.

Boil nearly one pint of new milk; take two small tablespoons of corn starch beaten with a little milk; to this add two eggs; when the milk has boiled, stir this in slowly with one scant teacup of sugar and one-half cup of butter, two teaspoons of lemon. Cakes: Three eggs, one cup of white sugar, one and a half of flour, one teaspoon of baking powder, mix it in flour; three table-spoons of cold water; bake in two pie-pans in a quick oven; split the cake while hot, and spread in the cream.

CREAM PIES.

Mrs. L. H. Holbrook.

One cup of flour, one cup of sugar, three or four eggs (the whites and yolks beaten separately and well); half a teaspoon of soda and one of cream of tartar; beat the eggs to a stiff froth; add the sugar, which should be of fine quality, and then the flour sifted with the soda and cream of tartar. Pour this into four common-sized pie tins and bake. It will be sufficient for two pies. Cream: Make a nice custard with one pint of milk, three eggs and one tablespoon of corn starch, cooking the custard in a tin kettle of hot water; before mixing in the corn starch wet it with milk, and add the eggs and sugar; then stir into the boiling milk; flavor to taste, and when cold spread between two layers of the crust.

CREAM PIE.

Mrs. S. Cornell.

Butter the size of an egg; one cup sugar and two eggs stirred together; then add one-third cup milk, two cups flour, with two teaspoons baking powder, stirred in before sifting into the mixture; bake in two pie tins for two pies. For the filling: One pint milk, taking out enough to wet one-half cup flour, and boil the rest, two-thirds cup sugar and yolks of two eggs; stir the filling mixture together and boil three minutes; when cold flavor with lemon or vanilla, and spread- between the upper and lower crusts, when cut smoothly apart. This makes two very delicious pies.

CREAM PIE.

Mrs. Bartlett,

One cup powdered sugar, one cup flour, one teaspoon cream tartar and one-half teaspoon soda, five eggs beaten separately, grated rind of lemon. Cream : Set in hot water one-half pint of milk ; when scalding hot add one-half cup sugar, a little salt and one egg beaten together; stir until thick, and when cool add one tablespoon vanilla put between crusts.

PHILADELPHIA BUTTER PIE.

Mrs. A. N. Arnold.

Cover a pie plate with crust, as for a custard pie; take a piece of butter the size of an egg, two-t█████ cup of sugar, one cup of sweet cream, one table██████ of flour; stir butter, flour and suga█ together ; then stir i█ the cream; pour in the plate; b██ until br███n.

SQUASH PIE.

Mrs. P. B. Ayer.

One crust, one small cup of dry map██ s██ █ssolved

in a little water, two cups of strained squash stirred in the sugar; add four eggs, two teaspoons of allspice, two cups of milk, one teaspoon of butter, and two of ginger, added last. This makes two pies.

SQUASH PIE.

Mrs. Rice.

One pint of squash, one pint of milk, three eggs, one-half of a nutmeg, one teaspoon of cinnamon, one teaspoon of vanilla, two cups of sugar; put everything into the squash, the milk last.

SQUASH PIE.

Mrs. L. H. Davis.

Two teacups of boiled squash, three-fourths teacup of brown sugar, three eggs, two tablespoons of molasses, one tablespoon melted butter, one tablespoon ginger, one teaspoon of cinnamon, two teacups of milk, a little salt. Makes two plate pies.

CUSTARD PIE.

Mrs. E. E. Marcy, Evanston.

Make a custard of the yolks of three eggs with milk, season to the taste; bake it in ordinary crust; put it in a a brick oven, that the crust may not be heavy, and as soon as that is heated remove it to a place in the oven of a more moderate heat, that the custard may bake slowly and not curdle; when done, beat the whites to a froth; add sugar and spread over the top, and return to the oven to brown slightly; small pinch of salt added to a custard heightens the flavor; a little soda in the crust prevents it from being heavy. Very nice.

WASHINGTON PIE.
Mrs. A. L. Chetlain.

One and one-half cups of sugar, one-half cup of butter, one-half cup of sweet 'milk, three eggs, two and one-half cups of flour, two teaspoons of baking powder; bake in three layers, in jelly cake tins; pare and grate two large apples; add one cup of sugar, grated rind and juice of one lemon; put this on the stove and let it steam until it forms a jelly; then take it off and stir in the yolk of one egg. When the cake and jelly are both cold put them together.

WASHINGTON PIE.
Mrs. D.

One cup of sugar, three eggs, one and one-half cups of flour, one teaspoon of baking powder; flavor to taste; bake as for jelly cake in layers, and spread between the layers raspberry jam.

COCOANUT PIE.
Mrs. E. P. Thomas, Rockford, Ill.

Grate fresh cocoanut; to one cup of cocoanut add one and one-half cups of sweet milk the yolks of four eggs, a little salt, and sweeten to taste; one tablespoon of melted butter; beat the whole five or six minutes; beat the whites of the eggs to a stiff froth, and put over the top just long enough to slightly brown before taking the pie from the oven. If you use dessicated cocoanut, soak it in the milk over night.

COCOANUT PIE.

Mrs. Taylor, Ft. Wayne.

One and one-half pints of milk, six eggs, one cocoa-nut, three cups sugar, one-half cup butter; mix sugar and butter, then the eggs, then the cocoanut, and lastly the milk.

POLISH TARTLETS.

Roll some good puff paste out thin, cut it into two and a half inch squares; brush each square over with the white of an egg, then fold down the corners so that they all meet in the middle of each piece of paste; slightly press the two pieces together, brush them over with the egg; sift over sugar; bake in a quick oven for a quarter of an hour; when they are done make a little hole in the middle and fill with jam or jelly.

LEMON TARTS.

Mix well together the juice and grated rind of two lemons, two cups of sugar, two eggs, and the crumbs of sponge cake; beat it all together until smooth; put into twelve patty pans lined with puff paste, and bake until the crust is done.

CUSTARDS CREAMS, ETC.

"They serve up salmon, venison and wild boars,
By hundreds, dozens and by scores,
Hogsheads of honey, kilderkins of mustard,
Plum puddings, pancakes, apple pies and custard."

MRS. GRAVE'S CUSTARDS.

Six eggs, one pint milk, one and a half cups sugar, one teaspoon of vanilla; beat sugar and eggs together, and stir into hot milk; when done, strain; cook very slowly, not boil; pour into cups.

ANOTHER WAY.— Instead of boiling, put the mixture into cups; set them in a dripping pan half full of water and bake in the oven till done.

RICE CUSTARD.

Mrs. G. M. Dickerman, Rockford.

To half a cup of rice, add one quart of milk, and a little salt; steam one hour, or until quite soft; beat the yolks of four eggs with four tablespoons of white sugar; add this just before taking off the rice; stir in thoroughly, but do not let it boil any more; flavor with vanilla. Beat the whites of the eggs to a stiff froth, with sugar; after putting the mixture into the pudding dish in which you serve it, put the whites over it, and let it slightly brown in the oven.

RICH CUSTARD.

Mrs. Morgan, Rockford, Ill.

One quart of cream, the yolks of six eggs, six ounces of powdered white sugar, a small pinch of salt, two table spoons of brandy, one tablespoon of peach water, half a tablespoon of lemon brandy, an ounce of blanched almonds pounded to a paste; mix the cream with the sugar, and the yolks of the eggs well beaten; scald them together in a tin pail in boiling water, stirring all the time until sufficiently thick; when cool, add the other ingredients, and pour into custard cups.

BOILED CUSTARD.

Mrs. T. Kingsford.

Two tablespoons of the corn starch to one quart of milk; mix the corn starch with a small quantity of the milk and flavor it; beat up two eggs. Heat the remainder of the milk to *near* boiling, then add the mixed corn starch, the eggs, four tablespoons of sugar, a little butter and salt. Boil it two minutes, stirring it briskly.

BOILED CUSTARD.

Mrs. R. M. Pickering.

One quart milk, eight eggs, one-half pound of sugar; beat to a good froth the eggs and sugar. Put the milk in a tin pail and set it in boiling water; pour in the eggs and sugar and stir until it thickens.

CHOCOLATE CUSTARD.

Mrs. Higgins.

Three ounces Baker's chocolate, three pints milk, four tablespoons white sugar, two tablespoons brown sugar; prepare a soft custard of the milk and the yolks of five eggs and the white of one; dissolve the chocolate in a cup of warm milk and heat it to boiling point; when cool, sweeten it with brown sugar and flavor with the extract of vanilla; pour the whole into a dish and cover with the whites of the five eggs beaten stiff, with a little sugar; brown slightly and serve cold.

SAGO CUSTARD.

C. D. Adams.

Three tablespoons sago boiled in a little water till clear; add one quart of milk, let it come to a boil, then add five or six well-beaten eggs and sugar to taste. Put the vessel containing the custard in a kettle of boiling water; stir it briskly till it thickens a little; flavor with vanilla after it is partly cool.

APPLE CUSTARD.

Mrs. F. B. Orr.

Pare, core and quarter one dozen tart apples, strew into it the grated rind of one lemon; stew until tender in very little water; then mash smooth with back of a spoon. To one and a half pints of strained apple add one and a quarter pounds sugar; leave it until cold; beat six eggs, light and stir alternately into one quart milk with the apples; put into cups or deep dish, and bake twenty minutes; to be eaten cold.

APPLE CUSTARDS.

Mrs. C. M. Dickerman, Rockford.

Take six tart apples, pare and quarter them, put into a baking dish with one cup water; cook until tender, but not to pieces, then turn them into a pudding dish and sprinkle sugar over to cover them; beat eight eggs with sugar, and mix with them three pints of milk, a little nutmeg; turn it over the apples, and bake twenty-five minutes.

CARAMEL CUSTARD.

Mrs. Perry Smith.

One quart of milk, one cup of white sugar, one cup of brown sugar, two tablespoons corn starch, four eggs and a pinch of salt and vanilla. Place the milk with the white sugar and salt in a farina kettle over the fire; if you have not such a kettle, a tin pail set in a pot of hot water will answer the purpose; beat the eggs without separating in a large bowl, and wet the corn starch with a little cold milk; put the brown sugar in a tin pan and set over the fire; stir until it is thoroughly scorched, but not burned; then turn the scalding milk on the eggs; put the mixture in the kettle again over the fire; stir in the corn starch until it thickens; lastly, stir in the scorched sugar and remove from the fire; then add a generous amount of vanilla. The scorched sugar falls into the custard in strings, but these will dissolve with vigorous stirring, after removal from the fire. Turn into custard glasses and serve cold,

RENNET CURD.

Take a piece of dried rennet two inches square, wash off the salt, put it into two quarts of lukewarm milk, with a thread attached to it so that it can be easily removed; let it remian in the milk until it begins to thicken, then remove it and place the milk where it will become cold and solid. To be eaten with rich cream, sweetened and flavored to taste.

APPLE SOUFFLE.

Mrs. A. N. Arnold.

Stew the apples; add a little grated lemon peel and juice; line the sides and bottom of the dish about two inches thick. Make a boiled custard with one pint of milk and two eggs; when it is cool, pour it into the center of the dish. Beat the whites of the eggs and spread it over the top; sprinkle sugar over it, and bake a few minutes in the oven.

FLOATING ISLAND.

Mrs. E. E. Marcy.

One-half package gelatine, one pint of water; soak twenty minutes; add two cups of sugar, set it on the stove to come to a boil; when nearly cold, add the whites of four eggs beaten stiff, the juice and rind of two lemons, and pour into a mould; turn over the form. Make a custard of the yolks of four eggs, a quart of milk, and a small tablespoon of corn starch, sweetened to taste.

FLOATING ISLAND.

From "In the Kitchen"—Mrs. E. S. Miller.

One tumbler of currant jelly, one pint of powdered sugar, five eggs; beat the whites of the eggs very stiff before putting in the jelly; then beat well; add the sugar gradually and beat it perfectly stiff; chill it thoroughly on the ice and serve in a glass dish half filled with cold milk; cover it with the island in spoonfuls standing in peaks. It is to be eaten with cream.

FLOATING ISLAND OF FRESH RASPBERRIES.

Adapted from "In the Kitchen."

Crush a pint of very ripe red raspberries with a gill of sugar; beat the white of four eggs to a stiff froth, and add gradually a gill of powdered sugar; press the raspberries through a strainer to avoid the seeds, and by degrees beat in the juice with the sugar and egg until so stiff that it stands in peaks. Serve as in the above rule.

APPLE FLOAT.

Mrs. O. L. Parker.

To one quart of apples, partially stewed and well mashed, put the whites of three eggs, well beaten, and four heaping tablespoons of loaf sugar; beat them together for fifteen minutes, and eat with rich milk and nutmeg.

ORANGE FLOAT.

Mrs. M. E. Kedzie, Evanston.

One quart of water, the juice and pulp of two lemons, one coffee cup of sugar; when boiling add to it four table-spoons of corn starch mixed in water; let it boil, stirring it fifteen minutes; when cool, pour it over four or five sliced oranges; over the top spread the beaten whites of three eggs, sweetened, and a few drops of vanilla. Eaten with cream.

WHIPPED CREAM.

Mix one pint of cream with nine tablespoons of fine sugar and one gill of wine in a large bowl; whip these with the cream dasher, and as the froth rises, skim into the dish in which it is to be served. Fill the dish full to top, and ornament with kisses or macaroons.

SPANISH CREAM.

Mrs. J. P. Booker.

One pint milk and one-half box gelatine, heated to-gether; yolks of three eggs, and five tablespoons sugar beaten together, added to the above; take off as soon as it thickens, then stir in the whites of three eggs beaten to a stiff froth; flavor with vanilla; to be served with cream and sugar.

SPANISH CREAM.

Mrs. J. H. Brown.

Boil one ounce of gelatine in one pint of new milk until dissolved, add four eggs well beaten and half a pound of sugar; stir it over the fire until the eggs thicken, take it off the fire and add a full wine-glass of peach water, and when cool pour it into moulds; serve with cream.

VELVET CREAM.

Mrs. R. Harris.

Nearly a box of gelatine, soaked over night in a cup of wine; melt it over the fire, with the sugar; when it is warm, put in a quart of cream or new milk and strain it into moulds. If the wine is too hot, it will curdle the milk.

CHOCOLATE CREAM.

Mrs. Spruance.

Soak one box of Coxe's English gelatine (in cold water sufficient to cover) one hour; one quart of milk boiled; scrape two ounces of French chocolate, mix with eight spoons of white sugar; moisten this with three spoons of the boiling milk; then stir in the gelatine and the yolks of ten well beaten eggs; stir three minutes briskly; take off, strain and add two teaspoons of vanilla; strain and put in moulds to cool. Serve with sugar and cream.

CHOCOLATE CREAM.

Mrs. King.

Half a cake of chocolate dissolved in a little hot water; put in a cup of milk and when it boils have five eggs well beaten and mixed with two cups of milk; pour the hot chocolate into the eggs and milk; stir well and boil all together for a few minutes; sweeten to your taste. To be eaten cold.

COFFEE CREAM.

Soak half an ounce of Coxe's gelatine in a little cold water half an hour; then place it over boiling water and add one gill of strong coffee, and one gill of sugar; when the gelatine is well dissolved, take from the fire; stir in three gills of cold cream and strain into your mould. Be sure that this has been previously wet with cold water.

ORANGE CREAM.

Make according to above rule, adding one gill of orange juice, and the grated rind of one orange which has been previously soaked in the orange juice while the gelatine is dissolving over the boiling water, and the beaten yolks of two eggs when you take off, and quite hot.

APPLE CREAM.

Mrs. Mann.

One cup thick cream, one cup sugar, beat till very smooth; then beat the whites of two eggs, and add; stew apples in water till soft; take them from the water with a fork; steam them if you prefer. Pour the cream over the apples when cold.

FRUIT CREAMS.

These consist of a rich cream; blanc mange poured over fruit and set on ice to chill.

PISTACHIO AND ALMOND CREAMS.

Make a nice vanilla ice-cream; have ready pistachio nuts, which have been prepared by pouring boiling water over them and letting them stand in it a few moments; then strip off the skins and pound to a paste in a mortar, and mix with the cream. Freeze.

BAVARIAN CREAM.

Mrs. Chas. Duffield.

One pint of milk, yolks of four eggs, one-fourth pound of sugar, one-half ounce of gelatine; put all over the fire, and stir until the gelatine is dissolved, then strain through a fine sieve, and when cool, add one pint of cold cream; flavor with vanilla.

ITALIAN CREAM.

E. V. Case, Elmhurst.

Take one quart of cream, one pint of milk sweetened very sweet, and highly seasoned with sherry wine and vanilla; beat it with a whip dasher, and remove the froth as it rises until it is all converted into froth. Have ready one box of Coxe's sparkling gelatine, dissolved in a little warm water; set your frothed cream into a tub of ice; pour the gelatine into it, and stir constantly until it thickens, then pour into moulds, and set in a cool place.

TAPIOCA CREAM.

Two tablespoons of tapioca dissolved very soft, three yolks of eggs beaten and sweetened to the taste; boil one quart of milk, when cool stir in the tapioca and flavor; beat the whites very light and mix all together; let boil ten minutes, pour into moulds.

TAPIOCA MERINGUE.

Mrs. Spruance.

One teacup of tapioca soaked in one and a half pints of warm water three hours; peel and core eight tart apples; fill apples with sugar, grating a little nutmeg or moistening with wine; one hour before needed, pour the tapioca over the apples and bake, serving in the dish baked in; the addition of the whites of four well beaten eggs spread over the top and browned slightly, improves it.

SPANISH MERINGUES.

M.

Take the whites of eight eggs; beat until stiff; add one-half pound of powdered sugar and a pinch of salt, and beat well; grease some paper and lay on a board; drop the meringues on it and bake in a slow oven; when done remove with a knife and place the two together; sprinkle with powdered sugar before baking.

SWEET MERINGUES.

M.

Use the same mixture as above, formed in a ring, using whipped cream with sugar and vanilla to taste, for the centre.

MELANGE.

Mrs. W. Guthrie.

Line a deep pie dish with pie crust, and spread on a thin layer of tart apple sauce, then a layer of buttered bread; on this another layer of apple. Bake until the

16

crust is done; when done, spread on the whites of two
eggs beaten to a froth and sweetened; brown slightly.
Serve with pudding sauce of butter and sugar stirred to a
cream, seasoned with lemon.

LEMON SPONGE.
Mrs. Lamkin.

Two ounces of gelatine; pour over one pint of cold
water; let it stand fifteen minutes; add half a pint of
boiling water, three-quarters of a pound of white sugar,
and the juice of four lemons. When the gelatine is cold,
before it begins to get firm, add the well beaten whites of
three eggs; beat the whole fifteen minutes, until the mixture is quite white, and begins to thicken; then put in a
mould first wet in cold water.

LEMON SPONGE.
Mrs. B.

Two ounces isinglass, one and three-fourths pints water,
three-fourths pound powdered sugar, juice of five lemons
and rind of one, whites of three eggs; dissolve isinglass
in water, strain, add sugar, lemon rind and juice; boil the
whole ten or fifteen minutes; strain again; let it stand
until it is cold and begins to stiffen; beat the whites of
the eggs, add them to the mixture; beat until quite
white, then mould and let it stand.

SNOW SOUFFLE.
Mrs. J. Louis Harris, Keokuk, Iowa.

Beat the whites of two eggs to a stiff froth; dissolve

one-half box of gelatine in a little more than a pint of hot water, two cups of sugar, and the juice of two lemons; when this is dissolved and cooled, stir into it the eggs you have beaten, beat the whole together until it is white and stiff; mould and pour around it soft custard.

SNOW PUDDING.
Mrs. L. H. Smith, Kenwood.

One-third box Coxe's gelatine, soaked ten minutes in one-half pint cold water, and afterwards add one-half pint of boiling water, juice of two good sized fresh lemons, one and a half cups powdered sugar; allow this to stand over a slow fire only a few moments; then strain it through a flannel bag into your pudding dish and set away to cool; then make a smooth custard of the yolks of five eggs with one and a half tablespoons corn starch; sweeten to taste and cook it a few minutes in a tin pail, set in a kettle of boiling water, stirring all the while; when sufficiently cooked and partially cooled, flavor with vanilla extract, and when entirely cold, pour this custard over the jelly already in the dish, and beat to a stiff froth the whites of the five eggs, adding a little sugar and pour over the top of the custard, and it is then ready to serve. This is considered an excellent and delicate dessert, if properly and carefully made.

SNOW PUDDING.
Mrs, Henry Stevens.

One-half box of Coxe's gelatine, dissolve in one pint of boiling hot water; when nearly cool, add one cup sugar, juice of one lemon; strain; add whites of three eggs beaten to a stiff froth; beat all thoroughly, and quickly pour into mould. Serve cold with soft custard made of the yolks of three eggs, and one-half teaspoon corn starch stirred in one pint of boiling milk; sweeten to taste.

APPLE CHARLOTTE.
Mrs. A. M. Gibbs.

Put a layer of bread, cut in thin slices and buttered on both sides, in the bottom of your pudding dish, and on this a layer of apples cut as for a pie, seasoning with sugar and a dust of cinnamon, alternating the bread and apples until the dish is filled, having a layer of bread on top. Bake one-half hour. If the bread is in danger of becoming too brown and hard, cover with a plate until the apples are cookod. To be eaten with cream.

CHARLOTTE RUSSE.
M.

One pint cream and whites of six eggs, beaten to a stiff froth separately; one-fourth ounce of gelatine soaked in one gill of milk; set on back of stove to dissolve. Mix cream and eggs, sweeten and flavor; stir in gelatine; when cool, place on sponge cake and set away to get firm; or you can use two eggs (whites) and one-half ounce gelatine. Good.

CHARLOTTE RUSSE.
Mrs. A. M. Gibbs.

Whip one quart rich cream to a stiff froth, and drain

well on a nice sieve. To one scant pint of milk add six eggs beaten very light; make very sweet; flavor high with vanilla. Cook over hot water till it is a thick custard. Soak one full ounce Coxe's gelatine in a very little water, and warm over hot water. When the custard is very cold, beat in lightly the gelatine and the whipped cream. Line the bottom of your mould with buttered paper, the sides with sponge cake or lady-fingers fastened together with the white of an egg. Fill with the cream, put in a cold place or in summer on ice. To turn out, dip the mould for a moment in hot water. In draining the whipped cream, all that drips through can be rewhipped.

CHARLOTTE RUSSE.

Mrs. J. P. Hoit.

Take one quart of thin cream, sweeten and flavor; whip the cream until all in froth; then take half box of gelatine, put in as little cold water as possible to soak, and set on the stove to melt; have the gelatine cool before putting into the cream; have a dish already lined with cake or lady-fingers, pour the cream into it and set on ice until ready for use.

CHARLOTTE.

Mrs. W. W. Kimball.

One quart rich cream, three tablespoons of Madeira wine, whites of two eggs beaten to a stiff froth, one teacup of powdered sugar, half a box of gelatine dissolved in half a cup of sweet milk; flavor with vanilla; beat the cream and wine together; add the eggs, then the sugar, and last, the gelatine.

RICE CHARLOTTE.

E. M. Walker.

Blanch one-fourth pound of rice, and boil in one quart of milk, with a little sugar and vanilla; when soft, let it cool, and then mix it with one pint of whipped cream; oil a mould and fill with a layer of rice and preserves, or marmalade, alternately; let it stand until stiff, and then turn it out.

FRUIT BLANC MANGE.

Mrs. T. V. Wadskier.

Stew nice fresh fruit (whatever you may please, cherries and raspberries being the best), strain off the juice, and sweeten to taste; place it over the fire in a double kettle until it boils; while boiling, stir in corn starch wet with a little cold water, allowing two tablespoons of starch for each pint of juice; continue stirring until sufficiently cooked, then pour into moulds wet in cold water; set them away to cool. This, eaten with cream and sugar, makes a delightful dessert.

BLANC MANGE — ARROWROOT.

Mrs. P. B. Ayer.

Boil one quart of milk, reserving one gill to wet up your arrowroot with; when it boils up, stir in two and a half tablespoons of arrowroot, and after a few minutes add one tablespoon crushed sugar, one tablespoon rosewater, and a little salt; pour into moulds.

CHOCOLATE MANGE.

S. D. F.

One box of Coxe's gelatine dissolved in a pint of cold water, three pints of milk; put over to boil, with one cup of French chocolate; when the milk is just scalded, pour in the gelatine; sweeten to taste; boil five minutes, then take from the fire, flavor with vanilla, pour into moulds. When cold, serve with powdered sugar and cream.

MOUNT BLANC.

Mrs. F. B. Orr.

One-third box of gelatine, grated rind of two lemons, two cups, of sugar, one pint boiling water; before the mixture gets stiff, stir in the whites of five eggs beaten to a stiff froth. Eat with custard, boiled, made with yolks of eggs and one pint of boiling milk. Sweeten to taste, flavor with vanilla. Excellent.

GELATINE BLANC MANGE.

C. D. Adams.

Soak one-half box Coxe's gelatine in one and a half pints of milk for an hour; put it over a kettle of boiling water, and when it comes to the boil, add the beaten yolks of three eggs and four tablespoons of sugar, stirring it briskly for a few moments; when partly cool, add the whites of the eggs, beaten very light; flavor with vanilla, cool in a mould and serve with sugar and cream.

A SIMPLE DESSERT.

A. S. Ewing.

Put a teacup of tapioca into sufficient cold water; boil until the lumps become almost transparent; squeeze the juice of two lemons partially into the mixture, then slice them into it, sweeten or not, then eat when cold, with cream and sugar.

JELLIED GRAPES.

Mrs. A. M. Lewis.

A very delicate dish, is made of one-third of a cup of rice, two cups of grapes, half a cup of water, and two spoons of sugar. Sprinkle the rice and sugar among the grapes, while placing them in a deep dish; pour on the water, cover close and simmer two hours slowly in the oven. Serve cream as sauce, or cold as pudding. If served warm as pudding, increase slightly the proportion of rice and sugar.

ICES.

Glittering squares of colored ice,
Sweetened with syrups, tinctured with spice;
Creams and cordials and sugared dates;
Syrian apples, Othmanee quinces,
Limes and citrons and apricots,
And wines that are known to Eastern princes.
*   *   *   *   *   *   *
And all that the curious palate could wish,
Pass in and out of the cedarn doors.
                                    — T. B. ALDRICH.

Use one part of coarse table salt to two parts of ice broken the size of a walnut. This should be firmly packed around the cream pail to the height of the freezer. For three pints of cream, one and a half pints of water should be poured over the ice in the freezer, and for every additional quart of cream one pint of water should be added to the ice after packing. When there is no ice-cream freezer· convenient, ices may be frozen by putting the cream to be frozen in a tin pail with a close cover. This ice and salt for packing may be put in a larger pail and packed firmly around the pail of cream to be frozen. Let this stand to chill for twenty or thirty minutes, then remove the cover and stir the freezing mixture within until stiff. Then re-pack, cover the whole closely with a woolen cloth or carpet and leave for an hour or two in a cool place.

CURRANT ICE.

One pint of currant juice, one pound of sugar, and one pint of water; put in freezer, and when partly frozen add the whites of three eggs well beaten.

ORANGE AND LEMON ICES.

The rind of three oranges grated and steeped a few moments in a little more than a pint of water; strain one pint of this on a pound of sugar and then add one pint of orange or lemon juice; pour in the freezer, and when half frozen add the whites of four eggs beaten to a stiff froth.

ORANGE ICE.

Juice of six oranges, grated peel of three, juice of two lemons, one pint of sugar, one pint of water, and freeze

STRAWBERRY ICE CREAM.

From "In the Kitchen."

Mash with a potato pounder in an earthen bowl one quart of strawberries with one pound of sugar, rub it through the colander and add one quart of sweet cream and freeze. Very ripe peaches or coddled apples may be used instead of strawberries.

STRAWBERRY ICE.

From "In the Kitchen."

Crush two quarts of strawberries with two pounds of sugar; let them stand an hour or more; squeeze them in a straining cloth, pressing out all the juice; add to this an equal measure of water, and when half frozen, the whisked whites of eggs in the proportion of three to a quart.

ICE CREAM.

M.

One pint milk, yolks of two eggs, six ounces sugar, one tablespoon corn starch; scald until it thickens; when cool, add one pint whipped cream and the whites of two eggs, beaten stiff; sweeten, flavor and freeze.

ICE CREAM.

Mrs. A. P. Iglehart.

Have ready two quarts of rich cream; take out three pints, and stir into the pint left one pound of white sugar; flavor with lemon or vanilla; after mixing this well add it to the three pints and freeze it.

ICE CREAM.

Mrs. W. H. Ovington.

Scald one quart of milk with one sheet of isinglass (broken), and a vanilla bean; when cool, strain, mix with one pint of cream whipped to a froth; sweeten to taste and freeze.

TUTTI FRUTTI.

From "In the Kitchen."

A rich vanilla cream with candied cherries, raisins, currants and citron. The fruit must be added when the cream is nearly frozen.

AN EXCELLENT DESSERT.

Mrs. J. Young Scammon.

One can or twelve large peaches, two coffeecups of sugar, one pint of water and the whites of three eggs; break the peaches with and stir all the ingredients together; freeze the whole into a form ; beat the eggs to a froth.

PEACHES A LA UDE.

From "In the Kitchen."

Make a syrup of a pound of sugar and half a pint of water; when boiled and skimmed place in it five or six large peaches peeled and halved with the blanched kernels. Let them boil gently until clear, being careful not to break them. Skim them from the syrup and leave them to drain. Squeeze the juice of six lemons and add to the syrup with gelatine, which has been soaked half an hour and melted over boiling water. It must be used in the proportion of one ounce to a quart of syrup; wet a mould, pour in the jelly to the depth of half an inch, and let it harden on the ice; then fill the mould with alternate layers of peaches and half formed jelly, and place on the ice. Do not disturb it until perfectly stiff.

MACEDOINE OF FRUIT.

From "In the Kitchen."

Wine jelly and fruit in alternate layers frozen together. The fruit may be of any and all sorts, and may be candied or preserved, or slices of pear, apple, etc.; may be boiled in syrup and then drained; the mould must be filled after the jelly has begun to form, but before it is stiff, and the first layer should be of jelly; when filled, place the mould in salt and ice prepared as for freezing ice cream; cover closely, and let it remain several hours.

FRUITS.

"Fruit of all kinds, in coat
Rough, or smooth rind, or bearded husk, or shell,
She gathers tribute large, and on the board
Heaps with unsparing hand."
                        —PARADISE LOST.

Bring me berries or such cooling fruit
As the kind, hospitable woods provide.
                        —COWPER.

Fruits for preserving should be carefully selected, removing all that are imperfect. They are in the best condition when not fully ripe, and as soon as possible after they are picked. Small fruits should not be allowed to stand over night after they are picked, when they are to be preserved. Use only the finest sugar for preserving. When fruit is sealed in glass cans, wrap paper of two or three thicknesses around the cans. The chemical action of light will affect the quality of the preserves when perfectly air-tight. With this precaution, glass cans are preferable to any other for preserving fruit. One-half a pound of sugar to a pound of fruit is a good rule for canned fruit, although many housekeepers use but one-quarter of a pound of sugar to a pound of fruit.

An excellent rule for canning the larger fruits, as

peaches, pears, etc., is to place them in a steamer over a kettle of boiling water, laying first a cloth in the bottom of the steamer; fill this with the fruit and cover tightly. Let them steam for fifteen minutes, or until they can be easily pierced with a fork, (some fruits will require a longer time.) Make a syrup of sugar of the right consistency. As the fruit is steamed, drop each for a moment in the syrup, then place in the cans, having each one-half full of fruit, and then fill up with the hot syrup, then cover and seal.

A SUGGESTION.

For canning all large fruits, where no other method is given by contributors, the directions for canning large fruits are given in the recipe for Preserved Peaches. For canning all of the small fruits, follow the directions given in Preserved Cherries. They are both excellent. If less sugar is preferred, use one-quarter of a pound of sugar to a pound of fruit. The syrup should be prepared by adding a pint of water in your preserving kettle to each pound and a half of sugar, let it boil up gently and skim until perfectly clear, when it is ready for the fruit.

SUGARED FRUITS.

Beat the white of the egg just enough to break, then dip fine stems of cherries or currants into the egg and then into powdered sugar, and dry on a sieve.

AMBROSIA.

Mrs. S. W. Cheever, Ottawa, Ill.

Take one dozen sweet oranges, peel off the skins and

cut them in slices; take a large sized fresh cocoanut, grate it on a coarse grater, then put alternate layers of the orange and grated cocoanut in a glass dish, and sprinkle pulverized sugar over each layer of the cocoanut. This makes a beautiful and palatable dish.

MOCK STRAWBERRIES AND CREAM.

Mrs. Bartlett.

Take any quantity of sound ripe peaches, and well flavored eating apples, say in proportion of three peaches. to one apple, peel the fruit nicely, cut a layer of peaches and then of apples, alternately; they should be cut (not sliced) about the size of a large strawberry. When finished, cover the top with a layer of crushed sugar, then pour over all two or three spoons of cold water. Let the whole stand about two hours; then mix the peaches and apples indiscriminately; let stand one hour longer, serve with or without cream. The flavor of strawberry is more perfect without cream.

BAKED APPLES.

Pare as many apples as you wish of some nice variety, neither sweet nor sour; core them by using an apple corer or a steel fork; set them in biscuit tins, and fill the cavities with sugar, a little butter, and some ground cinnamon, if you like; set them in the oven and bake until done.

BAKED PEARS.

Mrs. J. B. Stubbs.

Place in a stone jar, first a layer of pears (without paring); then a layer of sugar, then pears, and so on until the jar is full. Then put in as much water as it will hold. Bake in oven three hours. Very nice.

BAKED QUINCES.

One dozen nice quinces, cored and well rubbed. Put in baking pans, and fill the centre with pulverized sugar. Bake and serve cold, with or without cream.

PRESERVED QUINCES.

Mrs. Anna Marble.

As you peel and core the quinces, throw them in cold water; strain them out of the water and make a syrup. To a pint of water, put a pound of sugar to every pound of fruit. When the syrup boils, put in fruit and boil until soft. Boil the syrup down as usual with other preserves.

PRESERVED PEACHES.

Select peaches of fine quality and firm. If too ripe they are not likely to keep perfectly. Pare them and place them in a steamer over boiling water and cover tightly; an earthen plate placed in the steamer under the fruit will preserve the juices which afterwards may be strained and added to the syrup. Let them steam for fifteen minutes or until they can be easily pierced with a fork; make a syrup of the first quality of sugar, and as the fruit is steamed drop each peach into the syrup for a few seconds, then take out and place in the cans; when the cans are full, pour over the fruit the hot syrup and seal immediately. Inexperienced house-wives will do well

17

to remember, that the syrup should be well skimmed before pouring over the fruit. We prefer the proportions of half a pound of sugar to a pound of fruit for canning, although many excellent housekeepers use less. This rule is excellent for all of the large fruits—as pears, quinces, apples, etc.

PRESERVED PLUMS.

Jennie June.

Allow to every pound of fruit three-quarters of a pound of sugar; put into stone jars alternate layers of fruit and sugar, and place the jars in a moderately warm oven. Let them remain there until the oven is cool. If prepared at tea time let them remain until morning; then strain the juice from the plums, boil and clarify it. Remove the fruit carefully to glass or china jars, pour over the hot syrup and carefully cover with egg, tissue paper, or thick white paper pasted, or bladder tied closely down.

PRESERVED CHERRIES.

Jennie June.

Stone the fruit, weigh it, and for every pound take three-quarters of a pound of sugar. First dissolve the sugar in water in the proportion of a pint of water to a pound and a half of sugar; then add the fruit and let it boil as fast as possible for half an hour, till it begins to jelly. As soon as it thickens put in pots, cover with brandied paper, next the fruit, and then cover closely from the air.

CANNED CHERRIES.

Prepared in the same manner, allowing but half a pound of sugar to a pound of fruit; after putting the fruit into the syrup let it scald (not boil hard), for ten or fifteen minutes and then can and seal. A few of the cherry stones put in a muslin bag and put into the syrup to scald with the fruit imparts a fine flavor; they should not be put in the jars with the fruit. This method is excellent for use with all the small fruits, as strawberries, raspberries, and also plums.

PRESERVED ORANGE PEEL.

Mrs. A. N. Arnold.

Peel the oranges and cut the rinds into narrow shreds, boil till tender, change the water three times, squeeze the juice of the orange over the sugar; put pound to pound of sugar and peel; boil twenty minutes all together.

CITRON PRESERVES.

Carter.

Cut the citron in thin slices, boil in water with a small piece of alum until clear and tender, then rinse in cold water. Make a syrup of three-fourths pound of sugar to a pound of citron; boil a piece of ginger in the syrup; then pour the citron in and let it boil for a few minutes. Put in one lemon to five of the fruit.

SPICED PEACHES OR PEARS.

Mrs. Henry M. Knickerbocker.

To ten pounds good mellow peaches, use five pounds

sugar, one pint of good vinegar, and some whole cloves or cinnamon. Take the sugar, vinegar and cloves, and let them come to a boil, and turn over the fruit. This do three days in succession, and the last day put the fruit into the syrup, a few at a time, and let them just boil up.

CANNED PINE APPLE.
Mrs. F. L. Bristol.

For six pounds of fruit when cut and ready to can, make syrup with two and a half pounds sugar and nearly three pints of water; boil syrup five minutes and skim or strain if necessary; then add the fruit, and let it boil up; have cans hot, fill and shut up as soon as possible. Use the best white sugar. As the cans cool keep tightening them up.

CANNED STRAWBERRIES.
Miss Blaikie.

After the berries are pulled, let as many as can be put carefully in the preserve kettle at once, be placed on a platter. To each pound of fruit add three-fourths of a pound of sugar; let them stand two or three hours, till the juice is drawn from them; pour it in the kettle and let it come to a boil, and remove the scum which rises; then put in the berries very carefully. As soon as they come thoroughly to a boil, put them in warm jars, and seal while boiling hot. Be sure the cans are air tight.

CANNED CURRANTS.
Mrs. Wicker.

Put sufficient sugar to prepare them for the table, then boil them ten minutes and seal hot as possible.

TO CAN TOMATOES.

Mrs. Edward Ely.

Wash your tomatoes and cut out any places that are green or imperfect; then cut them up and put over to cook with a little salt; boil them till perfectly soft; then strain them through a colander; turn them back to cook, and when they have come to boiling heat, pour them into stone jugs (one or two gallon jugs as you prefer). They will keep a day or two in winter if all are not used at a time; put the cork in, and have some canning cement hot and pour over the cork. The jug must, of course, be hot when the tomatoes are poured in.

CRANBERRY SAUCE.

Mrs. Bartlett.

One quart cranberries, one quart water, one quart sugar, stew slowly.

PIC NIC LEMON BUTTER.

Etta C. Springer.

Grate the rind, add juice of three·lemons, one pound sugar, two ounces butter, three eggs ; mix together, let come to boil ; stir all the time.

LEMON BUTTER.

Mrs. D. S. Munger.

Beat six eggs, one-fourth pound butter, one pound sugar, the rind and juice of three lemons; mix together and set it in a pan of hot water to cook. Very nice for tarts, or to eat with bread.

PEACH BUTTER.

Mrs. M. L.

Take pound for pound of peaches and sugar; cook peaches alone until they become soft, then put in one-half the sugar, and stir for one-half an hour; then the remainder of sugar, and stir an hour and a half. Season with cloves and cinnamon.

TOMATO BUTTER.

Mrs. Johnson.

Nine pounds peeled tomatoes, three pounds sugar, one pint vinegar, three tablespoons cinnamon, one tablespoon cloves, one and one-half tablespoons allspice; boil three or four hours until quite thick, and stir often, that it may not burn.

APPLE JELLY.

Mrs. J. H. Brown.

Take nice green apples that will cook nicely; quarter the apples without paring, put them in a pan or kettle and cover over with water, and keep them covered; let them boil slowly until entirely done; then put in a bag and drain (not squeeze) them. Put a pound of white sugar to a pint of juice. This is very easily made in the winter; is best made day before using.

APPLE JELLY FOR CAKE.

Mrs. P. B. Ayer.

Grate one large or two small apples, the rind and juice of one lemon, one cup sugar; boil three minutes.

APPLE JELLY.

Mrs. N. P. Iglehart.

Take juicy apples (Ramboes, if possible); take the stem and top off, and wash them nicely, then cut up in quarters and put cold water on them, just enough to cover them; boil them soft, afterward strain them through a jelly bag; then take two pints at a time with two pounds of crushed sugar; boil twenty minutes, then do the same with the other juice; to be economical, pare and core the apples; don't strain so close, but that you can, by adding a little more water, use the apples for sauce or pies.

CRAB APPLE JELLY AND JAM.

Mrs. Ludlam, Evanston.

Remove stems and blossoms from the apples; let them scald and pour off the first water; next put them in plenty of water and let them cook slowly; as they begin to soften dip off the juice for jelly, straining it through flannel. One pound of juice to a pound of sugar for jelly. Next add more water; let apples stew very soft; strain through a sieve, which takes out cores and seeds; to this pulp add brown sugar, pound for pound; it needs careful cooking and stirring.

GRAPE JELLY.

Anonymous.

Allow fourteen ounces of sugar to a pint of juice; boil fifteen minutes alone; add sugar and boil five minutes.

LEMON JELLY.

Mrs. W. Guthrie.

One paper of gelatine; let it stand one hour in warm water; then add one quart of boiling water, the juice of three or four lemons and a pint and a half of sugar.

LEMON JELLY.

Mrs. P. B. Ayer.

Grate the outsides of two lemons, and squeeze the juice; add one cup sugar, one-half of butter, yolks of three eggs; beat the three last ingredients thoroughly, then add the juice and grated rind, and put it over your fire, stirring until thick; mould to fancy.

ORANGE JELLY.

Mrs. J. P. Hoit.

Soak one package of gelatine in one-half pint cold water for one hour; add the juice of three lemons, two pounds sugar and one quart boiling water; when all are dissolved add one pint of orange juice; strain carefully and set on ice till ready for use; eight oranges usually make it.

CURRANT JELLY.

Mrs. J. P. Hoit.

Jam and strain the currents; to each pint of juice add one pound sugar; boil the juice fifteen minutes without sugar, and the same time after it is in; strain into glasses.

When pouring hot fruit or jelly in cans or glasses, wring a towel out of cold water, lay it on a table, and set the

cold cans upon it, pouring the boiling fruit into them.
Care should be taken not to set two cans on the same spot
without first wetting the towel.

CURRANT JELLY.

Mrs. C. Wheeler.

Use the currants when they first ripen; pick them from
the stems and put them on the stove in a stone jar, bruis-
ing them with a wooden spoon ; then when warm, squeeze
through a coarse cloth or flannel, and put the juice on in
a new tin pan or porcelain kettle ; one quart of juice
requires two pounds of sugar, or a pound to a pint; boil
fifteen minutes; to be a nice color, the currants should
not come in contact with iron spoons or tin dishes, unless
new and bright; should be made quickly. It never fails
to jelly good if the currants are not too ripe. The same
method for jam, only do not strain the currants, but mash
them well. Currants should not be dead ripe for jelly or
jam.

GOOSEBERRY JELLY.

E. M. Walker.

Boil six pounds of green unripe gooseberries in six pints
of water (they must be well boiled, but not burst too
much); pour them into a basin, and let them stand covered with a cloth for twenty-four hours, then strain through
a jelly bag, and to every pint of juice add one pound of
sugar. Boil it for an hour, then skim it, and boil for one-
half hour longer with a sprig of vanilla.

LADY MARY'S JELLY.

From "In the Kitchen."

Put half a pint of calf's foot jelly in a mould that has been rinsed with cold water. When stiff and firm, place on it a small bunch of fine hot house grapes and above them two peaches and a nectarine, placing them very carefully, remembering that the whole is to be reversed when turned from the mould. When the fruit is tastefully arranged, add jelly that is partly formed; pour it in slowly on both sides of the fruit, being sure that it fills all the interstices; let it reach top of the fruit, and above this place two or three small glossy vine leaves and add a little jelly to keep them firm and fill the mould. It must be carefully turned out. To do this, either loosen from the mould with a knife, or wrap the mould a moment in a towel wrung from hot water. If in this last mode a little melted jelly should settle around the form absorb it with a soft napkin. The fruit may be varied at pleasure. Plums or strawberries, large and firm; nothing, however, from which the juice would come.

ORANGE JELLY.

From "In the Kitchen."

One box of Coxe's gelatine soaked one hour in one pint of cold water; add one pint of boiling water, one pound of sugar, and one pint of sour orange juice. 'Pour in moulds rinsed in cold water.

COFFEE JELLY.

From "In the Kitchen."

One pint of clear coffee as strong as it is generally

drank; sugar to taste. Pour one gill of cold water on half an ounce of Coxe's gelatine, and let it soak fifteen minutes; pour off the water and put the gelatine when well dissolved in the hot coffee; wet a mould and pour it through a strainer.

CIDER JELLY.

Mrs. George Frost, Detroit.

One package of gelatine (one and one-half ounces,) the grated rind of one lemon and the juice of three; add one pint of cold water, and let it stand one hour; then add two and one-half pounds of loaf sugar, three pints of boiling water, and one pint of cider, put into moulds and set in a cool place.

CORN STARCH JELLY.

One quart boiling water; wet five tablespoons corn starch, one teacup sugar, a pinch of salt, with cold water, and one teaspoon lemon or vanilla extract for flavoring; stir the mixture into the boiling water, boil five minutes, stir all the while; pour into cups previously dipped in cold water. This quantity will fill six or seven cups. If wished richer, milk may be used instead of water. Good for invalids.

TAPIOCA JELLY.

Mrs. O. F. Avery.

One cup tapioca, three cups cold water, juice of a lemon, and a pinch of the grated peel; sweeten to taste; soak the tapioca in water four hours; set within a sauce pan of boiling water; pour more lukewarm water over the tapioca, if it has absorbed too much of the liquid and heat, stirring frequently. If too thick after it begins to clear, put in very little boiling water. When quite clear, put in the sugar and lemon. Pour into moulds. Eat cold with cream, flavoring with rose water and sweetened.

GELATINE JELLY.

Dissolve one ounce package of sparkling gelatine in a pint of cold water for one hour; add the rind and juice of two or three large lemons, one and a half pounds of sugar, then pour on this mixture one quart of boiling water, add one pint of orange or raspberry juice, and pour into mould. This flavoring is very nice, and is to supersede the necessity of wine, which some consider indispensable in the same proportion.

RHUBARB JAM.

Mrs. T. W. Anderson.

Cut into pieces about an inch long, put a pound of sugar to every pound of rhubarb, and leave till morning; pour the syrup from it and boil till thickens; then add the rhubarb and boil gently fifteen minutes; put up as you do currant jelly in tumblers; it will keep good a year.

GOOSEBERRY JAM.

Take what quantity you please of red rough ripe gooseberries, take half this quantity of lump sugar, break them well, and boil them together for half an hour, or more, if necessary. Put into pots and cover with papers.

GRAPE JAM.

Mrs. S. W. Cheever, Ottawa, Ill.

Take your grapes, separate the skin from the pulp, keeping them in separate dishes, put the pulps in your preserving kettle with a teacup of water; when thoroughly heated, run them through a colander to separate the seeds; then put your skins with them and weigh; to each pound of fruit, put three-fourths of a pound of sugar; add merely water enough to keep from burning; cook slowly three-fourths of an hour. This is a delicious jam, and worth the trouble.

BLACKBERRY JAM.

M. A. T.

To each pound of fruit add three-fourths of a pound of sugar; mash each separately; then put together and boil from one-half to three-fourths of an hour.

RASPBERRY JAM.

To five or six pounds of fine red raspberries (not too ripe) add an equal quantity of the finest quality of white sugar. Mash the whole well in a preserving kettle; add about one quart of currant juice (a little less will do) and boil gently until it jellies upon a cold plate; then put into small jars; cover with brandy paper, and tie a thick white paper over them. Keep in a dark, dry and cool, place.

QUINCE JAM.

Mrs. P. B. Ayer.

Boil your fruit in as little water as possible, until soft

enough to break easily; pour off all the water and rub with a spoon until entirely smooth. To one pound of the quince add ten ounces of brown sugar, and boil twenty minutes, stirring often.

PINE-APPLE JAM.

Mrs. P. B. Ayer.

Grate your pine-apple; to one pound of the apple add three-fourths of a pound of loaf sugar; boil ten minutes.

ORANGE MARMALADE.

Mrs. J. Young Scammon.

One dozen Seville oranges, one dozen common oranges, one dozen lemons; boil the oranges and lemons whole in water for five hours; scoop out the inside, removing the seeds; cut the peel into thin slices with a knife, and add to every pound of pulp and peel a pint of water and two pounds of sugar. Boil twenty minutes.

ORANGE MARMALADE.

Mrs. Wm. Brackett.

Take seven oranges and five lemons; boil in water two or three hours; throw away the water, and open the oranges and lemons, taking out the seeds and preserving all the pulp and juice possible; cut the rinds in small strips or chop them, but cutting in strips is better; weigh it all, when this is done; then put three pounds of sugar to two of the pulp, and boil slowly till clear.

CANDY.

In order to understand the secret of candy making, it will be necessary to understand the action of heat upon · sugar. The first step in this process is the reduction of sugar to a syrup, and which is done by adding water to sugar in the proportion of a pint and a half of water to three and a half pounds of sugar. When this boils up in the kettle we have simple syrup. A few more minutes of boiling, reduces the water which holds the sugar in a perfect solution. At this stage, if the syrup is allowed to cool, the candy crystalizes on the sides of the dish, and we have rock candy. If, instead of allowing it to cool at this point, we allow it to reach a higher degree of heat, we shall find, in putting a spoon into the syrup, when drawing it out, a long thread of sugar will follow the spoon. It is at this point that confectioners bring the syrup for the greater number of candies produced. The greatest skill is required on the part of the operator to push the boiling sugar to this point without allowing it to reach the caramel state, when it becomes bitter and dark and is no longer fit to use as a confection. The proportion of sugar and water for candy making will be three

and one-half pounds of sugar to one and one-half pints
of water. To this add one teaspoon of cream of tartar,
which will prevent the tendency of the sugar to assume
the granular condition. To test the candy drop into cold
water. When this becomes at once hard and brittle the
vessel should be at once removed from the fire. Flat
sticks are formed by pouring the candy into long flat pans
and when cooling crease the mass which will readily break
into sticks when cold. To make round stick candy, when
cool enough to handle and while warm enough to mould,
roll into sticks with the hands. To color candies, take
small portions of the candy while cooling, and color, then
put together in stripes so twist slightly together.

LEMON CANDY.

Put into a kettle three and one-half pounds of sugar,
one and one-half pints of water and one teaspoon of
cream of tartar. Let it boil until it becomes brittle, when
dropped in cold water; when sufficiently done take off
the fire and pour in a shallow dish which has been greased
with a little butter; when this has cooled so that it can be
handled, add a teaspoon of tartaric acid and the same
quantity of extract of lemon and work them into the mass.
The acid must be fine and free from lumps. Work this
in until evenly distributed, and no more, as it will tend to
destroy the transparency of the candy. This method may
be used for preparing all other candies as pine apple, etc.,
using different flavors.

CREAM CANDIES.

Three and one-half pounds of sugar to one and one-half pints of water, dissolve in the water before putting with the sugar, one quarter of an ounce 'of fine white gum arabic and when added to the sugar put in one tea-spoon of cream of tartar. The candy should not be boiled quite to the brittle stage. The proper degree can be ascertained if, when a small skimmer is put in and taken out, when blowing through the holes of the skim-mer, the melted sugar is forced through in feathery filaments ; remove from the fire at this point and rub the syrup against the sides of the dish with an iron spoon. If it is to be a chocolate candy, add two ounces of chocolate finely siffed and such flavoring as you prefer, vanilla, rose or orange. If you wish to make cocoanut candy, add this while soft and stir until cold.

CANDY.

One pound sugar, one and a half cups water, three tablespoons rose-water ; boil twenty minutes ; then pull.

CANDY.

Carrie A.

One-half pound sugar, one-half cup syrup, butter the size of a walnut ; add little water to the syrup, and have the sugar thoroughly dissolved ; to try it, drop a spoonful in a glass of ice water, if brittle, it is done.

CANDY CARAMELS.

Mary H.

One pint cream, one pound sugar, one cup butter, one-fourth cup chocolate, one cup of molasses,

18

CHOCOLATE CARAMELS.

Etta C. Springer.

Two pounds sugar, two ounces butter, one cup of cream, boil over a good fire until the syrup is brittle; try in water as you do taffy; then pour it in pans, and when it is most cold cut it in squares.

CHOCOLATE CARAMELS.

One cup of fine granulated sugar, one cup of New Orleans molasses, one-fourth cup of milk, a piece of butter the size of an egg, one cup of chocolate after it is cut up, if made single quantity; if doubled, it is as well not to put the chocolate in till about done, and then the same quantity of this recipe will suffice, as it retains the flavor if not cooked as much. Boil till it will stiffen in water; pour into flat buttered pans to the thickness of half an inch. Use Baker's chocolate.

CHOCOLATE CARAMELS.

Mrs. P. B. Ayer.

Two cups of brown sugar, one cup molasses, one cup chocolate grated fine, one cup boiled milk, one tablespoon of flour; butter the size of a large English walnut; let it boil slowly and pour on flat tins to cool; mark off while warm.

CREAM CANDY.

One pound white sugar, one wineglass vinegar, one tumbler water, vanilla; boil one-half hour, and pull, if you choose.

COCOANUT DROPS.

Mrs. P. B. Ayer.

To one grated cocoanut, add half its weight of sugar and the white of one egg, cut to a stiff froth; mix thoroughly and drop on buttered white paper or tin sheets. Bake fifteen minutes.

KISSES.

E. S. P.

One egg, one cup sugar, one-half cup of butter, one-half cup milk, one teaspoon cream of tartar, one-half of soda, flour enough to make a stiff dough; drop on tins and sprinkle over with powdered sugar. Bake in a quick oven.

MOLASSES CANDY.

Mrs. Benham.

One cup molasses, two cups sugar, one tablespoon vinegar, a little butter and vanilla; boil ten minutes, then cool it enough to pull.

MOLASSES CANDY.

Julia French.

One cup molasses, one cup sugar, one tablespoon vinegar, piece of butter size of an egg; boil (but do not stir) until it hardens when dropped in cold water; then stir in a teaspoon of soda, and pour on buttered tins; when cool, pull and cut in sticks.

Or, two cups sugar, two tablespoons vinegar, boil, when done add a teaspoon soda, cool and pull, or cut in squares without pulling; do not stir while it is boiling.

BUTTER SCOTCH CANDY.

Four cups brown sugar, two of butter, vinegar to taste, two tablespoons water, and a little soda; boil half an hour; drop a little in hot water, and if crisp, it is done.

BUTTER SCOTCH.

Fannie Waggoner, Toledo.

Three tablespoons of molasses, two of sugar, two of water, one of butter; add a pinch of soda before taking up.

SUGAR TAFFY.

Mrs. Joseph B. Leake.

Three pounds best brown sugar, one pound butter, enough water to moisten the sugar; boil until crisp when dropped into cold water, then pour into pans, or upon platters, as thin as possible. It usually requires to boil fast, without stirring, three-quarters of an hour.

BREAD AND YEAST.

" There is scent of Syrian myrrh,
There is incense, there is spice,
There are delicate cakes and loaves,
Cakes of meal and polypi."
          —GRECIAN ODE.

" But I ate naught
Till I that lovely child of Ceres saw,
A large sweet round and yellow cake'; how then
Could I from such a dish, my friends, abstain ?"

GENERAL DIRECTIONS FOR MAKING BREAD.

In the composition of good bread, there are three important requisites :   Good flour, good yeast and strength to knead it well.   Flour should be white and dry, crumbling easily again after it is pressed in the hand.

A very good method of ascertaining the quality of yeast, will be to add a little flour to a very small quantity setting it in a warm place.   If in the course of ten or fifteen minutes it rises, it will do to use.   -

When you make bread, first set the sponge with warm milk or water, keeping it in a warm place until quite light. Then mould this sponge, by adding flour into one large loaf, kneading it well. Set this to rise again, and then when sufficiently light mould into smaller loaves, let it rise again, then bake. Care should be taken not to get the dough too stiff with flour; it should be as soft as it can be to knead well. To make bread or biscuits a nice color, wet the dough over top with water just before putting into the oven. Flour should always be sifted.

YEAST.
Mrs. E. S. Chesebrough.

Put two tablespoons of hops in a muslin bag and boil them in three quarts of water for a few minutes; have ready a quart of hot mashed potatoes, put in one cup of flour, one tablespoon of sugar, one of salt; pour over the mixture the boiling hop water, strain through a colander, put a pint or less of fresh baker's yeast, or two cakes of yeast in while it is warm, and set it in a warm place to rise. This yeast will keep three or four weeks, if set in a cool place. In making it from time to time, use a bowl of the same to raise the fresh with.

YEAST.
Mrs. Mary Ludlam, Evanston.

Six good potatoes grated raw, a little hop tea, one quart boiling water, three-fourths cup of brown sugar, one-half teaspoon salt; when cool, add yeast to rise; keep covered and in a cool place.

POTATO YEAST.
Mrs. J. B. Adams.

_Boil, steam and mash a few potatoes; pour slowly on

some boiling water, in which a bag of hops has been boiled; stir in immediately sifted flour enough to thicken; when lukewarm add compressed yeast (dissolved), or raise with potato or baker's yeast.

POTATO YEAST.

Boil a good handful of hops in one quart of water and pour it over two teacups of grated potatoes, while boiling hot, stir mixture until it just comes to a boil; add one-quarter teacup of salt, and one-half teacup of sugar, and let stand until it is cool; then add the usual quantity of good yeast to start it with; when raised put it into a jar, cover closely and set in a clean place; use one teacup for about four loaves of bread.

YEAST.

Mrs. W. C. Harris.

Boil in separate pans one-half cup of hops and two potatoes; strain both liquids boiling hot on a large cup of flour, one spoon of salt, half cup of sugar, and a cup of yeast. Pour it into a jug and set it in a cool place.

YEAST.

Mrs Freeman.

Boil two ounces of hops in four quarts of water twenty minutes, strain through a sieve and add one coffeecup of sugar to the hop water. When so cool as not to scald stir in one coffeecup of flour. Let this mixture stand in a warm place three days, stirring frequently. The third day boil three potatoes, press them through the colander and stir gradually into the hot water, adding a handful of salt; let it stand till next morning, then put into a jug. Shake well every time before using. Use a teacup full for six loaves. To your sponge next morning add three good-sized potatoes pressed through the colander, with the water they are boiled in.

GOOD YEAST.

S. S. Pierce.

Eight potatoes boiled and mashed fine, four tablespoons of flour put in with the potatoes, two tablespoons of salt, two of sugar; pour on one quart of boiling water; stir carefully while pouring, so as to dissolve, add one quart of cold water; then strain, and when cold add one cup of yeast and set it in a warm place to rise; as soon as it is light put in a jug or bottle and cork tight.

GOOD YEAST.

Mrs. Packard.

Grate six good sized potatoes (raw); have ready a gallon of water in which has been well boiled three handfuls of hops; strain through a cloth or sieve, while boiling hot, over the potatoes, stirring until well cooked, or the mixture thickens like starch; add one teacup of sugar, one-half cup of salt; when sufficiently cool, one cup of good yeast. Let it stand until a thick foam rises upon the top. Care must be taken not to bottle too soon, or the bottles may burst. Use one coffee cup of yeast to six loaves of bread. If kept in a cool place this yeast will last a long time, and housekeepers need not fear having *sour* bread.

YEAST THAT WILL NOT SOUR.

Mrs. J. B. Adams.

Boil two ounces of hops in two quarts of water; put one cup of brown sugar in a jar; boil and strain the hops and pour into the jar. Add one cup of flour stirred smooth; let it stand in a warm kitchen till it ferments. Add six potatoes boiled and mashed, and one cup of salt.

YEAST.

Mrs. Anna Marble.

Two quarts of wheat bran, one of Indian bran, two gallons of boiling water; simmer an hour or so; put in a handful of hops. As soon as the water boils, add one teacup of molasses and one tablespoon of ground ginger. When cold put in a teacup of yeast and cork tightly. Keep cool.

BREAD.

Mrs. E. S. Chesebrough.

Take four quarts of sifted flour and a teacup of yeast, a pinch of salt, and wet with warm milk and water stiff enough to knead. Work it on the board until it requires no more flour. If made at night the bread will be light enough to work over and put in pans early in the morning. This quantity will make two large loaves. One-third of the lump may be taken for rolls, which can be made by working in butter the size of an egg, and setting aside to rise again : when light the second time make out in oblong shapes; cover them with a cloth and let them rise again. As soon as they break apart bake in a quick

oven. They will not fail to be nice if they are baked as
soon as they seam. This is the great secret of white,
flaky rolls. Two or three potatoes will improve the bread.
Good housekeepers always have flour sifted in readiness
for use, and never use it in any other way.

BREAD.

M. E. B. Lynde.

The sponge is made over night in the center of a pan
of flour, with milk and warm water and a cup of home-
made hop and potato yeast to about four loaves. The
yeast is put in when about half the flour and water are
mixed, and then the remainder of the water is added and
the sponge beaten with a wooden spoon for fifteen minutes and left to rise over night in a moderately warm
place. In the morning, the bread-dough mixed and
kneaded for half an hour, adding flour to make a stiff
dough, and left to rise in a mass. It is then made into
small loaves, being kneaded with as little flour as possible,
and put in pans to rise the second time, all the while
kept moderately warm, and when light bake in a moderately hot oven. The important part of said recipe is the
beating of the sponge fifteen minutes, as given. Bread
made after this recipe received first premium at Wisconsin
State Fair, 1872.

EXCELLENT BREAD.

Mrs. Geo. W. Pitkin.

Four potatoes mashed fine, four teaspoons of salt, two
quarts of lukewarm milk, one-half cake compressed yeast

dissolved in one-half cup of warm water, flour enough to make a pliable dough; mould with hands well greased with lard; place in pans, and when sufficiently light, it is ready for baking.

SUPERIOR BREAD.
Mrs. D. C. Norton.

Scald one quart of sour milk; when cool enough, set your sponge with the whey; take about three quarts of flour, make a hole in the center, put in the whey about a good teaspoon of salt, one teacup of good hop yeast (home made is best), and stir quite stiff with a spoon; wrap in a thick cloth so as to keep as warm as possible (in cold weather), in summer it is not necessary. In the morning knead well, adding flour until stiff enough, and keep warm until light; then set it in pans to rise; no saleratus is needed. Bread made in this way will never fail to be good if good flour and yeast are used.

WHEAT BREAD.
Mrs. D. W. Thatcher, River Forest.

Take a pan of flour, and put in a small handful of salt and a bowl of soft yeast and one pint of lukewarm milk, mix stiff with flour and let it rise. Then knead it into pans, and let it rise, and if wanted very white, knead it down two or three times; this makes it whiter, but loses its sweet taste; bake forty-five minutes.

RICE BREAD.
Mrs. E. S. Chesebrough.

Boil a teacup of rice quite soft; while hot, add butter

the size of an egg, one and a half pints of milk, rather more than one-half pint of bolted corn meal, two tablespoons of flour, two eggs and a little salt. Bake just one hour. The bread should be about two inches thick.

MRS. FURLONG'S BROWN BREAD.

Three cups of corn meal, one cup of flour, one cup of syrup, one cup of sour milk, two cups of sweet milk, one teaspoon of soda, one teaspoon of salt; steam four hours.

BROWN STEAMED BREAD.

Mrs. G. B. Griffin.

Two cups corn meal, one cup Graham flour, one cup white flour, one cup molasses, two cups sour milk, one cup sweet milk, one teaspoon saleratus; steam four hours.

BROWN BREAD.

Mrs. J. M. Durand.

Scald two quarts of Indian meal; when sufficiently cool add two quarts of rye meal, one-half cup of yeast, one-half cup of molasses; add warm water, and stir hard as you can well with a spoon; set down to rise; when light stir well; put in pans to rise a second time. Steam one hour, and let bake from one-half to one hour.

BROWN BREAD.

Mrs. G. F. De Forrest, Freeport, Ill.

One and a half pints of thick sour milk, one and a half cups Graham flour, one and a half cups rye flour, two cups two-thirds full of Indian meal. one-half cup of molasses, salt, one heaping teaspoon soda beaten into the milk before adding the other ingredients. Steam five hours. Very fine.

STEAMED BROWN BREAD.
Mrs. C. G. Smith.

One pint of sweet milk, four tablespoons of molasses, one cup of Indian meal, two cups of rye or Graham flour. one teaspoon of salt, one of saleratus ; mix with a spoon. and steam three hours, and bake half an hour or more.

BROWN BREAD.
Mrs. Lamkin.

One and one-half cups of rye meal, one and one-half of Indian meal, one-half cup of molasses, two and one-half of cold water, even teaspoon of soda, a little salt ; steam four and a half hours, then put it in the oven for a very few minutes, just to take the moisture from the top.

BROWN BREAD.
Mrs. Banks.

Two cups of Graham flour, one of wheat flour, two large spoons of molasses, a little salt, one yeast cake or half cup of yeast, warm water enough to make a very stiff batter. Put it in the bake-tin, and when light enough, bake in a good oven three-fourths of an hour.

BOSTON BROWN BREAD.
Mrs. F. E. Stearns.

One and one-half cups of Graham flour, two cups of

corn meal, one-half cup of molasses, one pint of sweet milk, and one-half a teaspoon of soda; steam three hours.

BROWN BREAD

Mrs. Kent.

Three and one-half cups of Graham flour, two of corn meal, three of sour milk, one-half of molasses, one and one-half teaspoons of soda; steam two and one-half hours, and put in the oven for fifteen minutes.

BROWN BREAD.

Mrs. E. Wood.

One quart of Graham flour, one pint of wheat flour, one-half cup of brown sugar, one pint of yeast, a little salt; let rise; put in pans; stand short time to rise, and then bake.

BOSTON BROWN BREAD.

Mrs. L. Gilbert, Evanston.

Three teacups Graham flour, two teacups corn meal one-half teacup molasses, one pint sour milk, one pint water, one teaspoon soda, one teaspoon salt, put into a tin pail, covered tightly and boil four hours in a kettle.

BROWN BREAD TOAST.

Cut the bread in slices and toast. Put it in the dish for the table, take a bowl of thick cream, add a little salt, then pour over the toast; put it in the oven until it heats through.

BROWN JOE.

Mrs. O. L. Wheelock

Two cups of Indian meal, two of flour, one of molasses, one pint of milk, one teaspoon of soda, same of salt; steam six hours.

TRAVELER'S BREAD.

Take Graham flour (unsifted); and currants, figs, dates or raisins may be used by chopping them; stir quite stiffly with the coldest water as briskly as possible, so as to incorporate air with it; then knead in all the unbolted wheat flour you can; cut in cakes or rolls one-half inch thick, and bake in a quick oven.

STEAMED BREAD.

Sophia B. Irmberg.

One cup flour, one cup rye meal, one cup corn meal, one-half cup molasses, one and a half cups of sour milk, one egg, little salt, one teaspoon soda. Steam for three hours; then set the pan in the oven for ten or twenty minutes before sending it to the table.

STEAMED CORN BREAD.

Mrs. Jane Conger.

Take three cups of meal, and one of flour, scald two cups of the meal with boiling water, add the other cup of meal and flour, two cups of sour milk, one cup molasses, one teaspoon of soda, a little salt. Steam three hours.

OLD FASHIONED GRAHAM BREAD.

Mrs. Pulsifer.

One teacup of good yeast, one quart of warm water, one teaspoon of salt, two cups sugar, or less, one small teaspoon soda, stir in enough white winter wheat Graham flour to make it stiff enough to drop off the spoon readily, grease your bread pans, put in, and set to rise, let it get quite light, then bake in a moderate oven for three-quarters of an hour.

BROWN BREAD.

Mrs. Wm. Blair.

Take part of the sponge that has been prepared for your white bread, warm water can be added, mix it with Graham flour (not too stiff); and one cup of molasses for three loaves of bread.

FOR BROWN BISCUIT.—Take this Graham dough, as prepared for bread, working in a little butter. Butter the size of an egg is sufficient for two dozen biscuits.

CORN BREAD.

Mrs. Juliet L. Strayer, a Southern Lady.

One-half pint of buttermilk, one-half pint of sweet milk; sweeten the sour milk with one-half teaspoon of soda; beat two eggs, whites and yolks together; pour the milk into the eggs, then thicken with about nine table-spoons of sifted corn meal. Put the pan on the stove with a piece of lard the size of an egg; when melted pour it in the batter; this lard by stirring it will grease the pan to bake in; add a teaspoon of salt.

CORN BREAD.

Mrs. J. S. Gano, and Mrs. O. F. Avery.

One pint Indian meal, one pint sour milk or buttermilk, two eggs, whites and yolks beaten separately, whites put in last thing; two tablespoons sugar; one tablespoon melted butter, a little salt, half a teaspoon saleratus.

CORN BREAD.

Mrs. Wm. H. Low.

Two tablespoons of sugar, one tablespoon butter, two eggs; stir all together, add one cup of sweet milk, three teaspoons of baking powder, and three-fourths of a cup corn meal; flour to make it quite stiff.

INDIAN BREAD.

Mrs. G. H. L.

Five cups Indian meal, yellow, five cups sour milk, three cups rye flour, one-half cup molasses, one tablespoon saleratus.

INDIAN BREAD.

Mrs. A. T. Hall.

One pint of meal, one pint of flour, one pint of milk, one teacup of molasses, one teaspoon of soda, one-half of cream tartar; steam two hours and bake half an hour.

GRAHAM BREAD.

Mrs. B. J. Seward.

One pint sweet milk, one-half cup molasses, one teaspoon saleratus, one teaspoon salt. Mix thin enough to pour.

19

GRAHAM BREAD.

Mrs. J. B. Hobbs.

For one loaf, take two cups of white bread sponge, to which add two tablespoons of brown sugar, and Graham flour to make a stiff batter; let it rise, after which add Graham flour sufficient to knead, but not very stiff; then put in the pan to rise and bake.

GRAHAM BREAD.

Mrs. Ludlam, Evanston.

One cup wheat flour, three cups Graham flour, two tablespoons of molasses, one teaspoon salt, yeast enough to make it rise; mix and put in baking tins at night. It will be ready to bake in the morning.

GRAHAM BREAD.

Mrs. H. P. Stowell.

Set sponge of fine flour, same as for wheat bread; when sufficiently raised, instead of mixing with fine flour, mix with Graham to the usual consistency; mould with fine flour a little, raise once, then it is ready for the oven. Sweeten with syrup or sugar, if desired, though I think it better without either,

ROLLS.

Mrs. H. F. Waite.

To the quantity of light bread dough that you would take for twelve persons, add the white of one egg well beaten, two tablespoons of white sugar, and two table-spoons of butter; work these thoroughly together; roll out about half an inch thick; cut the size desired, and spread one with melted butter and lay another upon the top of it. Bake delicately, when they have risen.

PARKER HOUSE ROLLS.
Alice M. Adams, Mrs. J. P. Hoit, and others.

Two quarts flour, make a hole in the top, put in a piece of butter the size of an egg, a little salt, and a tablespoon of white sugar; pour over this a pint of milk previously boiled and cooled, and one-half teacup of good yeast. When the sponge is light, mould for fifteen minutes, let it rise again and cut into round cakes, butter on one side and turn over on itself, bake in a quick oven.

PARKER HOUSE ROLLS.
Mrs. A. H. Dashiell, Bricksburg, N. J.

One quart sifted flour, one-half cup yeast, two table-spoons of sugar, salt, two tablespoons butter and one of lard; pour one pint of boiling milk over the ingredients, except yeast, and add that when lukewarm; mix early in the morning, and knead at noon, adding sufficient flour to make as stiff as biscuit; when light knead into rolls; roll out rather thin, cut with a biscuit cutter and then roll oblong, spread a little butter on one end and fold over; let them rise on the pans before baking. They ought to bake in ten or fifteen minutes. In cold weather the sponge should be made at night.

PARKER HOUSE ROLLS.
Mrs. L. J. Tilton.

Boil one pint of sweet milk, and when partly cooled

melt in it half a cup of white sugar and one tablespoon of lard or butter; when lukewarm, add half a cup of yeast; make a hole in two quarts of flour and pour this mixture in. If for tea, set to rise over night, in the morning mix well and knead for half an hour, then set to rise again; about four o'clock knead again for ten or fifteen minutes; roll out thinner than for biscuit, rub melted butter upon half the surface and fold it upon the other; set to rise once more in pans, and when light bake twenty minutes in a hot oven.

DETROIT ROLLS.
Mrs. A. M. Gibbs.

Put one pint warm milk in the middle of two quarts flour, beat up a thick batter, a little stiffer than pancakes, and add one-half cake German compressed yeast. When light knead up like bread, kneading the dough out in a long roll and folding over like pie crust, doing this six or seven times. When again light, add a piece of butter size of a large egg, pulling it through the dough, then work in two eggs, and one tablespoon sugar that has been beaten together very light. Knead again same as before. Roll out on your bread board with rolling pin, cut with small round or oval cutters, dipping cutter occasionally in a cup of melted lard or drippings instead of flour, and put in pans to rise. When creamy light, bake, it will expedite the rising, to set the pans over hot water.

FRENCH ROLLS.
Mrs. Thos. Orton.

Take one-half cup of yeast, rub a small one-half cup of

butter in the flour (you will have to guess the quantity), then add the yeast, and water enough to wet; mix as for soda biscuit. Let it rise till morning. Roll in thin sheets, and cut into squares, spread a very little butter on each, and sprinkle a little flour on to roll up. Put in the pan when light, bake twenty minutes. Nice.

FRENCH ROLLS.

Etta C. Springer.

One quart flour, add two eggs, one-half pint milk, tablespoon of yeast, knead it well; rise till morning. Work in one ounce of butter and mould in small rolls; bake immediately.

BROWN ROLLS.

Mrs. Melancthon Starr, Rockford, Ill.

One quart Graham flour, milk enough to make a stiff batter, one-third cup of yeast, and mix over night; in the morning add two eggs, one large tablespoon of sugar, one-fourth teaspoon of soda, piece of butter half the size of an egg, and a little salt; put in cups, and let stand twenty minutes before baking.

CORN MEAL ROLLS.

Mrs. A. H. Dashiel, Bricksburg, N. J.

To one quart of mush, add, when hot, one-half cup unmelted lard, salt it well; when lukewarm, add one-half cup of yeast; make this at noon, and at night add a small teaspoon of soda, and knead in wheat flour as for biscuit. In the morning mould into biscuit, and let them rise in the pan before baking. Bake in a quick oven.

TREMONT BISCUIT.

Brought from Boston, by Mrs. O. B. Wilson.

One and a half pints of warm milk, one tablespoon lard, two tablespoons white sugar, a little salt, one yeast cake (Twin Bro.'s), or a cup of home made yeast or half a cake of compressed yeast as is most convenient; two quarts of sifted flour. To mix — make a hole in the flour and mix in all the ingredients to make a sponge; set in a warm place to rise; when quite light, work in all the flour and set the dough once more to rise; when well risen, work a little more, and roll out about one-third of an inch thick, and cut with a biscuit cutter. Moisten one edge with melted butter, then fold together in the middle like rolls. Place them in a bread-pan about one inch apart; set to rise for about half an hour in a warm place, and · when light, bake in a quick oven, allowing from ten to fifteen minutes if the oven is just right. Make up about ten o'clock in the morning if wanted for tea; if wanted for breakfast, make up about nine o'clock in the evening, and work in all the flour at the first fixing, then add as soon as you are up in the morning, one-half teaspoon of soda; mould your biscuit and they will be ready for baking when the oven is hot. With compressed yeast, about six hours all together is required. These are very delicate and delicious when properly made.

VIRGINIA BISCUITS.

Mrs. J. G. Hamilton.

Rub a teaspoon of lard into a quart of flour, put the flour into a sifter and sift a teaspoon of soda with the flour, one teaspoon of salt, and one pint of buttermilk to moisten the flour; after beating the mixture with a spoon until thoroughly mixed, turn it out on a biscuit board, work until smooth, cut it out with a cutter and bake with a steady heat.

GREEN MOUNTAIN BISCUITS.

Mrs. Lamkin, Evanston.

Three cups milk, two cups sugar, one cup butter; make a stiff batter at night with two tablespoons yeast, one-half the sugar and one-half the butter melted; in the morning add the other half of sugar and butter, and make it not quite as stiff as yeast bread; two hours before tea make up the biscuits and set them to rise.

GRAFTON BISCUITS.

Boil two large, white potatoes, mash and pour boiling water on until of the consistency of gruel; add one table-spoon of sugar and one teacup full of yeast when sufficiently cool; set away to rise; when light heat one pint of milk until warm enough to melt two tablespoons of butter, add salt and flour enough to make a thick batter; set to rise, when light work twenty minutes; set it to rise again, then roll out thin and spread melted butter over; cut out with a tumbler and lay one-half over the other prick in several places and set to rise; then bake twenty minutes.

FRENCH BISCUITS.

Mrs. Lind.

Two cups of butter, two cups of sugar, one egg, (or the

whites of two,) half a cup of sour milk, half a teaspoo'
of soda, flour to roll; sprinkle with sugar.

RAISED BISCUITS.

Hannah Johnson ; endorsed by Mrs. A. N. Sheppard.

Take one and one-half pints of milk, one spoon of lard,
two of white sugar, and one yeast cake or one-half a package of compressed yeast, and two quarts of flour; make
a hole in the flour and put in all the ingredients; set in a
warm place to rise until morning, then mix all together
and set to rise again; when well risen, roll out rather thin,
cut them out like biscuits, wet one edge with melted butter, and fold together like rolls ; when well risen, bake in
a quick oven about twenty minutes. If made with compressed yeast, six and one-half hours will be sufficient to
raise them in winter.

TEA BISCUITS.

Mrs. O. L. Parker.

Make a good soda or cream biscuit; mould it and roll
it out half the thickness of common biscuit; spread it
over with three or four spoons of melted butter; then
over this sprinkle half a coffee cup of best sugar ; roll up
as compactly as you would a roll of jelly cake ; slice your
roll off into inch thick slices; lay these flat on your tins
and bake as biscuits. They are very nice cold.

TEA BISCUITS.

Mrs. Norcross.

One cup of hot water, two of milk, three tablespoons

of yeast; mix thoroughly; after it is risen, take two-thirds of a cup of butter and a little sugar and mould it; then let it rise, and mould it into small cakes.

TO MAKE STALE BREAD OR CAKE FRESH.
Mrs. M. G. Adams.

Plunge the loaf one instant in cold water; lay it upon a tin in the oven ten or fifteen minutes. Cake and rolls may be thus made almost as nice as if just baked, but must be eaten immediately.

RAISED BISCUITS.
Mrs. C. H. Wheeler.

Make a sponge of one pint of milk, a little salt, and half a cake of compressed yeast (any other will do); when light, take a piece of butter the size of an egg, one quarter of a cup of sugar, and one egg; beat them up together and stir into the sponge, adding flour to make a stiff batter; stir it well and leave to rise; then take with a spoon the light dough just enough for each biscuit and work softly into shape; lay into pans and bake after standing a short time to rise again.

GRAHAM BISCUITS.
Mrs. A. W. D.

Three cups of Graham flour, one of wheat flour, one egg, butter the size of an egg, one tablespoon of sugar, two of cream tartar, one of soda; salt and milk to mix.

GRAHAM BISCUITS.

M.

One quart of Graham flour, three and one-half heaping teaspoons of baking powder, one teaspoon of salt, one of butter; make into soft dough with milk.

GRAHAM BISCUITS.

Mrs. Phelps.

Three cups of Graham flour, one cup white flour, three cups milk, two tablespoons lard, one heaping tablespoon white sugar, one saltspoon of salt, one teaspoon of soda, two teaspoons of cream tartar; mix and bake as you do the white soda biscuit.

RYE BISCUIT.

Mrs. Lamkin.

Two cups rye meal, one and a half cups flour, one-third cup molasses, one egg, a little salt, two cups sour milk, two even teaspoons saleratus.

BUNS.

Two coffeecups bread dough, two eggs, one cup sugar, spices, a few currants; mould like rusk and let them rise before baking.

BUNS.

M.

Take one large coffeecup of warm milk, one-quarter cake of yeast and salt; make sponge; let rise; when light work into a dough, adding one-half teacup of sugar.

6ne egg, butter twice size of an egg; let rise; roll into a sheet; butter it; cut into strips three inches wide and six inches long; fold, not quite in the middle; let rise again and bake; when in a dough, if it rises before you are ready, push it down. Excellent.

RUSKS.

Mrs. P. B. Ayer.

To one tumbler of warm milk add a half gill of yeast, three eggs and a coffeecup of sugar beaten together, two ounces of butter rubbed into flour, of which use only enough to enable you to mould it; let it rise over night; when very light, roll and put on tins to raise again, after which bake in a quick oven twenty minutes.

RUSKS.

Milk enough with one-half cup of yeast to make a pint; make a sponge and rise; then add one and a half cups of white sugar, three eggs, one-half cup of butter; spice to your taste; mould, then put in pan to rise. When baked, cover the tops with sugar dissolved in milk.

SODA BISCUITS.

M.

To each quart of flour add one tablespoon of shortening, one-half teaspoon of salt, and three and a half heaping teaspoons of Price's Cream Baking Powder; mix baking powder thoroughly through the flour, then add other ingredients. Do not knead, and bake quick. To use cream tartar and soda, take the same proportions without the baking powder, using instead two heaping teaspoons cream tartar and one of soda. If good they will bake in five minutes.

BAKING POWDER BISCUITS.
Mrs. M. G. Adams.

One quart flour, two teaspoons baking powder, one tablespoon butter (or lard), rubbed well together; mix with cold water, stirring quickly with a knife ; when well mixed add flour enough to mould out smoothly; roll about an inch thick, cut with a tumbler or tin cutter. place in pan and bake quickly in a well heated oven. If made properly they will be as light and white as foam.

CREAM BISCUITS.
Mrs. A. M. Gibbs.

Three heaping tablespoons of sour cream ; put in a bowl or vessel containing a quart and fill two-thirds full of sweet milk, two teaspoons cream tartar, one teaspoon of soda, a little salt; pour the cream in the flour, mix soft and bake in a quick oven.

STRAWBERRY SHORTCAKE.

Make good biscuit crust; bake in two tins of same shape and size; mix berries with plenty of sugar; open the shortcake, butter well and place berries in layers. alternated with the crust; have the top layer of berries and over all put charlotte russe or whipped cream.

STRAWBERRY SHORTCAKE.

Make a fine soda biscuit crust, and separate in three pieces, roll out about half an inch thick the size of your pans, which should be round (are best baked in jelly cake pans). As you place the crust in your pan, spread over melted butter, and then roll out another crust and place on this, butter this well and then roll out and put on your last crust, place in the oven and bake. As you take out the separate crusts may be lifted carefully; butter each crust again and place the berries on, covering again with the layer of crust and then a layer of berries quite thick. Serve with clear or whipped cream and sugar.

STRAWBERRY SHORTCAKE.

Make a fine sponge cake and bake in very small round pans. When baked put on one layer of berries quite thick with sugar, and then cover with a layer of sponge cake and sift sugar over. The pans in which these are baked should be the size around of a saucer, and served as above described; one cake to each person with cream handed.

ORANGE SHORTCAKE.

M.

Make a nice shortcake; spread in layers of sliced oranges with sugar and a little cream. To be eaten with sweetened cream.

ORANGE SHORTCAKE.

Mrs. A. A. Carpenter.

Prepare the crust as you would for strawberry short-

cake. Slice very fine and put down in sugar one dozen
nice oranges. When you separate the crust butter it
nicely and then add the oranges.

APPLE SHORTCAKE.

M.

Season apple sauce with butter, sugar, etc. ; make a nice
shortcake, open and butter it and put the apple sauce in
layers. Serve with sweetened cream.

ELLEN'S TEA CAKE.

Two eggs, two tablespoons sugar, beaten together, three
cups flour, one cup milk, one teaspoon soda, two of cream
tartar; add last two tablespoons melted butter. Bake
half an hour in square or round tin. To be eaten like
Sally Lunn, hot with butter.

SALLY LUNN.

Mrs. J. H. Brown.

One quart of warm milk, one-half cup of butter, one
of sugar, five eggs and one cup of yeast; flour enough
for stiff batter. Bake one hour.

SALLY LUNN.

M.

Take one pint of milk, three of flour, three eggs, a little
salt, two tablespoons of butter, and two of sugar. Yeast
enough to raise.

SALLY LUNN.

Mrs. C. H. Wheeler.

One pint of milk, a piece of lard or butter the size of an egg, warmed in the milk; take from the stove and add three well beaten eggs, three pints of flour, one cup of yeast; let it stand about three hours or until light; then pour into flat pans without working or kneading, and let it stand an hour before baking; when baked, split and butter; eat white hot.

SALLY LUNN.

Mrs. I. W. Preston, Highland Park.

One quart of flour, butter the size of an egg, two eggs, two cups of milk, three spoons of baking powder, a pinch of salt; rub the salt and baking powder dry with the flour; melt the butter in one cup of milk; add the other cold; break in the eggs without beating; stir all together hard, and bake twenty or thirty minutes in a hot oven.

SALLY LUNN.

Miss Annie Yocum, Cairo, Ill.

Three teacups of light dough from hop yeast, three teaspoons melted butter, one cup of sugar, three well beaten eggs, one-half teaspoon of soda dissolved and strained, a pinch of salt, and flour to make the dough stiff enough to knead well; set away to rise, and when light make out by rolling in cakes to fit your pans, one-half inch thick; place one in the pan, cover well with soft butter and lay another on top; when light bake and serve at once. If properly buttered the layers will separate when baked.

This bread we prize very highly for tea, warm, and any that may be left is good cold for breakfast.

SQUASH CAKES.

Miss C. Harris.

One cup squash, one pint sour milk, one egg, a little salt, half a teaspoon soda, flour for a batter thick enough to fry.

CREAM CAKES.

Six eggs, beaten separately, a half pint of sour cream, one pint of sweet milk, one and one-half teaspoons of baking powder, flour enough to make a thin batter; bake in cups.

BREAFAST CAKES.

Mrs. Rice.

One cup milk, one pint flour, three eggs, piece butter size of an egg, two teaspoons cream tartar, one teaspoon soda, one tablespoon butter.

TEA CAKES.

Mrs. E. S. Chesebrough.

One quart of sifted flour, one pint sweet milk, butter size of egg, two eggs, two teaspoons sugar, one of soda, two of cream tartar; bake in small patty-pans.

WHEAT GEMS.

Mrs. W. H. Ovington.

One pint milk, two eggs, flour enough to make a batter

not very stiff, two large spoons melted butter, yeast to raise them, a little soda and salt. Bake in gem irons.

GEMS.
Mrs. H. P. Stowell.

A heaping tea saucer of Graham flour, one-half teacup of white flour, mix with sweet milk or water until somewhat thicker than griddle-cake batter. In the meantime, have your gem-irons a little greased, heating on top of the stove. Bake in a hot oven and in twenty-five minutes you have a dish for your breakfast that is rightly named. Have tried them with and without salt, and we think the latter very preferable.

GRAHAM GEMS.
Mrs. E. R. Harmon.

One quart of sweet milk, one cup syrup, one teaspoon soda, two teaspoons cream tartar, little salt; mix cream tartar in Graham flour, soda in the milk, and make it as stiff with the flour as will make it drop easily from the spoon into muffin rings.

POP OVERS.
Mrs. Andrews.

One cup milk, one cup flour, one egg, beaten separately. Bake in cups, a tablespoon to each cup.

POP OVERS.
S. S. Pierce.

One cup flour, one cup milk, one egg, piece butter size of a walnut, a little salt; to be baked in scallops in a very quick oven This rule makes twelve.

20

POP OVERS.

Mrs. King.

Three cups of milk, three cups flour, three eggs, a little salt, one tablespoon melted butter put in the last thing; two tablespoons to a puff.

CORN POP OVERS.

Mrs. A. T. Hall.

One pint sweet milk scalded; stir into the hot milk a coffeecup of corn meal, a piece of butter half the size of an egg, a little salt, three eggs well beaten, and stirred in the last thing. No soda.

ROSETTES.

Mrs. A. S. Ewing.

Mix a quart of milk into a pint of flour, beat the whites and yolks of three eggs separately, one tablespoon of butter cut fine into the mixture, half teaspoon salt; add the stiffly beaten whites of eggs last of all. Bake in well warmed and greased rosettes or muffin pans.

PUFFS.

Mrs. Wren.

Two eggs beaten separately, two cups of milk, two cups of flour, butter the size of a walnut; drop into hot irons and bake quickly.

YPSILANTI COCOANUT PUFFS.

One grated cocoanut, a little over one-half pound pulverized sugar stirred in the whites of three eggs, beaten light; drop in small cakes on a dripping pan. Bake in a very quick oven,

PUFFS.

Four cups of milk, four cups of flour, four eggs, butter the size of two eggs; put in cups half full, and bake for tea or breakfast.

GRAHAM PUFFS.

Mrs. O. S. Wheelock.

One pint of Graham flour, one egg, teaspoon salt, one tablespoon baking powder; wet with milk or water.

FRITTERS.

Mrs. Brown.

One pint sweet milk, four eggs, one quart flour and three teaspoons baking powder sifted together. Serve warm with maple syrup.

FRITTERS.

Mrs. E. R. Harmon.

Four eggs, one quart of milk, a little salt; stir a little stiffer than pancakes, and fry in hot lard.

FRITTERS.

M.

One pint boiling water, one tablespoon butter, one pint flour, stirred into water while boiling; let it cool a little, and add four eggs, one at a time. Fry in hot lard when the steam rises,

FRITTERS OR PUFFS.

M.

One pint milk in sauce-pan ; when it boils, stir in flour until very thick; when cold, mix with six well-beaten eggs, one tablespoon sugar, one-half nutmeg, grated peel of small lemon, one tablespoon brandy. Beat well for fifteen minutes. It should be thicker than pancake batter. Drop into hot lard. Sprinkle with powdered sugar or spiced sugar.

FRENCH FRITTERS.

Beat the yolks of four eggs very light, add to them one pint of milk, cut some slices of baker's bread about an inch thick, cutting off all the crust and lay them in the milk about fifteen minutes. Have your griddle hot, and fry the slices a nice brown, using fresh lard for the purpose. Beat the whites of the eggs very light, and stir into them one cup of powdered sugar, and flavor with lemon ; to be used as sauce with the fritters. Some prefer liquid pudding sauce.

PARSNIP FRITTERS.

M.

One-half cup milk and a tablespoon of butter ; boil five or six medium sized parsnips till tender, mash very fine, add two eggs, three tablespoons flour and a little salt; fry a delicate brown in hot drippings. Serve on a hot dish, or napkin.

GREEN CORN FRITTERS.

Mrs. Andrews.

Twelve ears of corn grated, four eggs, tablespoon of butter, salt, very little flour; drop a spoonful of the batter into boiling lard.

APPLE FRITTERS.

M.

One teacup of sweet milk, one tablespoon of sweet light dough dissolved in milk, three eggs beaten separately, one teaspoon of salt, one and one-half teacups of flour, one tablespoon of sugar, and the grated peel of a lemon, peeled apples sliced without the core; drop into hot lard with a piece of apple in each one; sprinkle with powdered or spiced sugar. Let them stand after making and they will be lighter. Good.

SPICED SUGAR FOR FRITTERS.

M.

One tablespoon of finely powdered and mixed spices (sifted), three tablespoons of powdered sugar well mixed with spices (two-thirds cinnamon and one-third nutmeg and cloves).

GREEN CORN CAKES.

A. M. G.

Twelve ears of sweet corn grated, one teaspoon of salt, one egg and a little more than a good tablespoon of flour. If the corn is not young and milky, very little or no flour

need be used. Drop the cakes from the spoon into hot
lard or butter.

Oyster plant fritters may be made in the same way —
first boiling and mashing the oyster plant; six plants
would be sufficient for one egg.

GRAHAM MUFFINS.
S. L. S.

One coffee cup of sour milk, one tablespoon of sugar
or molasses, one egg, one scant teaspoon of soda, one-
half of salt, enough Graham flour to make a stiff batter;
sweet milk and two teaspoons of baking powder can be
used instead of sour milk and soda. Bake in muffin pans
twenty minutes.

MUFFINS.
Mrs. Wm. H. Low.

One tablespoon of butter, two tablespoons sugar, two
eggs — stir all together; add one cup of sweet milk, three
teaspoons of baking powder, flour to make a stiff batter.
Bake twenty minutes in a quick oven.

MUFFINS.
From a Southern Lady.

Beat four eggs into a full tablespoon of lard, mix into
them one and one-half pints sour milk, effervescing with
a teaspoon of soda; add enough flour to make the consistency of pound cake. Bake in heated rings.

MUFFINS.
Mrs. Rice.

Three cups flour, one-half cup sugar, two cups milk,

large spoon butter rubbed to a cream with the sugar, two eggs, one-half teaspoon soda, one teaspoon cream tartar, one teaspoon salt. Bake one-half hour.

MUFFINS.
Mrs. Bartlett.

One pint sweet milk, one-half cup yeast, one-half cup butter, one-half cup sugar, one teaspoon salt; stir a little thicker than fritters; set over night.

MUFFINS.
Mrs. C. M., Winnetka.

Butter size of an egg, three tablespoons of sugar, three eggs, (yolks beaten to a cream,) one-half cup sweet milk, flour to make a stiff batter; add whites of eggs well beaten. Bake in muffin pans in a hot oven.

MUFFINS.
M.

One-half cup sugar, one-half cup milk, two eggs, two tablespoons butter, two heaping teaspoons baking powder, flour enough to make thick as sponge cake.

MUFFINS.
Mrs. Hoge.

Five eggs, one quart flour, two small cups of milk, two tablespoons melted butter, four tablespoons sugar, three tablespoons baking powder and a little salt.

CINNAMON MUFFINS.
Mrs. N. C. Gridley, Evanston.

One teacup sour milk, one cup not quite half full sugar,

one teaspoon soda, one tablespoon cinnamon, one egg; stir thick with flour and bake in gem irons.

MUFFINS.

Mrs. P. B. Ayer.

No. 1. — One cup milk, three teaspoons baking powder, two tablespoons cream, one egg, flour enough to make a stiff batter; bake in rings.

No. 2. — Melt one-half teacup of butter in a pint and a half of milk, one gill of yeast, four eggs well beaten, and flour enough to make a stiff batter. When light, bake in rings.

GRAHAM MUFFINS.

Lake Forest.

One and a half pints of Graham flour, one-half pint wheat flour. Take a pint cup three-fourths full of sour milk; add sour cream until full, soda to sweeten, and little molasses and little salt. Bake in gem irons, and have the irons hot before turning in the mixture.

GRAHAM MUFFINS.

Mrs. L. Cornell.

One egg, butter half size of an egg, three cups Graham flour, three teaspoons baking powder, a pinch of salt, one-half pint milk, or milk and water; to be of thickness of ordinary cake batter. Corn cake may be made same way only use two cups of flour and one of meal, instead of the Graham flour, as above. Excellent.

GRAHAM MUFFINS.

Mrs. L. J. Tilton.

One egg, half a cup of sugar, piece of butter the size of an egg, one cup milk, three teaspoons baking powder, Graham meal to make a batter thick enough to drop in rings without spreading; thoroughly mix the baking powder with the meal; melt the butter and mix well with the sugar and egg; add the milk and gradually stir in the meal.

GRAHAM MUFFINS

Mrs. J. H. Brown.

One egg, one and a half cups of sour milk, one teaspoon saleratus, a little salt, two tablespoons of melted lard or butter, two tablespoons molasses; make stiff enough to drop from spoon. Bake fifteen minutes.

RYE MUFFINS.

Mrs. Bartlett.

Two cups of rye, one of flour, one of sugar, one egg, one teaspoon of soda, and a little salt; mix quite stiff with sour milk.

INDIAN MEAL MUFFINS.

Two cups of Indian meal scalded with as little water as possible, one coffeecup of flour, one teacup of sweet milk, one tablespoon of shortening, one-half cup of brown sugar, a small cup of yeast; mixed over night.

CORN MEAL MUFFINS.

Mrs. A. M. Gibbs.

Soak a pint of meal over night in sweet milk, just enough to wet it; in the morning dissolve half a teaspoon of soda in a tablespoon of boiling water, then fill the cup with buttermilk or sour milk; add this with the yolks of two eggs and a tablespoon of thick cream or melted butter to the meal, also half a teaspoon of salt, Have your rings or muffin frames hot, and bake twenty minutes. If preferred, a shallow pan can be used.

WAFFLES.

Yolks of three eggs, one quart milk, half cup melted butter, one heaping teaspoon baking powder. Afterwards add the whites of the eggs and flour enough to make a thin batter.

WAFFLES.

M.

One pint sour milk, three tablespoons melted butter .three eggs, beaten separately, one teaspoon soda, a little salt, flour enough to make a thick batter.

RICE CROQUETTES.

C. T. C., Evanston, Ill.

Boil one cup of rice in one quart of milk or water, till tender; while warm add a piece of butter the size of an egg, two eggs; make into rolls, dip them in cracker crumbs and fry them in lard or butter.

RICE CROQUETTES.
Mrs. N. C. Gridley, Evanston.

To about one quart of boiled rice, add the yolks of three eggs and a little salt; make it up into balls, roll them in flour and fry them in hot lard, as you would doughnuts.

RICE CROQUETTES.

One teacup rice, one pint milk, one pint water, a little salt; butter a tin, put in the mixture and swell on the stove, where it will not quite simmer. When dry, add two eggs, beaten light, with two tablespoons of sugar and one of butter. Have ready cracker crumbs spread on a board thickly. Make a roll of the rice in the crumbs; drop in hot lard and brown.

RICE CROQUETTES.
Mrs. Anna Marble.

Rice boiled in milk and flavored with lemon or orange flower water; add sugar and eggs; when cold, cut in small pieces; roll them in flour dipped in egg, then roll again in bread crumbs, fry in hot fat, as you would doughnuts.

CORN MEAL PONES.
Mrs. A. M. Gibbs.

Scald a quart of milk; stir into one pint of meal six eggs beaten separately, a little salt, one tablespoon flour, two teaspoons baking powder; bake in white cups or small bowls and send to the table in the cups, so they may be hot to be turned out on to the plate and eaten with butter or syrup. For tea or breakfast.

GOOD BREAKFAST CAKES.

Mrs. J. H. Brown.

Three eggs well beaten, two and a half teacups of flour, one pint of sweet milk, a little salt; make a batter of these, put in cups or rings and bake in a quick oven.

BANNOCKS.

M.

One pint corn meal, pour on it boiling water to thoroughly wet it; let it stand a few minutes; add salt and one egg and a little sweet cream, or a tablespoon melted butter. Make into balls and fry in hot lard.

INDIAN BANNOCKS.

R. A. Sibley.

One quart Indian meal, with a little salt, wet it quite soft with boiling water or milk—must be boiling; wet your hands; pat them out in small flat cakes; fry in hot lard, not enough to cover them. Cook one side first then turn. Cheap and good for breakfast.

STELLA'S CORN CAKE.

Mrs. F. M. Cragin.

No. 1.—One pint milk, one pint meal, two eggs, a piece of butter size of an egg, one and a half teaspoons cream tartar, three-fourths teaspoon soda, one-half teaspoon salt, a little sugar.

No. 2.—One pint sour milk, two eggs, one pint meal, one tablespoon melted butter, one teaspoon saleratus.

No. 3.—One pint sour milk, one-half pint water, one

quart meal, three tablespoons melted lard, one teaspoon saleratus, one teaspoon salt.

GREEN CORN CAKES.

Mrs. A. M.

One pint of grated sweet corn, three tablespoons milk, one teacup of drawn butter, one teaspoon salt, one-half teaspoon black pepper, if liked one egg. Drop by the tablespoon in hot butter. Fry from ten to twenty minutes.

CORN CAKES.

Mrs. B. F. Adams.

Three cups Indian meal, one cup flour, two cups sweet milk, one cup sour milk, one egg, teaspoon salt, teaspoon soda. Bake half an hour. This, with half a cup molasses and one cup suet, makes a nice pudding. Steam four hours.

CORN CAKES.

Mrs. Pulsifer.

One pint of milk, one-half pint of corn meal, two table-spoons of flour, two eggs, one tablespoon of lard or butter, three tablespoons of sugar, one-half teaspoon baking powder. Beat well.

CORN CAKES.

S. S. Pierce.

One pint meal, one pint flour, one cup white sugar, two eggs, piece of butter size small egg; melt the butter; teaspoon soda, two teaspoons cream tartar, salt, sweet milk; made as thick as griddle cakes.

GOOD CORN CAKES.

Mrs. Wm. C. Harris.

Scald about a pint of corn meal at night, adding a little salt; in the morning stir in one egg, and milk enough to make it thin enough to drop from a spoon on a tin.

CORN CAKES.

E. E. Marcy.

One and one-half cups of Indian meal, one-half cup fine flour, one-half of molasses, one of milk, one-half teaspoon soda, a little salt. For weak stomachs, it is an improvement to add a little ginger.

GREEN CORN GRIDDLE CAKES.

Mrs. C. M. Dickerman, Rockford, Ill.

Twelve ears corn grated, four eggs, one cup sweet milk (cream is better); one cup flour, three tablespoons butter, if you use milk, none if you use cream; a little salt. Bake on a griddle.

GRIDDLE CAKES.

Mrs. Orson Smith.

Two quarts warm water, one teaspoon salt, one cup flour, one cup corn meal, one-half teacup yeast, two eggs well beaten and added the last; raise over night.

RICE CAKES.

Mrs. Lunt, Evanston.

One cup soft boiled rice, add one-half cup milk, the yolks of three eggs, two tablespoons flour, a little salt;

then beat the whites to a stiff froth and mix with the rest. Fry on a buttered griddle as soon as possible after adding the whites of the eggs. Nice for invalids.

SQUASH GRIDDLE CAKES.

Mrs. Rice.

One cup squash, two eggs, one and a half pints milk, salt to flavor, flour to make it of a consistency for frying; add a little soda dissolved in milk.

QUICK BUCKWHEAT CAKES.

One quart of buckwheat flour, one-half a teacup of corn meal or wheat flour, a little salt, and two tablespoons of syrup. Wet these with cold or warm water to a thin batter, and add lastly four good tablespoons of baking powder.

BUCKWHEAT CAKES.

Lake Forest.

One quart buckwheat flour, four tablespoons yeast, one teaspoon salt, one handful Indian meal, two tablespoons molasses, not syrup. Warm water enough to make a thin batter; beat very well and set in a warm place. If the batter is the least sour in the morning, add a little soda.

CORN MEAL GRIDDDE CAKES.

Lake Forest,

Soak three-fourths of a pint of meal over night in three cups of sour milk and one of sour cream ; in the morning add one pint of flour, a little salt and two eggs; soda to sweeten the mixture,

CORN MEAL GRIDDLE CAKES.

M.

One pint of corn meal, two tablespoons melted butter, one teaspoon salt, two eggs, one tablespoon sugar, sour milk enough to make batter; saleratus (if you should get in a little two much it is easily remedied by adding a few drops of vinegar).

OAT MEAL GRIDDLE CAKES.

Mrs. J. M. Wetherell, Englewood, Ill.

One cup oat meal, one cup flour, one teaspoon sugar, one teaspoon baking powder, one-half teaspoon salt; sift the baking powder in with the flour; add cold water to make a batter of the consistency of buckwheat cakes; beat very well together and bake immediately. This recipe is sufficient for a family of three.

MUSH.

Indian or oat meal mush is best made in the following manner: Put fresh water in a kettle over the fire to boil, and put in some salt; when the water boils, stir in handful by handful corn or oat meal until thick enough for use. In order to have excellent mush, the meal should be allowed to cook well, and long as possible while thin, and before the final handful is added. When desired to be fried for breakfast, turn into an earthen dish and set away to cool. Then cut in slices when you wish to fry; dip each piece in beaten eggs and fry on a hot griddle.

OAT MEAL GRUEL.

Take two tablespoons of oat meal, pour on it a pint of

cold water; let it stand half a day, then pour it through a sieve and boil well one-quarter of an hour, stirring all the time; season according to taste. The coarse meal to be rejected. Good for invalids or children.

WEIGHTS AND MEASURES.

Ten eggs are equal to one pound.

One pound of brown sugar, one pound of white sugar, powdered or loaf sugar broken, is equal to one quart.

One pound of butter, when soft, is equal to one quart.

One pound and two ounces Indian meal is equal to one quart.

One pound and two ounces of wheat flour is equal to one quart.

Four large tablespoons are equal to one-half gill.

Eight large tablespoons are equal one gill.

Sixteen large tablespoons are equal to one-half pint.

A common sized wine glass holds half a gill.

A common sized tumbler holds half a pint.

Four ordinary teacups of liquid are equal to one quart.

CAKES.

But then my fare was all so light and delicate ;
The Fruit, the Cakes, the Meats so dainty frail,
They would not bear a bite — no, not a munch —
But melted áway like ice.

— HOOD.

SUGGESTIONS.

In making Cake, it is very desirable that the materials
be of the finest quality. Sweet, fresh butter, eggs and
good flour are the first essentials. The process of putting
together is also quite an important feature, and where
other methods are not given in this work by contributors,
it would be well for the young housekeeper to observe the
following directions : Never allow the butter to oil, but
soften it by putting it in a moderately warm place before
you commence other preparations for your cake : then put
it into an earthen dish (tin, if not new, will discolor your
cake as you stir it), and add your sugar ; beat the butter
and sugar to a cream ; add the yolks of the eggs, then the
milk, and lastly the beaten whites of the eggs and flour
Spices and liquors may be added after the yolks of the
eggs are put in, and fruit should be put in with the flour.

The oven should be pretty hot for small cakes, and

moderate for larger. To ascertain if a large cake is sufficiently baked, pierce it with a broom-straw through the centre; if done, the straw will come out free from dough; if not done, dough will adhere to the straw. Take it out of the tin about fifteen minutes after it is taken from the oven (not sooner), and do not turn it over on the top to cool.

ICING.

The following rules should be observed where boiled icing is not used:

Put the whites of your eggs in a shallow earthen dish and allow at least quarter of a pound or sixteen tablespoons of the finest white sugar for each egg. Take part of the sugar at first and sprinkle over the eggs; beat them for about half an hour, stirring in gradually the rest of the sugar; then add the flavor. If you use the juice of a lemon, allow more sugar. Tartaric acid and lemon juice whitens icing. It may be shaded a pretty pink with strawberry juice or cranberry syrup, or colored yellow by putting the juice and rind of a lemon in a thick muslin bag and squeezing it hard into the egg and sugar.

If cake is well dredged with flour after baking, and then carefully wiped before the icing is put on, it will not run and can be spread more smoothly. Put frosting on to the cake in large spoonfuls, commencing over the center; then spread it over the cake, using a large knife, dipping it occasionally in cold water. Dry the frosting on the cake in a cool, dry place.

FROSTING.

Mrs. Louise Dewey.

One pint of granulated sugar, moisten thoroughly with water sufficient to dissolve it when heated; let it boil until it threads from the spoon, stirring often; while the sugar is boiling, beat the whites of two eggs till they are firm; then when thoroughly beaten, turn them into a deep dish, and when the sugar is boiled, turn it over the whites, beating all together rapidly until of the right consistency to spread over the cake. Flavor with lemon if preferred This is sufficient for two loaves.

FROSTING FOR CAKE.

Ella Guild.

One cup frosting sugar, two tablespoons of water boiled together; take it off the stove and stir in the white of one egg beaten to a stiff froth; stir all together well; then frost your cake with it, and you will never want for a nicer frosting than this.

ICE CREAM ICING FOR WHITE CAKE.

Mrs. P. B. Ayer.

Two cups of pulverized sugar boiled to a thick syrup; add three teaspoons vanilla; when cool, add the whites of two eggs well beaten, and flavored with two teaspoons of citric acid.

ICING.

Mrs. H. P. Stowell.

One pound pulverized sugar, pour over one tablespoon

cold water, beat whites of three eggs a little, not to a stiff froth; add to the sugar and water; put in a deep bowl; place in a vessel of boiling water and heat. It will become thin and clear, afterward begin to thicken. When it becomes quite thick remove from the fire and stir while it becomes cool till thick enough to spread with a knife. This will frost several ordinary sized cakes.

CHOCOLATE FROSTING.

Mrs. C. H. Wheeler.

Whites of two eggs, one and one-half cups of fine sugar, six great spoons of grated chocolate, two teaspoons of vanilla; spread rather thickly between layers and on the top of cake; best when freshly made. It should be made like any frosting.

BLACK FRUIT CAKE.

Mrs. C. H. Wheeler.

Three-fourths pound butter, one pound sugar (brown), one pound flour, two pounds currants, three pounds raisins (seeded), one-half pound citron, one-fourth pound almonds, eight eggs, one nutmeg, cloves and cinnamon, one wine glass of brandy. The raisins are better to be soaked in brandy over night.

BLACK CAKE.

Mrs. G. F. DeForrest.

Two pounds of flour, two pounds sugar, two pounds butter, eight pounds raisins, four pounds currants, one pint brandy, two pounds citron, twenty-four eggs, two ounces nutmeg, two teaspoons of cloves; add a little molasses to make it more moist and black. This makes two very large loaves, baked in tin pans or hoops. For weddings. Splendid.

MOTHER DORCHESTER'S BLACK CAKE.
Mrs. Kate Johnson.

One pound sugar, one pound butter, one pound flour, ten eggs, three pounds raisins, three pounds currants, one-half pound citron, two teaspoons cinnamon, one teaspoon cloves, two teaspoons nutmeg, one wine glass of brandy or alcohol. Stone the raisins and pour the liquor over them, and cover tight over night. Brown the flour to darken the cake. Bake from two to four hours. Will keep good two or three years.

FRUIT CAKE.
Mrs. N. C. Gridley, Evanston.

One pound flour, one pound brown sugar, three-quarters of a pound of butter, three pounds seeded raisins, one pound currants, one pound citron, one-quarter pound almonds, blanched and powdered in rose water; one nutmeg, one wine glass brandy, ten eggs. Stir butter and sugar to a cream, then add whites and eight yolks of eggs, beaten separately. Stir in the flour, then spices, and add the fruit just before it is put in the pans. Bake slowly. This cake will keep two years.

CHEAP FRUIT CAKE.
Mrs. Earle, Peoria, Ill.

Three teacups flour, one coffee cup of sugar, three-quarters of a teacup of butter, three-quarters of a teacup of milk, three eggs, raisins and currants, one teaspoon of baking powder.

FRUIT CAKE.
Mrs. W. Guthrie.

Twelve eggs, one pound flour, one pound sugar, one pound butter, two pounds raisins, two pounds currants, one pound citron, two tablespoons cinnamon, four nutmegs, one cup sweet milk, one cup molasses, one teaspoon cream tartar, one teaspoon soda, one gill brandy. Bake two hours or more.

FRUIT CAKE.
Louisa Churchill.

One pound of sugar, one pound of butter, one pound flour, four pounds raisins, two pounds currants, one and one-half pounds citron, one gill brandy, one cup sour cream, one nutmeg, one teaspoon soda.

FRUIT CAKE.
Mrs. Creote.

One pound of flour, one pound sugar, one pound butter, three pounds raisins, three pounds currants, one pound citron, two grated lemons, ten eggs, three nutmegs, three ounces cinnamon, one gill brandy, one gill wine. Bake two and one-half hours in a ten quart pan.

FARMER'S FRUIT CAKE.
Mrs. W. P. Cragin.

Take three cups of dried apples, wash them and soak

over night in water. In the morning drain off the water and chop them; add two cups of molasses and let them simmer two hours, or until the molasses is all absorbed. Let them cool before adding them to the other ingredients, then take one cup of brown sugar, three-fourths cup butter, two eggs, one cup milk, one small teaspoon soda, one and one-half teaspoons cream tartar, one large tablespoon cloves, one of allspice, two of cinnamon, one nutmeg, the grated rind of two lemons and the juice of one, one-fourth pound of citron, one cup of raisins, flour enough to make it the consistency of cup cake. Bake in a moderate oven.

DRIED APPLE CAKE.
Mrs. G. W. Gage.

One cup dried apples soaked over night, then steamed till soft; put them into a cup of molasses and simmer slowly till well cooked; when cool add one egg, one-half cup of sugar, one-half cup of butter, one-half cup of milk, two and a half cups of flour, one teaspoon soda, two of cream tartar and spice to taste.

PHILADELPHIA PLUNKETS.
Mrs. J. A. Ellis.

One pound of sugar, one half-pound of butter, six eggs beaten separately; one pound of corn starch. Bake in small tins.

NEW ENGLAND ELECTION CAKE.
Mrs. John King, Jr.

Take three pounds sifted flour, leaving out a pint to put

in with fruit, and mix in warm milk till it is a stiff batter; weigh one and a half pounds of sugar, one pound butter; mix them to a cream, then mix one-half this with the batter of milk and flour, and one-half pint good home-made yeast; beat very thoroughly together; when light, which will take several hours in winter, better to mix at night and stand in a warm place till next morning, add the remainder of butter and sugar with six eggs and one pound raisins, one glass brandy, cinnamon, mace or nutmeg, as the taste, and a little soda; if in season of scarcity of eggs, it is very good without any; should rise the second time before pouring in pans for baking. The more such cake is beaten the finer and lighter it will be.

A PLAIN FRUIT CAKE.

Mrs. Ada Sturtevant, Delavan, Wis.

One cup of butter, three of brown sugar, three of sour milk, six of flour, two eggs, nutmeg, cinnamon and cloves, one and one-half teaspoons soda; two cups of raisins and currants improve it. Add the fruit the last thing. Bake in two tins.

FRUIT CAKE.

Mrs. E. H. Dennison,

One-half cup of butter, one-half cup of brown sugar, one-half cup of molasses, one-half cup of sour milk, the yolks of four eggs, one-half teaspoon of soda, one teaspoon cream tartar, one and one-half cups of flour, one cup of raisins chopped fine, one cup of currants; one teaspoon each of cloves, cinnamon and nutmeg; whites can be used for delicate cakes.

DOUGH CAKE.

Mrs. W. P. Nixon.

One pint bowl of dough as it is ready to mould into loaves, four eggs beaten separately, one cup of butter, two cups of white sugar, one tablespoon of cinnamon, one nutmeg, one-half teaspoon of soda, one pint bowl of stoned raisins; mix by hand; put the dough in a large bowl; first work in the butter well, then the sugar and spice, next the yolks, then the whites of the eggs, then the soda, first dissolved in a little warm water; lastly, the raisins. Bake about as long as you would bread. This quantity makes two loaves. Let it stand to rise after putting into the pans.

BREAD CAKE.

Mrs. W. H. Ovington.

Three teacups of light dough, three-fourths cup butter, two cups sugar, three eggs, small teaspoon soda dissolved in a little warm water, nutmeg or cinnamon for spice, a coffeecup of raisins or currants : mix all well together and let it raise before setting it in the oven.

RAISED LOAF CAKE.

Mrs. F. D. Gray.

Three cups of milk, two cups of sugar, one cup yeast, flour to make a thick batter. Stand till light; then add two cups sugar, two cups butter, two eggs, raisins and spices. Stand from one to three hours in the tins.

LOAF CAKE.
Mrs. John King, Jr.

Four pounds light dough, two pounds sugar, one pound butter, four eggs, one pound stoned and chopped raisins, (sliced citron if you like,) one wine glass brandy or wine, small teaspoon soda, mace or nutmeg; mix sugar and butter with the eggs, well beaten; then with the hands mix the dough to the ingredients, beating very thoroughly; add spices and fruit, and allow to rise before baking, after putting in the pans.

PLAINER LOAF CAKE.—Six cups light dough, three cups sugar, one and one-half cups butter, three eggs, small teaspoon of saleratus, spice and fruit as you please; mix as the fruit. Dough for cake should always be light, either bread or biscuit; if biscuit dough is used, a little less shortening is needed, and to insure light cake, the bread should be made from good home-made yeast.

LOAF CAKE.
Mrs. G. F. De Forrest, Freeport.

Four pounds flour, two pounds sugar, two and a half pounds butter (or one and a quarter pounds butter and three-quarters of a pound lard); three and a half pounds raisins, a little citron; add wine, brandy, four eggs, one teaspoon soda, and spice as you please; rub the butter and sugar together, then take half and work into the flour; add half a pint of domestic yeast; make the dough not quite as stiff as biscuit. When it has well risen, work in the other half of the butter and sugar, with the spices and brandy. When thoroughly light, add the eggs, beaten separately, and the fruit. Let it rise an hour in the tins; bake one and a quarter hours. It will keep all winter if frosted. This rule makes eight loaves.

LOAF CAKE.

Mrs. C. H. Wheeler.

Two cups light dough, one cup sugar, one cup chopped raisins, small half cup of soft butter, one egg, half a nutmeg, teaspoon of cinnamon; one-half a wine glass of wine or brandy can be added if desired; dissolve one-half teaspoon of soda in two tablespoons of milk; mix the butter and sugar well into the dough with the hand, before adding the rest of the ingredients; flour the raisins; a little flour may be added if the brandy is used and the cake seems too thin. Mix or stir very thoroughly, and raise about an hour or until it looks light.

QUICK LOAF CAKE.

Mrs. H. M. Buell.

One cup of sugar, one-half of butter, one of milk, one egg, two and one-half cups of flour, one-half teaspoon of soda, one teaspoon of cream tartar.

POUND CAKE.

Mrs. W. H. Ovington.

One pound of flour, one of sugar, ten eggs; beat the yolks and sugar together; add one pound of butter, putting in the whites beaten to a froth, and the flour last. Very nice baked in small patty pans and frosted.

WHITE POUND CAKE.

Mrs. G. S. Whitaker.

One pound sugar, one of flour, fourteen ounces butter, one cup sour milk, or sweet milk with soda or cream tartar mixed in milk, whites of twelve eggs; flavoring and citron.

IMPERIAL CAKE.

M. T.

One pound sugar, one of flour, one of butter, ten eggs, one pound almonds, three-quarters of citron cut fine, one glass of brandy and mace; put the fruit in the flour, and bake in thick loaves.

MOUNTAIN POUND CAKE.

Mrs. C. M. Dickerman, Rockford, Ill.

One pound sugar, one of flour, one-half of butter, six eggs (the whites and yolks beaten separately); three-fourths cup sweet milk, one teaspoon soda, two of cream tartar; sift the soda and cream tartar together into the flour, after sifting the flour; then rub butter and sugar to a cream, and add a part of the whites and yolks of the eggs, also a part of the flour, and then the milk.

IMPERIAL CAKE.

Mrs. De Forrest.

One pound sugar, one of flour, three-fourths of butter, one of almonds, blanched and cut fine, one-half of citron, one-half of raisins, rind and juice of one lemon, one nutmeg, ten eggs. This is very delicious and will keep for months. Elegant.

WHITE CAKE.

Elmina Meeker, Cortland, Ill.

Two cups of white sugar, one of cream (sweet); two of flour, one tablespoon of butter, the whites of five eggs, one teaspoon of cream tartar, one-half of soda. Flavor with lemon.

WHITE CAKE.

Marian Ely, Cortland, Ill.

One cup of sugar, one-half of butter, one-half of sweet milk, whites of two eggs, one teaspoon of cream tartar. one-half of soda, two and one-half cups of flour.

WHITE CAKE.

Mrs. C. H. Wheeler.

Two cups of sugar, one-half of butter, the whites of four eggs, one cup sweet milk, three of flour, three small teaspoons of baking powder sifted with the flour. Beat the sugar and butter to a cream, then stir in the milk and flour, a little at a time; add the whites last. All cake should be well stirred before the whites of the eggs are added. Never fails.

PRIZE WHITE CUP CAKE.

Mrs. Kate W. Hoge.

One cup of butter, four cups sifted flour or three of unsifted, two cups of white sugar, one of sour milk with one-half teaspoon soda, five eggs, beaten separately. Beat the yellow of the eggs until light, then add the sugar, and beat it well together, then add the whites of the eggs (beaten well beforehand) alternating with the flour (after being sifted.) Mix the whites of the eggs and flour very slowly and bake in a moderately heated oven at first, then finish with a hotter oven. Try it with a straw or knife; when the dough don't stick, it is done. Use flavoring to taste. This will make one large or two small cakes.

SNOW CAKE.
Mrs. Lamkin.

Three-fourths cup of butter, two cups sugar, one cup milk, one cup corn starch, two cups flour, one and one-half teaspoons baking powder. Mix corn starch, flour and baking powder together; add to the butter and sugar alternately with the milk; lastly, add the whites of seven eggs; flavor to taste. Never fails to be good.

DELICATE CAKE.
Mrs. Anson Gorton.

One coffeecup butter, two coffeecups sugar, four coffee-cups flour, one-half coffeecup milk. The whites of eight eggs, two teaspoons cream-tartar, even teaspoon of soda. Flavor to taste.

DELICATE CAKE.
Marian Ely.

The whites of four eggs well beaten, one cup white sugar, one-half cup butter, one-half cup sweet milk, two cups flour, one teaspoon cream tartar, one-half teaspoon soda.

DELICATE CAKE.

Mrs. J. A. Ellis.

One and a half cups powdered sugar, one-half of butter, one and a half of flour, one-half of corn starch, sifted with the flour, one-half of milk, the whites of six eggs beaten to a froth, one small teaspoon cream-tartar, one-half teaspoon soda; flavor with almond or vanilla. Bake in a moderate oven.

DELICATE CAKE.

Mrs. A. T. Hall.

One cup butter, two of sugar, one of sweet milk, whites of eight eggs, three cups flour one teaspoon of cream tartar, one-half teaspoon soda.

DELICATE CAKE.

Mrs. C. E. Browne, Evanston.

Two eggs, a trifle over half a cup of butter, one cup sweet milk, one and a half of sugar, and three teaspoons baking powder. Put together in the usual manner, and flavor with extract of almonds or lemon. Made with the whites of four eggs, it is admirable for cocoanut cake; or with yolks for chocolate. Use your judgment in adding flour. This recipe I have had in use for fifteen years, and while inexpensive, it is nice enough for most any occasion.

WHITE POUND CAKE.

Mrs. M. J. Woodworth.

One pound of flour, one pound sugar, three-fourths pound butter, the whites of sixteen eggs beaten to a stiff froth; flavor with bitter almond. Elegant.

FEATHER CAKE.

Mrs. A. P. Wightman.

One cup sugar, one cup flour, one egg, one tablespoon melted butter, one-half cup sweet milk, one teaspoon baking powder, pinch of salt, flavor to taste; put in the baking powder and run through a seive.

FEATHER CAKE.

Mrs. W. H. Ovington.

One cup sugar, three eggs beaten well together, butter the size of an egg, one cup flour, one teaspoon cream tartar mixed with flour, one-half teaspoon soda dissolved in eight teaspoons of water. Season to taste.

CREAM CAKE.

Mrs. M. J. Woodworth.

Three eggs, one and one-half cups flour, one cup sugar, two teaspoons baking powder, three tablespoons water, bake in jelly cake pans, making four cakes; cream, one pint milk, one egg, one and one-half tablespoons corn starch, two tablespoons sugar; flavor when cool. Very nice.

CREAM CAKE.

Mrs. James Wadsworth, Hyde Park.

Beat five eggs thoroughly, add two cups sugar, two table spoons cream, two cups flour in which has been mixed one and one-half teaspoons baking powder, a little salt, bake in five jelly tins, leaving about one-sixth of the batter, to this add one cup of milk, also lemon or vanilla;

22

boil till it thickens, stirring constantly; then spread it over the cakes as they are laid together.

CREAM CAKE.

Mrs. Chesebrough.

Four eggs, three teacups flour, not quite two of sugar, one teaspoon of soda, two of cream tartar, or three of baking powder; mix flour, sugar and cream tartar together; dissolve the soda in one cup good cream and add with the beaten eggs to the mixture. Flavor with lemon or _ vanilla. Bake twenty minutes. Is made quickly and very nice.

CORN STARCH CAKE.

Mrs. Dickinson.

One cup of butter, two cups sugar, one cup sweet milk, two-thirds cup corn starch and fill it up with flour, two cups flour, two teaspoons baking powder, whites of seven eggs.

CORN STARCH CAKE.

Lucy D. Fake.

One cup white sugar and one-half cup butter beaten together, one-half cup starch, the whites of three eggs beaten to a stiff froth, one cup milk, one cup flour, one teaspoon cream tartar, one-half of soda. Flavor with lemon.

LADY CAKE.

Mrs. Ewing.

One pound sugar, one-half pound butter, one pound of

flour, whites of sixteen eggs, one and one-half teaspoons soda, one and one-half teaspoons cream tartar. Rub butter and sugar together, then stir the whites of eggs into it. Sift the flour three times with cream tartar and soda in it, and add lastly.

LADY CAKE.

One cup of boiled milk, one-half cup butter, two cups powdered sugar, three cups flour, one even teaspoon cream tartar, one-half teaspoon soda, whites of two eggs; flavor with bitter almond.

LEMON CAKE.

Lake Forest, Ill.

Three cups of sugar, one cup butter, one cup milk, five eggs, four cups flour; stir the butter and sugar to a cream, beat the eggs separately, the whites to a stiff froth, and dissolve a little soda in the milk. Mix all together; sift the flour and put in by degrees, and add the juice and grated rind of a fresh lemon. This cake is delicious.

LEMON CAKE.

Mrs. H. B. Hurd.

Five cups flour, one cup butter, three cups sugar, one cup cream, five eggs, one teaspoon saleratus and the peel and juice of two lemons.

SPICE CAKE.

Mrs. A. T. Hall.

Two cups of sugar, two cups butter, six cups flour, one

cup molasses, one cup milk, six eggs, one glass brandy, two teaspoons cream tartar, one teaspoon soda, two teaspoons cloves, one nutmeg, two pounds raisins.

SPICE CAKE.

Mrs. J. C. Mooar.

One and one-half cups sugar, two-thirds cup butter, one cup raisins, two-thirds cup sweet milk, three cups flour, two eggs, one teaspoon cream tartar, one-half teaspoon soda, cinnamon, nutmeg and cloves to suit taste.

CURRANT CAKE.

Fanny L., Evanston.

One and one-half pounds flour, one pound sugar, three-fourths pound butter, seven eggs, one gill milk, one-half teaspoon saleratus, one pound currants.

POOR MAN'S CAKE.

Fanny L.

Two cups raised dough, one egg, one-half cup molasses, one cup sugar, butter size of an egg, one teaspoon soda; one cup raisins, flour to stiffen.

CLOVE CAKE.

Mrs. H. P. Merriman.

Four and one-half coffee cups of sifted flour, three cups sugar, one and one-half cups butter, one teacup cream or milk, one teaspoon saleratus, four eggs, one tablespoon cloves, one tablespoon cinnamon, one tablespoon nutmeg, one pound fruit and citron.

COFFEE CAKE.

Mrs. E. S. Chesebrough.

One cup butter, one of sugar, one of molasses, one of strong coffee, five of flour, one pound of raisins, one teaspoon of soda, one of cinnamon, one of allspice, one-half a nutmeg, three eggs (it can be made with one or two). Sift the soda in molasses. Excellent.

PUFF CAKE.

Mrs. A. M. Lewis.

One cup brown sugar, one-half of butter, two eggs, one-half cup sweet milk, two of Graham flour (sifted), one half teaspoon soda, one of cream tartar, or two teaspoons of baking powder, one cup of raisins.

MARBLE CAKE.

Mrs. J. Gilbert, Evanston.

WHITE PART. — One cup white pulverized sugar, one-half cup butter, one-half cup sweet milk, whites of four eggs, two and one-half cups flour, two heaping teaspoons baking powder, or one teaspoon cream tartar and one-half teaspoon soda. Stir butter and sugar together to a cream, and beat whites of eggs to a stiff froth, which are to be added the last of all ingredients, with the half cup of flour, which must contain the baking powder well mixed in the flour; season to taste. This is a very good recipe for delicate cake also.

DARK PART. — One cup brown sugar, one-half cup molasses, one-half cup sour milk, two and one-half cups flour, one level teaspoon soda dissolved in the milk and in the molasses, yolks of four eggs and one-half cup butter, to be rubbed well together with the sugar; add one-half teaspoon cinnamon, allspice and cloves.

Either of these make good cake used separately, or well mixed to represent marble.

CHOCOLATE CAKE.

C. A. Tinkham.

One cup butter, two of sugar, five eggs (leaving out the whites of two), one cup sweet milk, one teaspoon cream tartar, one-half of soda, both dissolved in the milk, three and one-half cups of flour, scant measure. For frosting: Take the whites of the two eggs, one and one-half cups of powdered sugar, six large tablespoons grated chocolate, two teaspoons vanilla; frost while the cake is hot.

COCHINEAL MARBLE CAKE.

Mrs. Anna Yocum, Cairo, Ill.

One cup butter, three cups pulverized sugar, five cups flour, one cup water, ten eggs (whites only), three teaspoons. yeast powder sifted with flour; cream the butter and sugar by stirring together; beat the whites of the eggs to a froth, and gradually add all together. Before beginning the cake, put a small teaspoon of cochineal to soak in two tablespoons of hot water; bruise it with a spoon, and strain through a piece of Swiss muslin into three-fourths teacup of the cake batter, and as you pour the batter into the cake tin, marble with the red dough. A little practice will produce very satisfactory results.

MARBLE CAKE.

Mrs. Frances M. Thatcher.

One-half cup sour cream, one-half cup butter, two and one-half cups flour, one cup white sugar, the whites of five eggs, two-thirds teaspoon soda; prepare another mixture, except substituting dark sugar for white, and the yolks instead of the whites; fill a tin with alternate layers of each and bake.

HICKORY-NUT CAKE.

Mrs. Hobbs.

One cup meats (broken), one and one-half of sugar, one-half of butter, two of flour, three-fourths of sweet milk, two teaspoons baking powder, the whites of four eggs well beaten; add the meats last.

HICKORY-NUT CAKE.

Mrs. C. C. Stratton, Evanston.

Two cups pulverized sugar, one cup butter, one cup new milk, four cups sifted flour (winter wheat flour), whites of eight eggs, one and one-half cups hickory-nut meats, one tablespoon vanilla, three heaping teaspoons baking powder; put the baking powder into the flour, and stir well before, using, beat and add the eggs the last; bake slowly one hour.

HICKORY-NUT CAKE.

Nellie Gould.

Not quite a cup of butter, one and one-half cups sugar, three-fourths cup sweet milk, three cups flour,

three teaspoons baking powder, whites of four eggs, one
cup hickory-nuts.

NUT CAKE.

Mrs. Taylor, Fort Wayne.

Two and a half cups sugar, one of butter, three and a
half of flour, one of sweet milk, five eggs, one pound
stoned raisins, one-half pound of citron, one-half of a
lemon peel, one-half of an orange peel, one pint hickory-
nut meats, one nutmeg, two teaspoons baking powder.

COCOANUT CAKE.

Mrs. Bartlett.

One pound of sugar; one pound of flour; one pound
of butter; whites of twelve eggs; one cocoanut; two-
thirds teaspoonful soda; half cup of wine.

WHITE CUP CAKE.

Mrs. A. S. Ewing.

Two cups of sugar, one-half of butter, four of flour,
one of sweet cream, one teaspoon soda dissolved in the
cream, two teaspoons cream tartar mixed through the
flour, whites of eight eggs.

COMPOSITION CAKE.

Mrs. H. F. Waite.

Five eggs, four cups sifted flour, two and one-half of
sugar, one of butter, one of milk, two teaspoons cream
tartar, one of soda. Beat sugar, butter and yolks of eggs
a long time, then add milk and part of the flour; with

the rest of the flour add the whites, beat very light; raisins or citron, if desired.

VANILLA CAKE.

A. E. W.

One-half cup of butter stirred into one cup of sugar till it is like cream, three eggs, one and one-half cups flour, two teaspoons vanilla; bake on tins, dropping.

REBECCA'S PLAIN CAKE.

Mrs. G. II. L.

One cup sugar, two of flour, one-half of butter, one-half of sour milk, one egg, one teaspoon saleratus. One loaf.

PLAIN CAKE.

Harriet N. Jenks.

One cup of Indian meal sifted, one of flour, one of sugar, one teaspoon soda, about a pint of sour milk, teaspoon of salt, one egg, piece of butter size of a common egg. Wholesome for children.

ONE EGG CAKE.

Mrs. P. B. Ayer.

One and a half cups sugar and one-half of butter beaten together, one egg, one cup milk, two and a half of flour, two and a half teaspoons of baking powder. This cake should have icing of some kind between, chocolate for example.

TIPSY CAKE.

Mrs. Gen. N. J T. Dana.

Take sponge cake and stick it full of almonds which have been blanched ; turn over it as much white wine as it will absorb; put it in a deep dish or glass bowl, and let it stand one hour, then pour over it as much soft custard as the dish will hold. Let it stand two or three hours. Very simple and very nice.

RUNAWAY CAKE.

Mattie Winslow, Aurora, Ill.

One egg, one teaspoon sugar, two tablespoons butter, one cup milk, two teaspoons cream tartar, one teaspoon soda, flour to make a little thicker than griddle cakes. This is very nice eaten hot with butter for breakfast and tea.

TUMBLER CAKE.

Mrs. Lamkin.

Four eggs, one tumbler sugar, one tumbler butter, one-half tumbler molasses, one-third tumbler milk, one teaspoon saleratus; spices to taste; one-half pound raisins, one-fourth pound currants, flour to make it the usual consistency. Bake one and one-fourth hours in a slow oven.

ADAMS' CAKE.

Mrs. H. P. Stowell.

One cup sugar, two-thirds cup butter, four eggs, one and one-eighth cups flour, very little soda. Very nice.

CLAY CAKE.

Mrs. Ada Sturtevant.

One cup butter, two and one-half cups sugar, one cup sweet milk, four cups flour, the yolks of five eggs and the whites of seven, two spoons cream tartar, one spoon soda, one spoon extract of lemon; stir the butter and sugar till it looks like cream; beat the yolks separately and well, the whites to a stiff froth, adding the whites and flour last, and beat all very thoroughly. This will make two cakes. If you lack time, and wish variety, by changing the flavoring and adding fruit to one, you will have two cakes entirely unlike, and very good.

HARRISON CAKE.

Mrs. B. F. Adams.

One and one-half cups butter, one cup sugar, one cup molasses, one cup sour milk, four eggs, one teaspoon - soda, flour to make as thick as pound cake; fruit and spice.

GOLD CAKE.

Mrs. Russell.

One and one-half cups sugar, one-half cup butter, one cup sweet milk, one teaspoon cream tartar, one-half teaspoon soda, nutmeg, three cups flour, yolks of six eggs.

SILVER CAKE.

Mrs. Russell.

One and one-half cups sugar, one-half cup butter, one cup sweet milk, one-half teaspoon soda, one teaspoon cream tartar, whites of six eggs beaten to a froth, and three cups flour.

GOLD CAKE.

Mrs. L. Bradley.

Take yolks of twelve eggs, five cups sifted flour, three cups white powdered sugar, one cup butter, one and a half cups of cream or sweet milk, one teaspoon cream tartar and half a teaspoon of soda.

SILVER CAKE.

Mrs. L. Bradley.

Take whites of one dozen eggs, five cups flour, three cups powdered sugar, one cup butter, one cup cream or sweet milk, one teaspoon cream tartar, half a teaspoon soda.

FRENCH SPONGE CAKE.

Mrs. James Wadsworth, Hyde Park.

Two eggs, two cups of sugar, one of milk, three of flour, two tablespoons butter, two teaspoons baking powder.

CREAM SPONGE CAKE.

Mrs. W. G. Morgan.

Break two large eggs into a teacup and fill it with sweet cream; add one cup white sugar, a little salt, and put in a pan; add two cups of sifted flour, two teaspoons baking powder, one of lemon essence; put in a square baking tin and bake fifteen minutes.

WHITE SPONGE CAKE.

Mrs. L. H. Smith.

One tumbler sifted flour, one and one-half of powdered sugar, one heaping teaspoon cream tartar, and a little salt; sift all together into a dish; beat the whites of ten fresh eggs, and stir (not beat) very carefully into the flour and sugar until well mixed. Bake with great care in a moderate oven, in one good sized round tin, with an opening in the center. Flavor with extract lemon, and put it in with the whites of the eggs. This is an excellent cake.

BERWICK SPONGE CAKE.

Fannie L.

Beat six eggs two minutes (yolks and whites together); add three cups sugar, and beat five minutes; two cups flour and one teaspoon cream tartar, and beat two minutes; add one cup cold water with one-half teaspoon saleratus dissolved in it, and beat one minute; add the grated rind and half the juice of a lemon, a little salt and two more cups of flour, and beat another minute, observing the time exactly. Bake in rather deep cake pans. Extract of lemon will answer.

LEMON SPONGE CAKE.

Mrs. Pulsifer.

Eight eggs, ten ounces of sugar, half pound of flour, the juice and grating of one lemon; separate the eggs, beat the yolks, sugar and lemon until thick and light; whisk the whites until dry, which add with the flour, half of each at a time; mix all together, but avoid beating; butter your pan well and bake in a moderate oven.

MRS. WILDER'S SPONGE GINGERBREAD.

In two cups molasses, sift two teaspoons soda and a dessert spoon ginger. Stir to a cream, then add four well beaten eggs, one cup butter melted, one cup sour milk in which is dissolved one teaspoon soda ; mix all together, then add flour to the consistency of pound cake. Two loaves.

BEST SOFT GINGERBREAD.

One cup molasses, one of sugar, one of milk, half of butter, five cups sifted flour, one tablespoon ginger, half teaspoon or rather more of soda, a little cloves can be added if liked. Melt the butter in molasses and sugar, allowing the mixture to become hot, then add spices, milk, with soda and flour. Persons measure flour so differently, if you would be quite sure to have it right, try a small cake first. If it falls add a little more flour.

HARD GINGERBREAD.

Mrs. J. A. Ellis.

One pound lard, one-half pound butter, beaten to a cream, one and one-half pounds brown sugar, three pints of West India molasses, ginger, cinnamon, allspice and cloves, enough flour to make a stiff dough ; roll out very thin and cut with a cutter.

MRS. HAMILTON'S GINGERBREAD.

Mattie M. Winslow, Aurora, Ill.

Two eggs, one cup molasses, one cup sour cream, two tablespoons ginger, one teaspoon soda. Stir quite thin.

LAYER CAKES.

GENTLEMAN'S FAVORITE.

Miss Anna M. Whitman, Indianapolis, Ind.

Seven eggs beaten separately, one-half cup butter, two cups white sugar, two cups flour, two tablespoons baking powder, two tablespoons water, one-half teaspoon salt; bake in jelly-cake pans in quick oven. The jelly for the cake : One egg, a cup of sugar, three grated apples and one lemon ; stir till it boils and becomes thick, let it cool before putting between the layers.

IMPROMPTU JELLY CAKE.

Mrs. P. B. Brown.

One cup butter, two cups sugar, three cups flour, four eggs; stir the sugar and butter to a cream, then add the yolks of the eggs, and lastly the beaten whites and flour. Have ready the jelly, made as follows: One grated apple, the grated rind and juice of one lemon, one cup sugar and one egg; boil until it jellies, stirring constantly; cool before using. Bake your cake in jelly-cake pans, or in thin layers, putting the jelly between each layer as in ordinary jelly cake.

JELLY CAKE.

Mrs. John Edwards.

One and one-half cups of sugar, one-half of butter, one-half of sweet milk, two and one-half of flour, three eggs, whites and yolks beaten separately, and add two teaspoons baking powder.

. THE JELLY.—One cup of sugar, one egg, grate the rind and use the juice of one lemon, one tablespoon of water, one teaspoon of flour; put your dish in a kettle of boiling water, and let it come to a boil; have your cake ready and put it together.

APPLE JELLY CAKE.

Mrs. W. G. Morgan.

Prepare and grate three large apples, (Greenings preferred,) the juice and rind of a lemon, half a cup of sugar, one egg well beaten; put the ingredients together in a tin basin; simmer until cooked, with constant stirring; set to cool until the cake is ready. Take three eggs, stir whites and yolks separately; to a cup and a half of white sugar, add half a cup sweet milk and a piece of butter the size of an egg; mix butter and sugar together, four cups of flour and three teaspoons of baking powder; divide in four equal parts, and put in baking tins or jelly pans; use the jelly as in other cases while the cake is hot.

JELLY CAKE—MADE WITH THE YOLKS OF EGGS.

Mrs. Brown.

One and one-half cups sugar, one-half cup butter, one-half cup milk, one egg and yolks of four; stir well, then sift in two cups flour and two teaspoons baking powder; bake in five cakes. This makes a delicious cocoanut cake by spreading between, and on the top of the cakes,

instead of jelly, a soft frosting, thickly strewn with dessicated cocoanut, which has been soaked half an hour in
warm milk.

CHOCOLATE CAKE.
Mrs. Monroe Frank.

One cup of butter, two cups sugar, four cups flour, four
eggs, three teaspoons of Royal Baking Powder, one cup
sweet milk.

FOR FROSTING.—One-half cake Baker's chocolate, one-
half cup sugar (pulverized); enough hot water to cover;
set in a pan of boiling water over the fire three minutes;
when cold, add one-half teaspoon vanilla. Spread the
same as for jelly cake.

WHITE MOUNTAIN CAKE.
Mrs. John Edwards, Rockford.

Two cups sugar, two-thirds cup butter, whites of seven
eggs well beaten, two-thirds cup sweet milk, two cups
flour, one cup corn starch, two teaspoons baking powder;
bake in jelly-cake tins.

FROSTING. — Whites of three eggs and some sugar
beaten together — not quite as stiff as for frosting;
spread over the cake; add some grated cocoanut, then
put your cakes together; put cocoanut or frosting for
the top.

YELLOW MOUNTAIN CAKE.
Nellie Spencer.

Yolks of ten eggs, one cup butter, two of sugar, one
of milk, three of flour, one teaspoon soda, two of cream
tartar.

23

COCOANUT MOUNTAIN CAKE.

Mrs. J. P. Hoit.

One cup butter, three cups sugar, one cup milk, three and a half cups flour, whites of ten eggs, one teaspoon cream tartar, one-half teaspoon soda, essence of almond; bake in sheets. Make an icing of the whites of three eggs and one pound sugar; ice each sheet, and sprinkle one grated cocoanut lightly over all.

COCOANUT CAKE.

Mrs. M. G. Hubbell, Shabbona, Ill.

Two eggs, one cup sugar, two-thirds cup of milk, one-half cup butter, two cups flour, two heaping teaspoons baking powder.

FROSTING.—Whites of two egg, eight teaspoons sugar, flavor to suit. Bake the same as jelly cake; spread a thin layer of frosting, sprinkled with prepared cocoanut, and frost the top and thickly sprinkle with the cocoanut.

ALMOND CAKE.

Mrs. Henry Stevens.

Two cups sugar, one-half cup butter, one cup sweet milk, two and one-half cups flour, whites of eight eggs, one teaspoon cream tartar, one-half teaspoon soda; mix butter and sugar to a cream; mix other ingredients alternately, putting in soda last; bake in layers like jelly cake; spread each layer with soft frosting, and add blanched split almonds about an inch apart on each layer.

BOSTON CREAM CAKE.

Mrs. E. S. Chesebrough.

One pint of water, one-half pound butter, three-fourth pound flour, ten eggs; boil the butter and water together; stir in the flour when boiling; when cool, add the eggs, and soda the size of a pea; drop by the spoonful on a buttered baking pan, leaving space so that the cakes will not touch when risen. Bake in a very quick oven about ten minutes. When cold, make an incision at the side and fill with the following cream: Six gills of milk, one and one-half cups flour, two cups sugar, six eggs; beat the flour, sugar and eggs together and stir into the milk while boiling. Flavor with the rind of a lemon.

CUSTARD CAKE.

· Mrs. James P. Clarke.

Two cups sugar, six tablespoons melted butter, six eggs beaten separately, two and one-half cups flour, one-half cup milk, one teaspoon soda, two teaspoons cream tartar.

CUSTARD FOR THE SAME.—One-half pint milk, two eggs, sweeten to taste, flavor with vanilla; bake on pie plates, and put custard between as jelly cake.

CUSTARD CAKE.

Mrs. F. M. Cragin.

Three eggs, one cup of sugar, two cups of flour, two teaspoons of melted butter, one teaspoon of cream tartar, one-half teaspoon of soda dissolved in two tablespoons of milk.

CUSTARD.—One egg, one-half cup of sugar, flavor with lemon; one-third cup of flour, beat and put it in one-half pint of milk. Cook in a pail or pitcher set in boiling water until it thickens ; when the cakes are cold, split and put this in. The above is enough for two cakes. This cake can be baked in layers.

ORANGE CAKE.
Mrs. S. W. Cheever, Ottawa, Ill.

Beat the whites of three and the yolks of five eggs separately; stir to a cream; two cups sugar, one-half cup butter; add one-half cup cold water, two and one-half cups flour with two teaspoons baking powder, grated rind of one orange and all the juice (except about one tablespoon), stirred into the cake. Bake in two square tins.

FROSTING.—Whites of two eggs, two small cups sugar, with a tablespoon of the orange juice sved from the cake. When the cake is cold, join them with this frosting and frost the tops.

ORANGE CAKE.
Mrs. A. M. Gibbs.

Two cups flour, one of corn starch, one tablespoon baking powder, one teaspoon of extract of lemon, one teaspoon of vanilla mixed with the flour and put all through the sieve together; one cup of butter, two cups of sugar stirred to a cream; add one teacup of milk and one-half of above ingredients; stir well, and add the whites of seven eggs well beaten, and then the rest of the flour mixture. Bake in jelly tins.

THE JELLY.—Whites of two eggs, one cup of pulverized sugar, juice and grated pulp of two oranges; meringue top adds to its appearance when piled on quite high.

LEMON HONEY CAKE.

Home Messenger, Detroit.

Two cups of sugar, two-thirds of a cup of butter, one cup of milk, one cup of corn starch, three cups of flour three teaspoons baking powder; rub the butter and sugar to a cream, then add the milk; lastly, the whites of eight eggs beated to a stiff froth, then the corn starch and flour, to which has been added the baking powder. Bake in jelly tins.

LEMON HONEY FOR THE CAKE.—One pound loaf sugar, yolk of eight eggs with two whole ones, the juice of six lemons and grated rind of two, one-fourth pound butter. Put the sugar, lemon and butter into a sauce pan, melt over a gentle fire; when all is dissolved, stir in the eggs which have been well beaten; stir rapidly until it is as thick as honey. Spread this between the layers of cake; set aside the remainder in a closely covered vessel for future use.

SMALL CAKES AND COOKIES.

CHESS CAKES.

Mrs. Lamkin.

Peel and grate one cocoanut, take one pound sugar, one-half pint water, and boil fifteen minutes; stir in the grated cocoanut, boil fifteen minutes longer, while warm stir in one-fourth pound butter, then add the yolks of seven well beaten eggs. Bake in patty pans lined with a rich paste, will keep some time, and mixes prettily in a basket of cake. The small oval patty tins are prettier than scallops.

FINGER CAKES.

Mrs. Lamkin.

Two eggs, beaten very light, to which add a cup of granulated sugar (excepting a tablespoonful); sift in a very small teaspoon cream tartar, half as much soda, a little salt; stir in flour enough for a stiff dough; roll very thin, and sprinkle with a tablespoon of sugar from the cupful, giving it a light roll; cut the dough in strips a finger width; do not let them touch in the pan. Bake in quick oven, watching them, as they readily scorch. Add a good size teaspoon of vanilla.

WINE CAKES.

Mrs. A. M. Chetlain.

One pint of sweet milk, three eggs well beaten, flour to make a thick batter, have hot lard and try as you would fried cakes; take a spoon of batter and let your hand shake as you drop into the lard. Serve warm with wine and sugar, or sweet cream.

OLD-FASHIONED YANKEE DOUGHNUTS.

Mrs. H. M..Riddle, Evanston.

One pint milk, one teacup yeast; put yeast in milk, stir in flour and let it rise over night; in the morning add two teacups sugar, one teacup lard, two eggs, one tea-spoon soda; work in flour and let it rise very light; add nutmeg or cinnamon to suit taste.

DOUGHNUTS.

Mrs. Benham.

Two cups milk, one cup sugar, one-half cup butter, one-half cup lard, one cup sponge yeast, two eggs; add flour to make a stiff dough; let it rise; when light roll it out, and after they are cut out let them. stand on the moulding board until light. Fry in hot lard, and when hot dip them in pulverized sugar.

DOUGHNUTS.

Mrs. H. W. Loomis, Rockford, Ill.

One quart new milk, four eggs, one cup of yeast, one cup of butter, two cups of sugar, one large nutmeg; at night, take one quart scalding milk, and stir in your flour until very thick; beat the eggs with one cup of sugar, and add the butter as soon as it can be done without scalding the eggs; then add the cup of yeast and let it rise until morning. In the morning add the butter and sugar that has previously been stirred; then the nutmeg, with flour enough to make it as stiff as soft biscuit; let it rise again. When very light, roll out three-fourths of an inch thick, and cut with a small cake cutter; let them stand two hours before frying. Roll in sugar when nearly cold.

DOUGHNUTS.

Mrs. L. H. Clement.

One cup of sugar, one and one-half of sour milk, one-half of butter, two eggs, and one teaspoon of soda; flavor with nutmeg.

FRIED CAKES.

Mrs. B. J. Seward.

One cup of sugar, four tablespoons of butter, three eggs, one cup sweet milk, one teaspoon soda, two of cream tartar, or three teaspoons baking powder; roll half an inch thick after mixing soft, and fry in hot lard.

FRIED CAKES.

Mrs. A. Kesler, Evanston.

Two quarts unsifted flour, two teaspoons soda. four of cream tartar, two of salt, two eggs, one-half cup shorten-ing, two of sugar, milk to mix.

CRULLERS.

Ella Waggoner, Toledo.

. .Eight heaping tablespoons sugar, four eggs, four table-spoons melted butter, two tablespoons milk, and two of wine (or four of milk), and a pinch of soda dissolved in water. Fry in hot lard; sprinkle sugar over when hot.

CRULLERS.

Mrs. Fred. A. Arnold.

Three eggs, two cups sugar, one-half cup butter, one cup of sweet milk, three teaspoons baking powder; spice to taste.

RUSK COOKIES.

Mrs. E. A. Forsyth.

One cup melted butter, one and a half cups sugar, one

cup of tepid water, two teaspoons Dr. Price's baking powder mixed well with sifted flour; roll out very thin, and cut with a round cake cutter, baking in a quick oven.

WATER COOKIES.
Mrs. F. D. Gray.

One cup of sugar, one-half of butter, one-half of water, caraway seed, wet hard and roll very thin, indeed; sprinkle with sugar after putting them in the tins.

LEMON COOKIES.
Ella J. Roe.

One pint sugar, one cup butter, one teaspoon soda, juice and grated rind of one lemon. Roll soft and·thin, and bake quickly.

VANILLA COOKIES.
Mrs. C. S. Bartlett.

One cup of butter and two cups of sugar, beaten well; one cup of cold water, one teaspoon of soda, two teaspoons of vanilla, flour to make a very stiff dough. Roll very thin and bake brown.

BOILED COOKIES.
Mrs. F.

Boil one cup of milk, two of sugar, three of flour; cool it off; then add one teaspoon of soda, the yolks of three eggs; cut in rounds and bake in a quick oven.

EVERLASTING COOKIES.
Mrs. John Edwards, Rockford.

Two cups sugar, one of butter, three-fourths of sweet

milk, two teaspoons baking powder; season to taste; rub butter- and sugar together; then add two eggs, milk and flour to make a soft dough; roll thin, sprinkle a little sugar over the top, and bake in quick oven.

COOKIES.

Mrs. Russell.

One cup butter, two of sugar, one of sour cream, one teaspoon soda, two of cream tartar, three eggs, three tablespoons caraway seed, a little nutmeg, flour enough to form a soft dough; roll out thin and bake in a quick oven.

COOKIES.

Mrs. Solomon Thatcher, Sr.

Two cups of sugar, one of butter, one of sour cream, three eggs, beat separately, one teaspoon of soda; beat cream and yolks well together, the mix soft and roll out very thick; bake in a quick oven.

COOKIES.

Virginia West, Evanston.

Two eggs, two teacups sugar, one teacup butter, one teacup milk, one nutmeg, one teaspoon cream tartar, one-half teaspoon soda; flour to roll.

WHIG JUMBLES.

Mrs. W. H. Ovington.

One teacup and a half of butter; three teacups of sugar, one cup of sour cream, four eggs, one teaspoon of

Soda dissolved in it, six cups of flour, nutmeg; drop in heaping teaspoons on buttered paper in pans.

JUMBLES.

Mrs. W. H. Ovington.

One pound of butter, one pound of sugar, six eggs, grated peel of a fresh lemon, flour sufficient to make a soft dough; put in teaspoons in papered pans; on top of each cake put a blanched almond, and some coarse lumps of crushed sugar before baking.

RICH JUMBLES.

Mrs. Kate Johnson.

One-half pound butter, one-half pound sugar, two eggs well beaten, three-quarters pound flour; have plenty of rolled sugar on the board, and work little lumps of the dough (which is very soft) in it; make into little rings, and turn them over into buttered pans and bake with care; they will keep for two or three months.

EXCELLENT JUMBLES.

Mrs. J. H. Brown.

One cup butter, two cups sugar, one cup cream, one teaspoon soda, one egg, a little bit of nutmeg, flour enough to stiffen it so as to bake in rings; bake quickly.

COCOANUT JUMBLES.

Mrs. F.

Two cups of sugar, one of butter, two eggs, small teaspoon of soda, mixed with the flour, two cups of cocoanut.

JACKSON JUMBLES.

Mrs. C. A. Rogers.

One cup of butter, one cup cream, three cups of sugar, five eggs, five cups of flour.

SAND TARTS.

Mrs. W. H. Ovington.

One pound sugar, three-fourths pound of butter, two eggs, flour enough to make very stiff: roll them out and wet the tops with whites of eggs, then put two almonds on each one; sprinkle over them cinnamon and sugar.

SUGAR DROPS.

Mrs. H. M. Buell.

One pound flour, three-fourths pound of sugar, one-half of butter, four eggs, a gill of rose water. To be baked on paper. This will make sixty drops.

COCOANUT DROPS.

Mrs. H. M. Buell.

The meat of one cocoanut, pared and grated, weight of the same in sugar, one-half cup of flour, white.

NO MATTERS.

M. A. Bingham.

Three cups sour milk, three tablespoons of cream or butter; one cup of sugar; roll about the size of a plate, fry in hot lard, cover each with nicely seasoned apple sauce; lay over each other.

CINNAMON WAFERS.

Mrs. Beyer.

Two and a half cups of sugar, one-half cup butter, three eggs, one tablespoon cinnamon, one-half teaspoon soda; put in enough flour to roll out.

GINGER CAKE.

Mrs. Mann, Freeport.

One half cup butter, one of molasses, one of sugar, one of cold water, one heaping teaspoon soda, one quart of flour. Ginger and salt to taste; drop on the tins and bake in a quick oven.

GINGER COOKIES.

Mrs. J. O. Knapp.

One cup of sugar, one of butter, one of molasses, two tablespoons ginger, and two teaspoons saleratus dissolved in three tablespoons of hot water. Bake quickly.

GINGER SNAPS.

Miss Gilbert, Evanston.

One cup molasses, one-half of sugar, two-thirds of butter, one-half of water, one tablespoon ginger, one-half teaspoon of alum dissolved in hot water, two teaspoons saleratus, dissolved in the molasses; mix the whole, with flour enough to roll out nicely.

GINGER SNAPS.

Mrs. John Edwards, Rockford.

One cup of molasses; let it come to a boil, then add

two teaspoons of soda, when cool; mix one cup of butter, three-fourths of sugar, and two eggs well together; then add your molasses and two tablespoons of water, two tablespoons ginger, some cinnamon, and some cloves, and allspice; add flour and roll very thin; bake in a quick oven.

DRINKS.

The bubbling and loud hissing urn
Throws up a steaming column ; and the cups
That cheer, but not inebriate, wait on each ;
So let us welcome peaceful evening in.
— COWPER.

TEA.

When the water in the tea-kettle begins to boil, have
ready a tin tea-steeper ; pour into the tea-steeper just a
very little of the boiling water, and then put in tea, allowing one teaspoon of tea to each person. Pour over this
boiling water until the steeper is little more than half full ;
cover tightly and let it stand where it will keep hot, but
not to boil. Let the tea infuse for ten or fifteen minutes
and then pour into the tea urn, adding more boiling water,
in the proportion of one cup of water for every teaspoon
of dry tea which has been infused. Have boiling water
in a water pot, and weaken each cup of tea as desired.
Do not use water for tea that has boiled long. Spring
water is best for tea, and filtered water next best.

TEA A LA RUSSE.

Pare and slice fresh, juicy lemons ; lay a piece in the

bottom of each cup, sprinkle with white sugar and pour hot, strong tea over. Or the lemon may be sent around in slices with the peel on. No cream is used.

ICED TEA A LA RUSSE.

To each glass of tea add the juice of half a lemon fill up the glass with pounded ice and sweeten.

COFFEE.

Cleanse the coffee, dry and roast the berries evenly but quickly, until they are browned to the centre, and are of a dark chestnut color. Grind as you use it, keeping the rest in a closely covered glass can. Allow one heaping tablespoon of ground coffee for every person, and one or two over. Mix with the grounds, a part or whole of an egg, according to the amount of coffee used. Pour boiling water in the coffee-pot before using, and scald it well; then put in the coffee and pour over half as much water as will be used. Let the coffee froth up, stir down the grounds, and let it boil for about five minutes; then stand the coffee-pot where it will be hot (but not to boil the coffee), for five or ten minutes longer. Mocha is the richest and most delicate flavored coffee. Old Government Java is an excellent coffee, and more economical than Mocha. An excellent authority in coffee making allows to one pound of Mocha coffee, five quarts of water made after the above recipe.

CHOCOLATE.

Scrape Baker's chocolate fine, mix with a little cold water and the yolks of eggs well beaten; add this to equal parts of milk and water, and boil well, being careful that it does not burn. Sweeten to taste and, serve hot.

SODA CREAM.
M. G. Rand.

Two and one-half pounds white sugar, one-eight pound tartaric acid, both dissolved in one quart of hot water; when cold, add the beaten whites of three eggs, stirring well; bottle for use. Put two large spoons of this syrup in a glass of cold water, and stir in it one-fourth of a spoon of bicarbonate of soda. Any flavor can be put in the syrup. An excellent drink for summer.

RASPBERRY ACID.
Mrs. G. W. Pitkin.

Dissolve five ounces of tartaric acid in two quarts of water; pour it upon twelve pounds of red raspberries in a large bowl; let it stand twenty-four hours; strain it without pressing; to a pint of this liquor add one and a half pounds of white sugar; stir until dissolves. Bottle, but do not cook for several days, when it is ready for use. Two or three tablespoons in a glass of ice water will make delicious beverage.

RASPBERRY VINEGAR.
Mrs. W. S. Walker.

To four quarts red raspberries, put enough vinegar to cover, and let them stand twenty-four hours; scald and strain it; add a pound of sugar to one pint of juice; boil it twenty minutes, and bottle; it is then ready for use and will keep years. To one glass of water, add a great spoonful. It is much relished by the sick. Very nice,

24

RASPBERRY VINEGAR.

Mrs. Joseph B. Leake.

Fill a jar with red raspberries picked from the stalks. Pour in as much vinegar as it will hold. Let it stand ten days, then strain it through a sieve. Don't press the ber‍ries, just let the juice run through. To every pint add one pound loaf sugar. Boil it like other syrup; skim, and bottle when cold.

BLACKBERRY SYRUP.

Mrs. Bausher.

To one pint of juice, put one pound of white sugar, one-half ounce of powdered cinnamon, one-fourth ounce mace, and two teaspoons cloves; boil all together for quarter of an hour, then strain the syrup, and add to each pint a glass of French brandy.

LEMON SYRUP.

Mrs. De Forrest.

Pare off the yellow rind of the lemon, slice the lemon and put a layer of lemon and a thick layer of sugar in a deep plate; cover close with a saucer, and set in a warm place. This is an excellent remedy for a cold.

SPLENDID GINGER BEER.

Mrs. H. L. Bristol.

Five gallons of water, one-half pound ginger root boiled, four pounds sugar, one-eighth pound cream tartar, one bottle essence of lemon, one ounce of tartaric acid, one quart of yeast.

HOP BEER.

Mrs. Dickinson.

One handful of hops, boil an hour, strain, and add one pint of molasses, and enough water to make two gallons. When milk-warm, add one cup or cake of yeast; let it stand over night; skim' and pour it off from the yeast carefully; add one tablespoon of wintergreen, and bottle for use.

MISCELLANEOUS.

What does cookery mean? It means the knowledge
of all fruits and herbs and balms and spices, and of all
that is healing and sweet in fields and groves, and savory
in meats. It means carefulness, and inventiveness, and
watchfulness, and willingness, and readiness of appliance.
It means the economy of your great grandmother and the
science of modern chemists. It means much tasting and
no wasting; it means English thoroughness, and French
art, and Arabian hospitality; and it means, in fine, that
you are to be perfectly and always ladies — loaf givers;
and as you are to see imperatively that everybody has
something pretty to put on, so you are to see even yet
more imperatively that everybody has something nice to
eat. — RUSKIN.

GENERAL HINTS.

It is a matter of great convenience to have a covered
tub or pail of sifted flour ready for use. It will save
half the time in an emergency.

Always sift soda, when not dissolved in hot water,
through a fine wire sieve.

Sugar for fried cakes should be dissolved in the milk,
to prevent the cake from absorbing the lard while frying.

Two kinds of coffee mixed, (Java and Mocha,) are better than one alone ; but should be browned separately.

Tea should never be boiled, but be sure that the water boils that you use for steeping. From three to five minutes is sufficient time; if it stands longer the tea is apt to lose its aroma and have the bitter taste of the leaf.

An old housekeeper of fifty years' experience thinks the very best way of making coffee, is to use the National Pot, no egg; nothing to settle is required, simply use a muslin bag and let the water boil around it ten or fifteen minutes. A very important advantage is, that none of the aroma is lost by standing. If the "gude mon" of the home is late to breakfast, his coffee is just as nice and hot as when first made.

When bread is like a honey comb all through, is the time to make it up in loaves. When the 'loaves do not retain the dent of the finger, it is ready for the oven.

When meats are put in to roast, have no water in the pan. When they begin to brown is time enough for water.

Chicken for salad is nicer cut with a knife than chopped in a bowl, and the celery should always be cut with a knife.

If you would be a true economist, do not burn letters, envelopes, etc., but tear them across once or twice, and put them in the scrap bag for the rag man.

A silver spoon put into a glass jar, will temper it so that it can at once be filled with anything hot, even to the boiling point.

Marion Harland says that putting old and new milk

into cake will have a tendency to injure the quality of the cake.

A caution is given by an excellent authority not to put glass goblets that have held milk, into hot water, as this causes the milk to penetrate the glass and can never be removed.

In furnishing your house, have conveniences for put-ting away food for preservation. The greatest of the many advantages to be derived from modern cookery are the many palatable dishes which can be made with the remains of cold meat, a few bread crumbs, combined with other simple ingredients. It has often been observed that a French housekeeper can supply a family, with pleasing and nutritious food, of that which forms the waste of an ordinary American household.

We cannot recommend too strongly to young house-keepers the policy of mixing the sponge for bread at night, as the bread will thus be ready for baking early in the morning. Otherwise bread-making becomes the dread of the housekeeper and the anxiety of the whole day. Prepare the potatoes for the sponge at dinner, or tea-time, having the flour sifted in the bread pan. If the yeast is rapid, and the weather warm, do not mix the sponge until late in the evening. In cool weather this should be done at tea-time.

Coffee sacking cut into the shape of mats, and em-broidered about the borders in simple patterns with bright worsted, are very pretty and useful ornaments, especially for bed-room service, to lay in front of dress-ing bureaus, tables, stands, lounges, etc., thus preventing the wear of carpets. They should have the border threads of the sacking drawn out, to form a fringe, and are best lined with a piece of old carpet.

Very pretty coverings for chair covers are made of Turkish toweling, trimmed with fine colored skirt braid, stitched neatly on and embroidery each side, forming stripes alternately of braid and embroidery; or a border, with embroidery, each side of the braid, and a monogram, or small piece of simple embroidery in the center.

Many pretty fancies may be produced from these materials, as slipper pockets, comb and brush pockets, etc.

An oil cloth on the kitchen floor will save a good deal of Bridget's time. It is easily kept clean and does not absorb dirt and grease.

The floors of all closets through the house should be covered with oil cloth. Dust and moths are not thus harbored as when carpets are used, and are much prettier than a bare or painted floor.

Instead of the custom so common of putting fresh newspapers on closet and pantry shelves, we would recommend the pretty marbled oil cloth, which is used for " splashers," " stand covers," etc. This is easily cleaned, and when the edge is finished with a crocheted border of some bright colored worsted, it has a pretty effect hanging over the edge of the shelf.

An excellent method of preserving a table-cloth clean for the longest time is to lay a clean towel under any spots immediately after clearing the table, then washing the table-cloth with a fresh clean cloth in clean soap suds, then rinse it with clear water, dry it as much as possible with a clean dry towel, then fold and lay it under a heavy weight. In this way a table-cloth may be made to last clean for a long time.

The tea-table is the only meal where the table may be laid without a cover. An excellent fancy are the pretty crocheted mats for every dish, preserving the polished surface of the table from being defaced. When these are used a large oval mat for the tea service is appropriate.

Do not use a salver for the tea service. Fringed napkins are the choice for this meal.

LIME WATER.

Mrs. E. B. Lynde, Milwaukee.

One of the most useful agents of household economy, if rightly understood, is lime water. Its mode of preparation is as follows : Put a stone of fresh unslacked lime about the size of a half-peck measure into a large stone jar or unpainted pail, and pour over it slowly and carefully, (so as not to slacken too rapidly,) a teakettle full (four gallons,) of hot water, and stir thoroughly; let it settle, and then stir again two or three times in twenty-four hours. Then bottle carefully, all that can be poured off in a clear and limpid state.

USES.—It is often sold by druggists as a remedy for children's summer complaints, a teaspoon being a dose in a cup of milk, and when diarrhœa is caused by acidity of the stomach, it is an excellent remedy, and when put into milk gives no unpleasant taste, but rather improves the flavor.

When put into milk that might curdle when heated, it will prevent its so doing, and can then be used for puddings and pies. A little stirred into cream or milk, after a hot day or night, will prevent its turning when used for tea or coffee.

It is unequaled in cleansing bottles or small milk vessels, or babies' nursing bottles, as it sweetens and purifies without leaving an unpleasant odor or flavor.

A cupful, or even more, mixed in the sponge of bread or cakes made over night, will prevent it from souring.

PRESERVING AUTUMN LEAVES.

Mrs. C. H. Wheeler.

These may be easily preserved and retain their natural tints, or nearly so, by either of the following methods: As they are gathered they may be laid between the leaves of a magazine until the book is full, and left with a light weight upon them until the moisture of the leaves has been absorbed; two or three thicknesses of paper should intervene between the leaves. If the leaves are large or in clusters, take newspapers, lay them on a shelf and use in the same manner as above. Then dip the leaves into melted wax (such as is used for moulding fruits, etc.) into which you have put a few drops of turpentine and lay upon newspapers to harden perfectly. This will make the leaves pliable and natural and gives sufficient gloss. Great care should be taken that the wax is of right temperature. This can be ascertained by the first leaf which is dipped in. Draw out gently over the pan both sides of the leaf and hold it up by the stem. If the wax is too hot the leaf will shrivel — if too cool it will harden in lumps on the leaf.

Another method is to iron each leaf with a middling hot iron until the moisture is all out of them. Are best without varnish.

SKELETON LEAVES.

Boil the leaves in equal parts of rain water and soft soap until you can separate the pulp from the skin ; take them out into clear water ; lay the leaf to be cleaned on glass, the upper side of the leaf next to the glass; then with a tooth-brush remove all pulp and skin, turn the leaf and repeat the process; when thoroughly done, put the leaf to bleach in this solution: One pound sal soda, dissolved in five pints rain water; one-half pound chloride of lime, in three pints water; allow twenty-four hours for the latter to dissolve. Strain out the sediment, and pour the clear solution of lime into the solution of sal soda. The result will be a thick butter-milk solution, otherwise the lime was not strong enough. Filter this until it is perfectly clear. For leaves, use one part of solution to one part of water; for ferns, use the solution full strength. When perfectly white, remove to clear water; let stand for several hours, changing two or three times; the last water should be a little blue; float out on paper, press in books when nearly dry. In mounting use mucilage made of five parts of gum arabic, three parts white sugar, two parts of starch; add a very little water, boil and stir until thick and white.

FOR CRYSTALIZING GRASS.

Mrs. Ludlam, Evanston.

Take one and one-half pounds of rock alum, pour on three pints of boiling water; when quite cool, put into a wide-mouth vessel, hang in your grasses, a few at a time. Do not let them get too heavy, or the stems will not support them. You may again heat alum and add more grasses. By adding a little coloring, it will give variety.

CAMPHOR ICE.

Mrs. A. M.

One ounce of lard, one ounce spermaceti, one ounce camphor, one ounce almond oil, one-half cake of white wax; melt and turn into moulds.

CAMPHOR ICE.

Mrs. Bartlett.

One-half ounce each of camphor gum and white wax, spermaceti and sweet oil; melt slowly the hard ingredients and then add the oil.

COLD CREAM.

Mrs. Anna Marble.

Four ounces sweet almond oil, two of rose water, two of white wax, two of cocoa butter, two of spermaceti; put a bowl in a pan of boiling water; cut the spermaceti, white wax and cocoa butter in small pieces; put them in the bowl, also the oil and rose water. When melted, stir contents until cold.

TO BEAUTIFY TEETH.

Dissolve two ounces of borax in three pints of boiling water, and before it is cold, add one teaspoon of spirits of camphor; bottle it for use. A teaspoon of this with an equal quantity of tepid water.

HAIR TONIC.

Mrs. A. M.

One-half ounce sugar of lead, one-half of lac sulphur, one quart of rose water, six tablespoons castor oil.

FOR CLEANING HAIR BRUSHES.

Mrs. C. H. Wheeler.

Use spirits of ammonia and hot water; wash them well and shake the water out, drying on a coarse towel; they will look white and clean as new; little or no soap is needed.

TO CLEAN HAIR BRUSHES.

E. A. Forsyth.

Do not use soap, but put a tablespoon of hartshorn into the water, having it only tepid, and dip up and down until clean; then dry with the brushes down, and they will be like new ones. If you do not have ammonia, use soda; a teaspoon dissolved in the water will do very well.

JAPANESE CLEANSING CREAM.

One-fourth pound white castile soap, three ounces ammonia, one of ether, one of spirits of wine, one of glycerine; cut the soap fine and dissolve in one quart rain water; then add four quarts rain water, and then all the ingredients. For cleansing silks.

FOR CLOTHES THAT FADE.

One ounce sugar of lead in a pail of rain water. Soak over night.

TO WASH CALICO.

Mrs. Edward Ely.

Blue calicoes or muslins will retain their color if one small teaspoon of sugar of lead is put into a pail of water and the articles washed in the water.

BLACK CALICOES.

Wash black percales or calicoes as usual, rinse in water with a strong solution of salt. This will prevent black from running, and also colors.

TO WASH WOOLEN BLANKETS.

Mrs. J. A. Packard.

Dissolve soap enough to make a good suds in boiling water, add a tablespoon of aqua ammonia; when scalding hot, turn over your blankets. If convenient, use a pounder, or any way to work thoroughly through the suds without rubbing on a board. Rinse well in hot water. There is usually soap enough from the first suds to make the second soft; if not, add a little soap and ammonia; and after being put through the wringer, let two persons, standing opposite, pull them into shape; dry in the sun. White flannels may be washed in the same way without shrinking.

TO WASH WOOLEN.

E. A. Forsyth.

To every pail of water, add one tablespoon of ammonia, and the same of beef gall; wash out quickly, and rinse in warm water, adding a very little beef gall to the water. This will remove spots from carpets, making them look fresh.

TO WASH CARPETS.

E. A. Forsyth.

Spread the carpet where you can use a brush; take Irish potatoes and scrape them into a pail or tub of water and let them stand over night, using one peck to clean a large carpet; two pails of water is sufficient to let them stand in, and you can add more when ready to use; add two ounces of beef gall and use with a brush, as to scrub a floor; the particles of potato will help cleanse; when dry, brush with a broom or stiff brush.

WASHING FLUID.

Mrs. A. P. Iglehart.

Nine tablespoons unslacked lime, two pounds of sal soda, four quarts water; let this simmer half an hour, then bottle up. Take a small teacup to a boiler of water.

WASHING FLUID.

Mrs. A. W. D.

One pound sal soda, one pound potash, each dissolved in one gallon of water (separately); then mix together and bottled.

TO MAKE GOOD STARCH.

Mrs. D.

Mix the starch with cold water, add boiling water until it thickens, then add dessert spoon of sugar, and a small piece of butter. Makes a stiff and glossy finish equal to laundry.

AN EXCELLENT HARD SOAP.

Mrs. Kate Johnson.

Pour twelve quarts soft boiling water on two and one-half pounds of unslacked lime; dissolve five pounds sal soda in twelve quarts soft hot water; then mix and let them remain from twelve to twenty-four hours. Pour off all the clear fluid, being careful not to allow any of the sediment to run off; boil three and one-half pounds clean grease and three or four ounces of rosin in the above lye till the grease disappears; pour into a box and let it stand a day to stiffen and then cut in bars. It is as well to put the lime in all the water and then add the soda. After pouring off the fluid, add two or three gallons of water and let it stand with the lime and soda dregs a day or two. This makes an excellent washing fluid to boil or soak the clothes in, with one pint in a boiler of water.

CLEANING SILVER.

Mrs. O. L. Parker.

Never put a particle of soap about your silver if you would have it retain its original lustre. When it wants polish, take a piece of soft leather and whiting and rub hard. The proprietor of one of the oldest silver establishments in the city of Philadelphia says that housekeepers ruin their silver in soap suds, as it makes it look like pewter.

POLISH FOR ZINC OR TIN.

Mrs. Thos. A. Hill.

To three pints of water add one ounce of nitric acid, two ounces of emery, and eight ounces of pumice stone; shake well together. Any druggist will fill it for fifteen cents.

STOVE POLISH.

Mrs. O. L. Parker.

Stove lustre, when mixed with turpentine and applied in the usual manner, is blacker, more glossy, and more durable than when mixed with any other liquid. The turpentine prevents rust, and when put on an old rusty stove will make it look as well as new.

TO EXTRACT INK.

To extract ink from cotton, silk and woolen goods, saturate the spot with spirits of turpentine and let it remain several hours; then rub it between the hands. It will crumble away without injuring either the color or texture of the article.

TO TAKE INK OUT OF LINEN.

Dip the spotted part in pure tallow, melted; then wash out the tallow and the ink will disappear.

PATENT SOAP.

Mrs. Ludlam.

Five pounds hard soap, one quart ley, one-fourth ounce pearl-ash ; place on the fire and stir well until the soap is dissolved; add one-half pint spirits turpentine, one gill spirits hartshorn and stir well. It is then fit for use. The finest muslin may be put to soak in this suds, and if left for a time will become beautifully white. A small portion of soap put into a little hot water, and a flannel cloth will save hard labor and a brush in cleaning paint. One who has tried it thinks it worth the price of the book.

FOR BLEACHING COTTON CLOTH.

Mrs. C. H. Wheeler.

One pound chloride of lime, dissolved and strained; put in two or three pails water; thoroughly wet the cloth and leave it in over night; then rince well in two waters. This will also take out mildew, and is equally good for brown cotton or white that has become yellow from any cause, and will not injure the fabric.

TO REMOVE TAR.

Rub well with clean lard, afterwards wash with soap and warm water. Apply this to either hands or clothing.

JAVELLE WATER FOR MILDEW STAINS.

One pound of chloride of lime, two of washing soda, two gallons of soft water; pour one gallon of boiling water to the ingredients to dissolve them, adding the cold water when dissolved.

25

COLORING COTTON CARPET RAGS.

Mrs. S. I. Parker, Channahon, Ill.

BLUE.—For five pounds of cloth, take five ounces of copperas, with two pails of water in a tin or copper boiler; set it over the fire till the copperas is dissolved and it begins to heat, then put in the cloth, stirring it frequently till it boils, one-half or three-fourths of an hour; then remove the cloth where it can drain; pour away the copperas water and take two ounces of prussiate of potash in about two pails of water in the same vessel; when it is well dissolved and hot, put in the cloth from the copperas water, stirring it thoroughly till it boils, one-half an hour, then remove the cloth; add (with care and caution, on account of the spattering which ensues,) one tablespoon of oil of vitroil, and stir it well in the dye; replace the cloth, stirring it briskly till it has boiled one-half an hour. Should be well rinsed and washed in clear water to prevent the dye from making it tender after coloring.

YELLOW.—For five pounds of cloth, dissolve one-half pound of sugar of lead in a tub of warm water and twelve ounces of bichromate of potash in another tub of cold water; soak, rinse, and wring the cloth in the lead water first, then in the other, and return from one to the other till the right shade of color is obtained.

ORANGE.—Dip the yellow colored cloth into strong lime water—if it should not turn, boil it, rinse all well.

GREEN.—Put your blue cloth in the yellow dye in the same manner as for coloring yellow. Old calico will take a darker shade of blue or green in the same dye with the white cloth.

TO BOIL CORN BEEF.

Mrs. E. A. Forsyth.

Put into boiling water when you put it on to cook, and do not take it out of the pot when done, until cold. This will leave the meat juicy, instead of dry, when cold.

TO PREVENT RED ANTS.

Put one pint of tar in an earthen vessel, pour on it two quarts of boiling hot water, and place it in your closet.

FOR PRESERVING EGGS.

Mrs. B. F. Adams.

To one pint of unslaked lime and one pint of salt, pour one pail of boiling water; when cold, pour over the eggs, having placed them in a jar or tub, with the small end of the egg down.

CLEANING MARBLE.

Mrs. Gray.

Dissolve a large lump of Spanish whiting in water which has previously dissolved a teaspoon of washing soda, take only sufficient water to moisten the whiting, and it will become a paste; with a flannel cloth rub the marble well, leaving it on for a while and repeating the process two or three times, if necessary. Wash off with soap and water, then dry the marble well and polish with a soft duster.

FURNITURE POLISH.

No. 1. Shellac varnish, linseed oil and spirits of wine, equal parts. No. 2. Linseed oil, alcohol, equal parts,

No. 3. Linseed oil five ounces, turpentine two ounces, oil of vitriol one-half ounce.

CLEANING WHITE PAINT.

Mrs. C. H. Wheeler.

Spirits of ammonia, used in sufficient quantity to soften the water and ordinary hard soap, will make the paint look white and clean with half the effort of any other method I have ever tried. Care should be taken not to have too much ammonia, or the paint will be injured.

HARD SOAP.

Mrs. Mary A. Odell.

Six pounds of clean grease, six pounds of sal soda, three pounds of stone lime; slake the lime and put it into four gallons of soft water; add the sal soda, and when dissolved let it settle. Pour off the water into an· iron kettle, and add the grease melted, and boil. If the soap does not come after boiling a few minutes, add more soft water till it is of the consistency of honey. Wet a tub and· pour the hot soap into it. When cold, cut it into pieces and lay it away to dry. Always make soap in ar iron kettle.

THE SICK ROOM.

EGG GRUEL.—Boil eggs from one to three hours until hard enough to grate; then boil new milk and thicken with the egg, and add a little salt. Excellent in case of nausea.—MRS. BARTLETT.

GRUEL FOR INFANTS.—To make a gruel for infants suffering from marasmus, take one pint of goat's milk and the yolks of two eggs boiled sufficiently hard to reduce to an impalpable powder; add a pint of boiling water, a little salt or sugar, and administer by a nursing bottle.—DR. SMALL.

BEEF TEA.—To one pound of lean beef add one and one-half tumblers of cold water; cut the beef in small pieces, cover and let it boil slowly for ten minutes, and add a little salt after it is boiled. Excellent.

BEEF JELLY FOR INVALIDS.—Three small onions, three small or one and one-half large carrots, a few whole cloves and black pepper, one small teaspoon of sugar, one slice of ham, two calf's feet, one and a half pounds of beef. Put in the onions and other ingredients in succession. Place the ham on top, then the calf's feet, and lastly the beef; no water; put on the side of the range, and let it stand until reduced to a soft mass, then add a quart of water and let it boil one hour; strain and let stand until cold, when take off the fat. Use by dissolving a little in hot water.—MRS. J. A. ELLIS.

PANADA.—Two thick slices of stale bread half an inch in thickness; cut off the crust, toast them a nice brown, cut them into squares of two inches in size, lay them in a bowl, sprinkle a little salt over them and pour on a pint of boiling water.

REMEDY FOR CANCER.—Col. Ussery, of the Parish of De Soto, informs the editor of the Caddo *Gazette*, that he fully tested a remedy recommended by a Spanish woman, native of the country. Take an egg and break it, pour out the white, retaining the yolk in the shell; put in salt, mix with the yolk as long as it will receive it; stir them together until the salve is formed; put this on a piece of sticking plaster and apply it to the cancer twice a day.

A citizen of Philadelphia using a weak solution of car, bolic acid as a wash to neutralize the offensive odor aris-ing from a cancer, discovered that the latter was removed by the application. The solution consisted of one-fourth of an ounce of acid diluted in a quart of water.—MRS. R. A. SIBLEY.

FEVER AND AGUE.—Four ounces galangal root in a quart of gin, steeped in a warm place; take often.—MRS. R. A. SIBLEY.

SMALL POX REMEDY.—The following remedy a friend tried in Ohio in a case of confluent small pox, when the doctor had little hope of saving the patient, and it saved the woman's life. The remedy is sure in scarlet fever. "I herewith append a recipe which has been used to my own knowledge in a hundred cases. It will prevent or cure the small pox, even though the pittings are filling. When Jenner discovered cow pox in England, the world of science hurled an avalanche of fame upon his head, and when the most scientific school of medicine in the world (that of Paris), published this panacea for the small pox, it passed unheeded. It is unfailing as fate, and con-quers in every instance. It is harmless when taken by a well person. It will also cure scarlet fever. Take sul-phate of zinc, one grain; fox glove (*digitalis*) one grain; half a teaspoon of water. When thoroughly mixed, add four ounces water. Take a spoonful every hour, and either disease will disappear in twelve hours. For a child, smaller doses, according to age."

FOR HYDROPHOBIA.—Franklin Dyer, a highly respec-table farmer of Galena, Kent county, Md., gives the fol-lowing as a sure cure for the bite of a mad dog. He has tested it with most gratifying results: Elecampane is a plant well known and found in many gardens. Imme-diately after being bitten, take one and a half ounces of the root of the plant, the green root is preferable. The dried, to be found in drug stores, will answer; bruise it, put it in a pint of fresh milk, boil down to half a pint, strain, and when cold, drink it, fasting at least six hours afterwards. The next morning repeat the dose, fasting, using two ounces of the root. On the third morning, take another dose prepared as the last, and this will be suffi-

cient. After each dose, nothing to be eaten for at least
six hours. I had a son who was bitten by a mad dog
eighteen years ago, and four other children in the neigh-
borhood were also bitten. They took the above, and are
now alive and well. I have known many who were cured.
It is supposed that the root contains a principle, which,
being taken up by the blood in its circulation, counteracts
or neutralizes the deadly effect of the virus of hydrophobia. I feel so much confidence in this simple remedy
that I am willing you should give my name in connection
with this statement.

FOR FELON.—Take common rock salt, as used for
salting down pork or beef, dry in an oven, then pound it
fine and mix with spirits of turpentine in equal parts;
put it in a rag and wrap it around the parts affected; as
it gets dry, put on more, and in twenty-four hours you are
cured. The felon will be dead. No harm to try it, as I
have with success.

CURE FOR NEURALGIA.—A friend who suffered horrible
·pains from neuralgia, hearing of a noted physician in
Germany who invariably cured the disease, went to him,
and was permanently cured after a short sojourn. The
doctor gave him the remedy, which was nothing but a
poultice and tea made from our common field thistle.
The leaves are macerated and used as a poultice on the
parts affected, while a small quantity of the same is boiled
down to the proportion of a quart to a pint, and a small
wine glass of the decoction drank before each meal. Our
friend says he has never known it to fail of giving relief·

while in almost every case it has effected a cure. God gave herbs for the healing of the nations.

FOR HOARSENESS.—Squeeze the juice of half a lemon in a pint bowl, add loaf sugar (two tablespoons), one full teaspoon of glycerine, and one full tablespoon of whisky; pour over this boiling hot water to nearly fill the bowl, and drink hot just before going to bed.

FOR SORE THROAT.—Cut slices of salt pork or fat bacon; simmer a few moments in hot vinegar, and apply to throat as hot as possible. When this is taken off, as the throat is relieved, put around a bandage of soft flannel. A gargle of equal parts of borax and alum, dissolved in water, is also excellent. To be used frequently.

HEALING LOTION.—One ounce glycerine, one ounce rose-water, ten drops carbolic acid. This preparation prevents and cures chapping of the skin, and at the same time bleaches it. It is also excellent for sore lips and gums. I consider it an indispensable adjunct to the toilet table.—MRS. A. YOCUM, Cairo, Ill.

TO STOP BLEEDING.—A handful of flour bound on the cut.—MRS. A. M.

TO PREVENT CONTAGION FROM ERUPTIVE DISEASES.— Keep constantly, in plates or saucers, sliced raw onions in the sick room, if possible. As fast as they become discolored, replace by fresh ones. During any epidemic of skin diseases that are eruptive, onions, except those taken fresh from the earth, are unsafe, as they are peculiarly sensitive to disease.

TO RESTORE FROM STROKE OF LIGHTNING.—Shower with cold water for two hours; if the patient does not show signs of life, put salt in the water, and continue to shower an hour longer.

FOR TOOTHACHE.—Of powdered alum and fine salt, equal quantities; apply to the tooth and it will give speedy relief.—MRS. BARTLETT.

FOR HEADACHE.—Pour a few drops of ether on one-half ounce of gum camphor and pulverize; add to this an equal quantity of carbonate ammonia pulverized; add twenty drops peppermint; mix and put in an open-mouthed bottle and cork.—MRS. A. M. GIBBS.

SALVE FOR CHILBLAINS.—Fry out nicely a little mutton tallow; into this while melted, and after it is nicely strained, put an equal quantity of coal oil; stir well together while it is cooling.

TO REMOVE DISCOLORATION FROM BRUISES.—Apply a cloth wrung out in very hot water, and renew frequently until the pain ceases. Or, apply raw beefsteak.

CURE FOR WASP STING.—Apply a poultice of saleratus water and flour, and bind on the sting. Apply slices of raw onion for a bee sting.

CURE FOR SUMMER COMPLAINT.—Two ounces tincture rhubarb, one of paregoric, one-half of essence of peppermint, one-half of essence of annis, one-half of prepared chalk. Dose for adult, one teaspoon in a little water; take as often as needed.—MRS. L. BRADLEY.

THE BEST DEODORIZER.—Use bromo-chloralum in the proportion of one tablespoon to eight of soft water; dip cloths in this solution and hang in the rooms; it will will purify sick rooms of any foul smells. The surface of anything may be purified by washing well and then rubbing over with a weakened solution bromo-chloralum.

A weak solution is excellent to rinse the mouth with often, when from any cause the breath is offensive. It is also an excellent wash for sores and wounds that have an offensive odor.

TO DESTROY BED BUGS, MOTHS AND OTHER VERMIN. —Dissolve alum in hot water, making a very strong solution; apply to furniture or crevices in the walls with paint brush. This is sure destruction to these noxious vermin, and invaluable because easily obtained; is perfectly safe to use, and leaves no unpleasant traces behind. When you suspect moths have lodged in the borders of carpets, wet the edges of the carpets with a strong solution; whenever it reaches them, it is certain death.

BILLS OF FARE.

In the accompanying Bills of Fare, the arrangement of the various courses will be suggested by the form in which they are given :

MENU. .

BREAKFAST.—No. 1.

Fine Hominy.	Buttered Toast.
	Beefsteak.
French Rolls.	Potatoes a la Creme.
	Buckwheat Cakes.
Tea.	Coffee. Chocolate.

BREAKFAST—No. 2.

Broiled Spring Chickens.
Parker House Rolls.   Saratoga Potatoes.
Scrambled Eggs.   Fried Oysters.
Rye and Indian Loaf.
Coffee.   Tea.   Chocolate.

BREAKFAST—No. 3.

White Fish.   Potatoes.
Muffins.
Fried Ham.   Egg Omelette.
Coffee.   Tea.   Chocolate.

LUNCHES.

LUNCH PARTY—No. 1.

Beef Tea, served in small porcelain cups.
Cold Chicken and Oyster and other forms of Croquettes.
Chicken Salad.   Minced Ham Sandwiches.
Escalloped Oysters.
Tutti Frutti.   Chocolate Cream.
Cake Basket of Mixed Cake.
Mulled Chocolate.
Mixed Pickles.   Biscuits, etc.
Ice Cream and Charlottes can either be added or substituted.   For twenty guests, allow one gallon.

(396)

LUNCH PARTY—No. 2.

Oyster Pie.   Boiled Partridge.   Cold Ham.
Sweet Pickles.   Sandwiches.
Pound and Fruit Cake.   Pyramids of Wine Jelly.
Blanc Mange.   Snow Jelly.
Pineapple Flummery.
Kisses.   Macaroons.   Ice Cream.

DINNERS.

DINNER—No. 1.

FIRST COURSE.

Oyster Soup, with Celery.

SECOND COURSE.

Roast Turkey.
Croquettes of Rice.   Sweet and Irish Potatoes.

THIRD COURSE.

Quail on Toast.
Vegetables.   Pickles.   Escalloped Tomatoes.
Macaroni.   Jelly.

DESSERT.

Almond Pudding.
Mince Pie.   Lemon Pie.
Cheese.   Fruits.   Nuts.
Coffee.

DINNER—No. 2.

FIRST COURSE.

Raw Oysters.
White and Brown Soup.

SECOND COURSE.

Boiled White Fish, with Sauce and Sliced Lemon.

THIRD COURSE.

Roast Beef.

FOURTH COURSE.

Roast Turkey.   Ducks.
Vegetables in season.   Croquettes of Rice or Hominy.
Cranberry Sauce.   Currant Jelly.

DESSERT.

Cream Custard.   Lemon Pie.
Fruits.   Nuts.
Coffee.

TEA COMPANY

TEA COMPANY — No. 1.

Tea. Coffee. Chocolate.
Biscuits.
Oyster Sandwiches. Chicken Salad.
Cold Tongue.
Cake and Preserves.
Ice Cream and Cake later in the evening.

TEA COMPANY — No. 2

Tea, Coffee, or Chocolate.
Escalloped or Fried Oysters. Muffins.
Sliced Turkey and Ham.
Cold Biscuits.
Sardines and Sliced Lemons.
Thin slices of Bread, rolled. Sliced Pressed Meats.
Cake in variety.

SUPPERS.

SUPPER — No. 1.

Cold Roast Turkey. Chicken Salad.
Quail on Toast.
Ham Croquettes. Fricasseed Oysters.
Charlotte Russe. Vanilla Cream.
Chocolate Cake. Cocoanut Cake.
Mixed Cakes.
Fruit.
Coffee and Chocolate.

SUPPER — No. 2.

Cold Roast Partridges or Ducks.
Oyster Patties. Cold Boiled Ham. Dressed Celery,
Oysters or Minced Ham Sandwiches.
Raw Oysters. Chicken Croquettes or Fricasseed Oysters.
Wine Jelly. Ice Cream. Biscuit Glacé. Cakes.
Fruits. Chocolate. Coffee.
Pickles and Biscuits,

ALLOWANCE OF SUPPLIES FOR AN ENTERTAINMENT.

In inviting guests, it is safe to calculate that out of one hundred and fifty, but two-thirds of the number will be present. If five hundred are invited, not more than three hundred can be counted upon as accepting.

Allow one quart of oysters to every three persons present. Five chickens [or, what is better, a ten pound turkey, boiled and minced], and fifteen heads of celery. are enough for chicken salad for fifty guests ; one gallon of ice cream to every twenty guests ; one hundred and thirty sandwiches for one hundred guests ; and six to ten quarts of wine jelly for each hundred. For a company of twenty, allow three chickens for salad ; one hundred pickled oysters ; two moulds of Charlotte Russe ; one gallon of cream ; and four dozen biscuits.

COLD LUNCHES FOR WASHING DAYS, OR OTHER DAYS OF EXTRA LABOR.

LUNCH No. 1.—Cold corn beef, nicely sliced ; baked potatoes ; bread, butter and pickles. Dessert — mince pie and cheese.

LUNCH No. 2.—Chicken pie , baked potatoes ; rolled bread or biscuit. Dessert — cake and custard.

LUNCH No. 3.—First course : Raw oysters, with lemon and crackers. Second course : Cold veal, with jelly and Saratoga potatoes ; bread and butter. Dessert — cherry pie with cheese.

LUNCH No. 4.—Casserole of fish, with mushroom cutsup ; bread and butter. Dessert — pie with cheese.

ECONOMICAL DINNERS.

SUNDAY.—Roast beef, potatoes and greens. Dessert — pudding or pie, cheese.

MONDAY.—Hashed beef, potatoes and bread pudding.

TUESDAY.—Broiled beef, vegetables, apple pudding.

WEDNESDAY.—Boiled pork, beans, potatoes, greens, and pie or rice pudding.

THURSDAY.—Roast or broiled fowl, cabbage, potatoes, lemon pie, cheese.

FRIDAY.—Fish, potato croquettes, escalloped tomatoes, pudding.

SATURDAY.—*A la mode* beef, potatoes, vegetables, suet pudding and mince pie, cheese.

www.ingramcontent.com/pod-product-compliance
Lightning Source LLC
Chambersburg PA
CBHW022258280326
41932CB00010B/905